Contents

Introduction to the fifth edition

In this fifth edition of *Studying the Novel* there is more extensive discussion of the novella in Chapter 3. Two new chapters are included: one concerned with fiction and the electronic media (Chapter 5) and one concerned with versions and adaptations that pays particular attention to the issues raised by film adaptations of works of fiction (Chapter 8). The section on using computers in Chapter 7 has been expanded, and this chapter also contains additional advice on writing essays and examination answers. The Glossary has also been expanded, and now contains an extended definition of cyberpunk and cyberfiction.

As in previous editions, I have tried to keep referencing to a minimum, omitting sources for many standard critical and fictional works.

Throughout the book I attempt to highlight the distinction between historical and structuralist or narratological approaches to the study of the novel – starting with some comments following.

I am grateful to those many friends and colleagues who have commented on ideas and drafts while I have been writing this new edition, especially Jakob Lothe and Paul Goring. They are not responsible for any errors or inadequacies in the final result.

■ History and structure

It is the discipline of modern linguistics that we have to thank for making us aware that many 'objects of study' can be approached in two fundamentally different ways – either as entities that evolve over time or as states or systems that can be studied 'as they are' at a particular instant of time. The individual who is generally given the credit for making us aware of the fundamental difference between these approaches is the Swiss linguistician Ferdinand de Saussure, whose *Course in General Linguistics* was put together from notes taken in his lectures by students, and was published after his death in 1915. Saussure is often dubbed the father of modern linguistics because he distinguished between what he termed 'static' and 'evolutionary' linguistics (nowadays the terms 'synchronic', or structuralist linguistics, and 'diachronic', or historical linguistics, are generally preferred).

Why should this be of concern to the student of the novel? Saussure's work persuaded scholars in many different fields to approach their chosen 'objects of study' synchronically rather than (or as well as) historically. The theory known as structuralism attempts to generalize such work, and structuralism is the theory that has contributed most to what is known as narrative theory, or narratology. Because some of the most important narratives in our culture are those that we call novels and short stories, many of the tools (concepts, terms, methods) that we use to analyse novels and short stories come to us from structuralism via narratology. Structuralists in general and narratologists in particular are interested not in how things evolve and change over time but in how they work at a particular moment of time, and they typically model their approach upon the synchronic study of language. Thus a narratologist interested in the concept of 'plot' is not primarily concerned with how novelists over many centuries refined their ideas about what a plot should be or do, but in how plot is one component in the system that is the novel (or, in some applications, in the system that is *a* novel), and in how it interacts with other components. Many of the terms included in the glossary at the end of this book come from structuralist narratology, an approach that is not just based on structuralist linguistics but that actually draws parallels between language and narrative and applies terms developed in the study of language to the study of narratives.

At this point a comparison may be useful. If you are a mechanic trying to work out how a car engine functions you do not need to know anything about the different stages of development through which the internal combustion engine has passed from the start of the twentieth century. But knowing something of this history *will* help you to understand why car engines today are as they are. Similarly, knowing how a car engine works will tell you nothing about how the internal combustion engine evolved, but such knowledge *will* make it easier to study this process of evolution. Synchronic and diachronic approaches complement each other, so that it should not be assumed that the development of narratology has put an end to the historical study of the novel. Indeed, the dimension of history probably remains more present in writing about the novel than in writing about drama or poetry. The odds are that in any general discussion of the novel the word 'history' will appear quite early on: of all the three main literary genres, the novel seems most fundamentally linked in our minds to the dimension of history.

Some of the chapters that follow – Chapter 2, for example, 'History, genre, culture' – outline a primarily historical approach. Others – most notably Chapter 6, 'Analysing fiction' – owe more to the synchronic approach of narratology than to the historical study of the novel. The distinction is not an absolute one by any means; you will note for example that, when discussing dialogue in Chapter 6 on p. 128, I refer to historical changes in the ways in which novelists represent dialogue. You should certainly not assume that the mapping of historical change in the novel cannot involve analytical detail, nor that the close analysis of fictional prose is unable to engage with historical processes or formal changes. Indeed, I do myself believe that histories of the novel that fail to engage with how the novel (as either a single work or a system at a point in time) works cannot but be superficial – just as I also believe that close analysis of fictional prose that is unresponsive to the detail of historical contexts and movements is arid.

1
Fiction and the novel

Preview

This chapter deals with:
- some preliminary definitions: novel, fiction, narrative
- the universality of fiction and the distinctiveness of literary fiction
- imaginary characters and real life
- prose and narrative
- showing and telling
- characters, action, plot
- novel, short story, novella: some preliminary comments

If we are going to be using terms such as 'novel', 'fiction', 'narrative', and so on, we need at least some preliminary sense of what we mean by these terms: some working definitions. Such definitions inevitably raise the issue of history: if the novel is a genre that develops over time, then no single or short definition can exhaustively capture what it is at all times and in all places. Working definitions do nevertheless allow us to narrow down the field of possibilities and to home in on those characteristics that have continued to distinguish the novel from other literary genres, and from other examples of narrative.

According to the *Oxford English Dictionary*, a novel is 'a fictitious prose narrative or tale of considerable length (now usually one long enough to fill one or more volumes) in which characters and actions representative of the real life of past or present times are portrayed in a plot of more or less complexity'. This may sound a bit like stating the obvious, but there are some important points contained in this very concise definition. Let us consider some of its component parts.

■ The universality and the distinctiveness of fiction

Gregory Currie has commented that fiction 'is one of those concepts like goodness, color, number, and cause that we have little difficulty in applying but great difficulty in explaining' (Currie 1990, 1). 'Telling stories' is a function that is so central to our culture that we pay it little analytical attention. From a very early age we learn to distinguish not just between true and untrue reports, but also between different sorts of untrue reports – 'lies' and 'stories' for example. Fiction is much wider than the novel or, indeed, than prose fiction: jokes, imitations and parodies, songs and narrative poems can all be described as fictions – and wider, non-literary usages include such things as legal fictions and (perhaps) folk tales and urban myths (fictions do not have to take the form of a story or a narrative). Fiction has its historical and cultural dimensions; if fiction seems to be universally present in the lives of all human beings, it nevertheless assumes different forms in different ages and different societies. Not all fictions are novels, then, but the specific tradition or set of traditions which we refer to as 'the novel' is made possible by a far more widespread and fundamental reliance upon fiction in human society.

We can start with a number of seeming paradoxes: fictions are not true, but they are not lies; they typically describe that which is not real but which is nonetheless not totally unreal; they can include references to real people and events without jeopardizing their fictional status; they are designed to get readers or listeners to respond 'as if', but not (normally) to deceive them; even though readers are aware that fictions describe people who do not exist or events which have not happened, they nonetheless produce real emotions, important reflections, and even altered behaviour in the real world.

In their book *Truth, Fiction, and Literature: A Philosophical Perspective*, Peter Lamarque and Stein Haugom Olsen provide us with a number of useful distinctions with which to approach this complex topic. First, they differentiate between what they call the 'object' and the 'description' senses of the term 'fiction', arguing that a fictional character is a fiction in the object sense while a work of fiction is a fiction in the description sense:

> *To say of a thing that it is fictional is to suggest that it does not exist, the implied association being between what is fictional and what is* unreal. *To say of a description that it is fictional is to suggest that it is not true, the implied association being between what is fictional and what is* false. *(Lamarque and Olsen 1994, 16)*

Second, they distinguish between fictional content and fictional mode, illustrating the difference by reference to Konrad Kujau's forgery which was presented to the world as Hitler's (genuine) diaries. As they remark, while it would be reasonable to refer to the content of this forgery as fictional, 'we should surely hesitate to call the finished product a "work of fiction" given the mode of its presentation' (17). These distinctions allow them to focus not on the structural or semantic properties of sentences 'but on the conditions under which they are uttered, the attitudes they invoke, and the role that they play in social interactions' (32). Such an approach leads to a stress on fictional storytelling as a convention with institutional resources or, to put it another way, as a more or less universally understood custom or family of customs within a culture.

If fiction is in one sense universal, those fictions that we call novels and short stories are arguably possessed of certain unique features. In her book *The Distinction of Fiction* (1999), Dorrit Cohn approaches the definition of fiction from a narratological perspective, and makes an impressively energetic case for the distinctiveness of *literary* fiction. Cohn suggests that literary fictions can be distinguished from other non-fictional narratives in three ways. First, the distinction between *story* and *plot* (in her terminology story and discourse) does not have the same validity for 'texts that refer to events that have occurred prior to their narrative embodiment'. You will find this point easier to understand after having read the discussion of story and plot on p. 111. Second, only in fictional narratives can narrators enter the consciousness of persons apart from themselves. Third, in non-fictional narratives the distinction between author and narrator does not make the same sort of sense as it does when applied to fictional texts (1999, 130).

In the 1950s the London *Evening Standard* ran a regular feature entitled 'Did it Happen?' The newspaper would publish an account of a striking experience, then ask readers to decide whether the experience really did happen, with the truth being revealed the following day. The authors ranged from Stevie Smith and Angus Wilson to Gerard Hoffnung and Benny Hill, and their contributions were gathered together and published as a book in 1956 (*Did It Happen?: Stories*). Reading through the contributions it is interesting to see what a writer has to do to leave the reader in doubt as to whether he or she is reading fact or fiction. All of the accounts are in the first person, and in no case does the narrator enter the consciousness of another person. No account suggests a distinction between author and narrator. Once we know whether the account is fact or fiction we can indeed recognize as Cohn suggests that the distinction between author and narrator, and that between story and plot, make a different sort of sense for the two types of account. But these are retrospective judgements. It is the entering of the consciousness of a person other than the narrator that seems to suggest most strongly that a narrative is fictional, and the authors of the 'fictional' accounts seem instinctively to have recognized this.

■ Fiction, play, fantasy

Anyone who has watched a child grow and mature will know that he or she attempts to understand and master the world and his or her relation to it through modelled performances which we call play. However much we may like to think of play as sharply distinguished from the real, workaday world, relegated to 'free time' or 'relaxation', there seems little doubt that the rules of games can function as a model of the social and material restraints which we meet with in the world, and that play can help us to internalize these aspects of the world and of our operating within it.

Fictional stories, too, present us with models of (especially) the social world which we can empathize with and observe because we are not constrained to act. According to Lamarque and Olsen (1994), readers 'often fantasize with fictive content, "filling in" as the whim takes them, and no doubt some genres of fantasy actively encourage this kind of whimsical response'. This is rather stern, and it becomes more so as the two authors then insist upon the need to distinguish between authorized and non-authorized responses – with 'the content itself and its presentation' as the source of this authority (89).

I call this a rather stern pronouncement in spite of the fact that as a university teacher I spend a lot of time telling my students that they need to be able to justify their responses and interpretations by reference to textual and other evidence. I do this because although academic discussion of literature has to insist upon such standards in order to establish ground-rules for discussion and debate, I do not think that readers (as against students or critics) of novels are − or ever have been − obliged to remain within the boundaries of the academically authorized. Indeed, were it possible to render 'whimsical responses' impossible, then I suspect that novel-reading would be a lot less popular than it is today. I agree that certain aspects of literary response are like those forms of play which are bound by very rigid rules: football or chess, for example. But reading novels also resembles the child's make-believe games, those games where it is the imagined roles and situations which offer the only constraints. To a certain extent Peter Lamarque himself clearly accepts this point, as in a later book he argues that fictive storytelling 'disengages standard conditions of assertion, it invites imaginative rather than belief-based involvement, it creates worlds and characters, and it encourages participation, not a concern for correspondence with the facts' (Lamarque 1996, 144).

This is not to argue that works of fiction impose no constraints on what we imagine while we are reading them. Indeed, it is precisely because our responses, our imaginings, have to confront and negotiate with what cannot be changed in a novel that the reading of fiction is able to model what it is like to live in the social and material world. We cannot read on through Emily Brontë's *Wuthering Heights* (1847) pretending that Catherine does not really die but is only hiding somewhere, so that she can re-emerge outside Lockwood's window and give him a shock. One of the things which games do, though, is to allow us to act out *alternative* moves, modes of behaviour, or whatever, in a way that is impossible in the real world where we often have to act quickly and irrevocably − and this, I believe, is also true of novels and short stories. Thus, although I would reach for my red pen if I received an essay from a student which argued that Catherine never really died but lived on the moor as a hermit, it seems to me that wondering what would have happened had Catherine not died, or wondering 'how I would have behaved in Catherine's position', is an absolutely normal − indeed essential − part of reading a novel such as *Wuthering Heights*. One implication of the fact that novels stimulate our fantasy is that there can be no single, final, true, authorized response to a complex novel. Response is interactional, and in every new reading one of the interacting elements is different.

Remember, however, that 'response' is not the same as 'interpretation'; my response may be different from yours, but we can try to reach agreement about our interpretation of a given work. Now this book is called *Studying the Novel*, not *Responding to the Novel*, and my emphasis throughout it is on those institutionally approved ways of categorizing, analysing and interpreting novels and short stories. I am concerned, in other words, with the ways in which those private, individual and utterly varied reading responses people have can be introduced into society and allowed to converse to others. If our talk to others about novels is to be more than a semi–comprehensible outpouring of our highly idiosyncratic reading experiences then we have to anchor it to things that we can all share: textual details, scholarly procedures, and so on. We should however be very careful to avoid the assumption that such public and 'objective' information is all that matters.

Just as our account of a dream is not at all the same as our experience of actually dreaming, so too reading fiction produces responses and mental processes which are too complex ever to be fully captured in the discussion we have when we have finished reading. This does not make such discussion pointless: learning to study the novel helps us to refine and extend our reading experiences, and it allows us to turn the experience of reading into knowledge and self-knowledge through ordered and rational discussion. That said, we should never be ashamed to admit that the reading of stories is a mysterious process, only a part of which can be held on to and brought into the light of day through analysis and interpretative discussion.

■ Imaginary characters and real life

The novel depicts imaginary characters and situations. A novel may include reference to real places, people and events, but it cannot contain *only* such references and remain a novel. Even though its characters and actions are imaginary they are in some sense 'representative of real life', as the dictionary definition has it; although fictional they bear an important resemblance to the real. What exactly this resemblance is has been a matter of much discussion and dispute among literary critics, and it is arguable that it varies in kind from novel to novel. Even so, this resemblance to *real* life is one of the features that distinguishes the novel from other forms such as the epic and the romance (see the Glossary and also the discussion on p. 14), however much we recognize that 'real life' is a problematic concept. Later on in Chapter 4 we will see that the term 'realism' is one that, although arguably indispensable to discussion of the novel, requires careful definition and use.

As the dictionary definition puts it, a novel is concerned with 'the real life of past or present times'. There are of course many works which we would not hesitate to call novels which are set in the future – and this was also the case at the time that the *OED* definition was written. It is probable that it is the novel's association with what seems 'real' to us, with a recognizable human life in existing or past cultures, that has prompted the exclusion of 'the unreal' (however defined) from the dictionary definition. Even novels which have a significant dependence upon the fantastic typically seem still to direct our attention to the real life of past or present times more than do works belonging to genres such as epic or romance, although this is a more controversial matter and I will look at some dissenting views in Chapter 2.

It is common knowledge that people can 'lose themselves' in a novel. Even if the novel generally presents us with a recognizable, 'non-fantastic' world, we exercise our fantasy and our imagination to live within this world for short periods of time. But although readers can and do lose themselves while reading a novel this does not mean that they are unable to mull over and learn from their reading experiences once they return to their everyday reality after finishing a novel.

The world of the novel is so familiar to us that we can on occasions recognize its distinctive qualities only by contrasting it to other genres. The Russian critic Mikhail Bakhtin points out, for example, that '[t]he world of the epic is the national heroic past', it is based upon a 'national tradition (not personal experience and the free thought that grows out of it)', and 'an absolute epic distance separates the epic world from contemporary reality'. The novel, 'by contrast, is determined by experience, knowledge and practice (the future)' (Bakhtin 1981, 13, 15). The novel presents us with stories, experiences that are new; whereas those who experienced the epic knew what was to occur, when we pick up a novel we hope that our curiosity will be aroused by our wanting to know 'what happens'. As I will argue in Chapter 2, this difference has a lot to do with the different sorts of society from which these two genres emerge.

■ Prose and narrative

The novel is in *prose* rather than verse, although the language of novels may often strike us as very 'poetic' on occasions. It would nonetheless be a serious mistake to assume that the language of a novel is identical to that of ordinary speech or of most non-literary writing. Even so, the fact that the novel is in prose helps to establish that sense of 'real life' – of recognizable, everyday, 'prosaic' existence – that is the preserve of the genre. Generalization is dangerous, but prose has the potentiality of being a more transparent medium than, for example, verse. Reading a novel, our attention is not naturally drawn to considering the language as language. The tendency is more for us to 'look through' the language of the novel at what it describes and evokes than to 'look at' it – although novelists can write prose that arrests our attention as language, and many novelists are known for the manner in which they draw the reader's attention to their use of language. In the course of studying novels we must learn to pay more overt attention to their language than does the average casual reader.

The novel is a *narrative*: in other words it is in some sense a 'telling' rather than an 'enacting', and this distinguishes it in an important sense from the drama. One useful way to define narrative involves reference to what Seymour Chatman has called 'double chronology' (1990, 114): the things that happen in a novel happen in a particular order, and the telling of what happens also takes place in a particular order. Importantly, these two 'orders' or chronologies are not necessarily the same, and the interaction between them constitutes a fundamentally important aspect of the novel and the short story. You will find more about narrative's double chronology in the discussion of story and plot on p. 111. Double chronology is a necessary but not a sufficient condition of a narrative, as it may apply also to plays and films (*Citizen Kane* opens with the depiction of events which take place after the events that are recounted in the bulk of the film have taken place: the order-in-which-things-take-place is not the same as the order-in-which-we-witness-what-takes-place). What *is*, I would argue, central to narration is the element of telling: events in a piece of prose fiction come to us mediated through a retailing and organizing consciousness that puts them into words.

What this means is that built into the very fact of narrative is an act of looking back, of *recounting*. As the first-person narrator of Javier Marías's novel *Tomorrow in the Battle Think on Me* remarks: 'in fact, the person telling the story always tells it later on, which allows him to add things if he wants, to distance himself: "I have turned away my former self, I am not the thing I was nor the person I was, I neither know nor recognize myself. I did not seek it, I did not want it"' (Marías 1997, 308). Even though some theorists have pointed out that plays and films come to us via the organizing of a director – which is undeniable – what we see on stage or on screen 'is happening', while what we read in a novel is what someone *tells us* 'happened'.

Even though it is easy to make a distinction between prose fiction and drama, we often feel that novels contain very dramatic scenes, scenes that grip us with their immediacy. Reading such scenes, we may forget that what we learn of character and event is not experienced directly through a presentation or an enactment (as in the theatre or the cinema) but mediated through a particular telling, a narrative source. Take the opening of Henry James's short story 'The Lesson of the Master' (1888):

> *He had been told the ladies were at church, but this was corrected by what he saw from the top of the steps – they descended from a great height in two arms, with a circular sweep of the most charming effect – at the threshold of the door which, from the long bright gallery, overlooked the immense lawn.*

If our first impression is that we are witnessing a scene directly, a second glance will confirm that we are actually being *told* about the scene. The telling is such that we can visualize what is described – that is often the mark of an accomplished narrative – but we see what is first selected and then pointed out to us by a narrator or a narrative voice or source. Of course, this selection and presentation are fictional: the author is actually *creating* rather than selecting what we see. Nevertheless, as we read we are given the sense that the scene's potentially infinite complexity is reduced, ordered and explained to us through the organizing and filtering consciousness of a narrator. Imagine that we were presented with a filmed version of the above scene. Would we necessarily think of the ladies as forming 'two arms'? Would we find the effect of the 'circular sweep' 'most charming'? I will say more about the difference between film and prose narrative in Chapter 8.

One word of caution is needed at this point. You should be aware that the term 'narrative' can be used both with a narrow and specific meaning and also with a rather wider one. The narrower meaning restricts narrative to the telling of events, the recounting of things that happen. (Clearly events can just as well be mental as physical: a sudden dawning of insight is as much an event as is the outbreak of the First World War.)

The words 'tell' and 'recount' are both related to the action of counting, or enumerating (think of a bank teller, who counts money). As 'tell' is etymologically related to 'tale' we can say that behind the act of narrative itself lies the idea of communicating things that can be counted. (Compare the French *conte*, for which a brief definition is provided in the Glossary.) If we limit ourselves to such a narrow definition of narrative, therefore, we must remember that not everything in a novel is narrative. *Description* (of a beautiful scene) or *argument* (about, say, the existence of God) are neither of them examples of narrative in this strict sense; they do not involve the telling or enumerating of discrete events or countable entities. However, the term 'narrative' is also used in a wider sense to include everything that comes within the purview of a particular telling or recounting. From this perspective a novel is a narrative even though it contains passages of description and argument. If you think about it, much the same is true of our use of the word 'fiction'. After all, many statements in novels are literally true, yet we do not restrict use of the word 'fiction' to only those parts of novels that are untrue.

■ Characters, action, plot

The novel has *characters*, *action(s)* and a *plot*: it presents the reader with individuals who do things in a defining context or 'secondary world' (see p. 18) ruled over by some sort of connective logic: chronology, cause and effect, or whatever. In most novels we also find a connection between these three elements such that they form some sort of unity. A poem does not have to contain characters or a plot — or, indeed, any action — but it is only very rare novels which dispense with one of these elements, and in such unusual cases it is often a matter of dispute as to whether the net result is recognizable as a novel. Some recent narrative theorists have preferred to talk of *actors* rather than characters, pointing out that a work of science fiction might be based on roles filled by non-human participants.

We have of course to give the term 'action' a relatively broad meaning in the present context. Much recent fiction involves significant concentration upon what has been termed 'inner action': events taking place in a character's consciousness rather than in the social and physical worlds outside. It is nevertheless revealing that there are few novels that consist only, or mainly, of inner action. It is as if our view of the novel requires that it contain a significant amount of action more traditionally defined.

In Chapter 6, I will be talking about the important distinction between 'story' and 'plot' (see p. 111); at this stage I will limit myself to stating that the concept of plot involves some sense that the actions we have talked about represent a whole rather than merely a succession of unconnected events.

Here again care is needed, for, as my comments on the picaresque novel in the Glossary make clear, certain novels are characterized by a very *episodic* structure. Jerome J. McGann makes the interesting comment that '[Dickens's] early work is far more episodic than the later, so much so that many would be reluctant to call *Pickwick Papers* [1836–7] a novel at all' (McGann 1991, 82). It seems that nowadays readers tend to like their novels to have plots that unfold to reveal some principle of unity rather than episodes that merely succeed one another in an order that is without significance.

Ian Watt has argued that the novel is distinguished by the fact that unlike the works of the great English and Classical poets and dramatists, its plots are generally not taken from traditional sources (Watt 1963, 14). If we compare the modern novel with the prose fictions of antiquity, or the medieval romance, Watt's point is certainly justifiable. On the other hand even the modern novel has recourse to certain recurrent plots and story-lines (see the more extended discussion of plot on p. 111). As a result, many modern novels manifest an important and productive *tension* between their fidelity to the random and unpredictable nature of everyday life, and their patterning according to the demands of certain predetermined but widely different structures, from 'tragedy' to 'repetition' or 'the journey'. Novels can be written within traditions that are highly *formulaic* – that is, written to conform with a particular, pre-existing pattern. The popular romance of today with its shy blonde heroine who is finally appreciated by the good-looking hero after he has seen through the strikingly attractive but treacherous dark anti-heroine is but one in a long line of formulaic sub-genres that can be traced back to the folk tales of oral cultures.

■ Novel, short story, novella

Finally, the novel is of a certain length. A poem can be anything from a couplet to a thousand pages or more, but we feel unhappy about bestowing the term 'novel' on a tale of some forty or fifty pages. Of course it is not just a question of length: we feel that a novel should involve an investigation of an issue of human significance in such a manner as allows for complexity of treatment, and by common consent a certain length is necessary to allow for such complexity. In practice, therefore, we now usually refer to a prose narrative of some twenty or thirty pages or fewer as a short story, while a work that seems to hover on the awkward boundary between 'short story' and 'novel', having a length of between forty or fifty and a hundred pages, is conventionally described as a novella (plural: novelle or novellas). I say 'now', because some of these conventional categorizations are relatively recent, particularly so far as the short story and the novella are concerned, and some of the issues raised by dividing prose fiction into three main categories in this way are discussed more fully in Chapter 3.

In my next chapter I will discuss the case made by a number of recent literary historians that terms such as 'novel' and 'romance' achieved a fixity of meaning only in the nineteenth century. We need to remember that the same is true of terms such as 'novella' and 'short story' in the twentieth century. Moreover because the novel's rejection of traditional forms and conventions and its ability to respond to and incorporate aspects of the changing world around it into itself are fundamental to its existence, the novel is *generically* characterized by a permanent revolution of both its form and its content.

Topics for discussion

■ What elements *must* a novel contain to be a novel?
■ Is literary fiction different from other fictions? If so, in what ways?
■ Do you read novels to escape from 'the real world', or to learn more about it?
■ Does your reading ever make you see the real world differently, and behave differently in it?
■ Why do we classify novels and short stories as narratives?

2
History, genre, culture

Preview

This chapter deals with: ■ the problem of deciding *when* (and if) the novel was born
■ the relationship between the novel and the romance
■ the contribution of literacy, printing, a market economy and individualism to the novel
■ the novel, secularism and urban experience
■ the novel as a force for cultural centralization
■ the novel: an imperialist and masculine genre?

■ When was the novel born?

In the first two editions of this book I referred to the 'running debate' between those who see prose fiction as 'a universal and ancient form with a continuous history' (Novak 1991, 8), and those who prefer to emphasize the distinctiveness of the prose fiction which emerged in the early eighteenth century, and who speak of the novel as a new form which had its birth then. Even so, my account implied that although 'the novel' as category might be fuzzy round the edges, and might be in a state of permanent development and self-reconstruction, nevertheless this new literary genre emerged in the Europe of the late seventeenth and early eighteenth centuries and was clearly different from earlier forms such as that of the romance.

This, it has to be said, remains the consensus view. It is not without its opponents though, and recently the 'running debate' has heated up somewhat, especially following the publication of *The True Story of the Novel* (1996), a weighty study written by Margaret Anne Doody. Doody reminds her readers that the distinction between novel and romance is one that is not reflected in all languages in the way that it is in English, and she proposes that it 'has outworn its usefulness, and that at its most useful it created limitations and encouraged blind spots' (1996, xvii). For her, the novel 'as a form of literature in the West has a continuous history of about two thousand years', a fact which recent scholarship has denied or obscured (1996, 1). In order to press her case she advances a rather wider and more all-embracing definition of the novel from that which I quoted from the *OED* at the start of my first chapter; for her, a work is a novel if 'it is fictional, if it is in prose, and if it is of a certain length' (1996, 16).

A less extreme attack on the view that the novel emerges with Defoe, Richardson and Fielding is provided by J.A. Downie, who draws attention to the fact that 'writings calling themselves novels had been appearing in print in English for about a hundred and fifty years before the publication of *Robinson Crusoe* [in 1719]', and that while Richardson's *Pamela* did indeed lead to a sustained increase in the demand for fiction, Defoe's work did not (Downie 2000, 311, 325).

There is no doubt that, if one defines the novel as Doody recommends, then it is quite correct to see it as a literary form with a continuous history of two thousand years, and it is certainly the case that the term 'novel' did not emerge for the first time in the eighteenth century. It is also the case that we should avoid falling into the trap of believing that the works on modern literature syllabuses were the only ones read by and exerting influence on readers and writers, and that (as I have already suggested) we need to be aware that there are continuities and lines of tradition that cut across the sharp dividing lines posited by talk of 'the birth of the novel'.

Such provisos notwithstanding, I still believe that what happened to prose fiction in the course of the eighteenth century in Europe represents such a radical change that what to avoid debate we can call 'the modern novel' merits and repays separate study. As Michael McKeon points out, it was the first modern 'novelists' themselves who affirmed that 'a distinct new form' had emerged: Richardson believed he had introduced a new 'species' of writing while Fielding claimed a new 'kind' or 'province' (McKeon 1987, 410).

Discovering exactly how the modern novel did emerge is not a simple matter. In some ways it is a little like reading one of those historical accounts of the emergence of the human species; all sorts of near-misses occur, dead-ends of development peter out, and then – miraculously – all the required ingredients come together and human beings emerge. Just as researchers are still arguing about 'disputed ancestors' of the human species (are we or are we not descended from this particular ape-like creature, and do these fossil remains stem from a human being or something else?), so too literary critics and historians are by no means in total agreement about who the ancestors of the novel are, or, indeed, quite when the novel came into existence. (The argument about when apes end and humans begin is paralleled by arguments about whether various forms of early narrative should or should not be described as 'novels', while other texts are like the poor Neanderthals – almost there, but doomed to extinction.)

The 'running battle' I mention above involves, among other things, detailed debates about the extent to which those 'novel' works produced by writers such as Defoe, Richardson and Fielding in the first half of the eighteenth century were in direct line of descent from the chapbooks and the French fiction of the late seventeenth century, hundreds of which were translated into English and published in England at this time (Novak 1991, 8). Even those who concur with the view that the modern novel emerges as a new literary genre in the eighteenth century concede that it still owes much to traditions and works, literary and non-literary, from earlier times. No serious student of the novel would deny, for example, that its development in the eighteenth century was profoundly influenced by works such as François Rabelais's *Pantagruel* and *Gargantua* (1532 and 1534) and Miguel de Cervantes's *Don Quixote* (1605–15) – whether or not one agrees to describe these works as novels.

∎ Ancestors and close relations

As with the problems attendant upon tracing the emergence of *Homo sapiens*, claims concerning parentage are often controversial. One of the things which sets the novel apart from many other literary genres is its ability to incorporate the most disparate elements from human life and experience. It would be a serious mistake to assume that to trace the novel's descent we need to examine only a sequence of written forms, or of oral and written narratives. We should rather picture a family tree in which certain lines of descent involve various written forms, certain involve a succession of oral narrative forms, but others involve a wide range of very different elements: introspective self-analyses, both in diary and in unrecorded form; joke-telling; sermons; travel accounts; letters. What distinguishes the novel is, among other things, the heterogeneity of its ancestry, a heterogeneity that Mikhail Bakhtin has argued is mirrored in the variety of different 'voices' to be found in any single novel. He claims (and this is by no means uncontroversial) that, however many contradictions and conflicts are developed in a poem, the world of poetry is always illuminated by 'one unitary and indisputable discourse'. The novel, in contrast, is he argues characterized by that 'variety of individualized voices' that is 'the prerequisite for authentic novelistic prose' (Bakhtin 1981, 286). It should be noted that the term 'voice' has more than a physical reference for Bakhtin, and includes ideological and existential elements too.

One of the impulses that often moves those who compile family trees is a desire to prove that all the discovered ancestors were respectable and legitimate. In the case of the novel, we have to be prepared to accept that many of its ancestors were neither. As J. Paul Hunter has put it:

> *I join the debate here by arguing that the emerging novel must be placed in a broader context of cultural history, insisting that popular thought and materials of everyday print – journalism, didactic materials with all kinds of religious and ideological directions, and private papers and histories – need to be seen as contributors to the social and intellectual world in which the novel emerged. (Hunter 1990, 5)*

Fictional narratives can be found almost as far back as we have written records, but these lack many of the characteristics that today we associate with the modern novel. First, they are often in verse rather than prose. Second, they do not concern themselves with 'the real life of past or present times' but portray the experiences of those whose lives can only be said to resemble 'real life', however it is defined, in extremely convention-governed and indirect ways (gods or mythical heroes, for example). Third, their characters tend not to be individualized – to the extent that even the use of our familiar term 'character' is problematic. (We do not feel too comfortable calling a purely stereotyped or conventionally portrayed individual a character precisely because today the term 'character' is associated with *distinctive* traits, with some particularity or individuality.)

The etymology of 'character' is very revealing: the word comes from a Greek word for an instrument used for marking or engraving, just as 'style' is etymologically related to the word stylus and is also associated with a cutting instrument. As a result, the word's literal meanings – as the *OED* will confirm – are related to marks that distinguish and represent individuality (think of the obsolescent use of the word to mean a person's handwriting). From this we get the familiar *OED* definition: 'A personality invested with distinctive attributes and qualities, by a novelist or dramatist.' Our sense of human individuality, this etymology suggests, is closely related to making marks – to *writing*. Writing allows human beings to develop individualities, to be and to know themselves to be different, particular, unique.

■ Novel and romance

There is no better example of the problems attendant upon generic classification than those connected with the *romance*, universally agreed to represent one of the most important traditions contributing to the emergence of the novel. (The term 'roman', as Margaret Anne Doody reminds us (see p. 11) is the equivalent of 'novel' in many modern European languages. Etymologically the two terms tell different stories; while the word 'novel' comes from the Italian 'novella' – 'small new thing' – the word 'romance' evolves from a word denoting a concern with the Romans. Even in modern usage this sense of the novel looking forward to the new and the romance looking back to the old can be detected.)

The traditional chivalric romance which developed in twelfth-century France depicted not epic heroes but a highly stylized and idealized courtly life founded upon rigid but sophisticated conventions of behaviour. Like the epic (which it displaced) it often involved supernatural elements – another factor which in general terms distinguishes it from the modern novel. The distinction with which we are familiar is first commented upon in the eighteenth century, the century in which, I have argued, the novel appears in its recognizable modern form in England. Geoffrey Day quotes the following from a review of Frances Burney's novel *Camilla*, which appeared in *The British Critic* of November 1796:

> *To the old romance, which exhibited exalted personages, and displayed their sentiments in improbable or impossible situations, has succeeded the more reasonable, modern novel; which delineates characters drawn from actual observation, and, when ably executed, presents an accurate and captivating view of real life. (Day 1987, 6)*

As Day notes, 'throughout the eighteenth century "romance" was seen by many as a term suggesting excessive flights of fancy' (1987, 6), and he quotes a number of examples of such a usage. He goes on to point out that this neat definition, one which served to distinguish the romance from the novel, was not universally accepted: many writers tended to lump the two terms together relatively uncritically. He comments:

> [T]hough there is a tradition of clarity of definition, there is vastly more evidence to show that those works now commonly referred to as 'eighteenth-century novels' were not perceived as such by the readers or indeed by the major writers of the period, and that, far from being ready to accept the various works as 'novels', they do not appear to have arrived at a consensus that works such as Robinson Crusoe, Pamela, Joseph Andrews, Clarissa, Tom Jones, Peregrine Pickle and Tristram Shandy were even all of the same species. (1987, 7)

(In case we should be tempted to feel superior to these dull individuals who were incapable of recognizing the birth of a new genre, it is salutary to stop and think about the enormous formal variety that this list of works represents.)

In an extract from a letter written by the eighteenth-century man of politics Lord Chesterfield to his son, we can detect both the familiar novel–romance distinction and also a sense that the two categories overlap to a considerable extent.

> I am in doubt whether you know what a Novel is: it is a little gallant history, which must contain a great deal of love, and not exceed one or two small volumes. The subject must be a love affair; the lovers are to meet with many difficulties and obstacles, to oppose the accomplishment of their wishes, but at last overcome them all; and the conclusion or catastrophe must leave them happy. A Novel is a kind of abbreviation of a Romance; for a Romance generally consists of twelve volumes, all filled with insipid love nonsense, and most incredible adventures.
>
> . . .
>
> In short, the reading of Romances is a most frivolous occupation, and time merely thrown away. The old Romances, written two or three hundred years ago, such as Amadis of Gaul, Orlando the Furious, and others, were stuffed with enchantments, magicians, giants, and such sort of impossibilities, whereas the more modern Romances keep within the bounds of possibility, but not of probability. (Carey 1912, 90; the original letter is in French, and is probably written 1740–1)

Geoffrey Day points out that in his *Dictionary* (1755), Samuel Johnson also insisted on the importance of length, defining a novel as 'A small tale, generally of love'. Today Samuel Richardson's *Clarissa* (1747–8) is uncontroversially defined as a novel, but it is certainly *not* a 'small tale'; at the same time, Johnson's own small tale *Rasselas* (1759) cannot comfortably be assimilated into what we now think of as a novel. It is arguably only in the early years of the nineteenth century that our present understanding of what a novel is starts to emerge as a consensus view.

Although the development of the English novel is generally associated with a concern with the everyday and a rejection of the supernatural, those aspects of the romance that were repressed as the novel defined itself did not disappear from fiction altogether. Freudians claim that the repressed always returns, and the history of prose fiction would seem to confirm this: the fantastic, the super-natural, the other-worldly (whether defined in religious or in astronomical terms) constitute the novel's dogged shadow. Sometimes this family of repressed elements emerges within what we can call mainstream fiction in hints and suggestions (madness, dreams and fevered hallucinations are a favoured way of introducing the supernatural into fiction without directly challenging a realistic framework). At the same time this family of excluded romance com-ponents also survives in what we can call sub-genres such as the modern romance or the ghost story. As I will argue later on, it is noticeable how some of the elements excluded from what I have termed mainstream fiction suddenly reappear in forms associated with the electronic media. There are clear and, I think, undeniable lines of descent from the medieval romance through the gothic novel to fantasy games such as 'Dungeons and Dragons' and computer games such as *Tomb Raider* (for more discussion of this, see Chapter 5).

However, even if fantastic and romance elements survive in the novel, there is no doubt that an emphasis upon the this–worldly is fundamental to the novel's emergence as a major genre, and at the time of the birth of the modern novel in the early and mid-eighteenth century this emphasis was widely believed by contemporary readers to distinguish the novel from the romance. Geoffrey Day cites another useful contemporary definition that again defines the novel by contrasting it to the romance, from Samuel Johnson's fourth *Rambler* essay (1750). Johnson clearly has in mind what we now call the novel in these comments, but by labelling what we would now call the novel 'the comedy of romance', he defines it in relation to the traditional romance.

> *The works of fiction, with which the present generation seems more particularly delighted, are such as exhibit life in its true state, diversified only by accidents that daily happen in the world, and influenced by passions and qualities which are really to be found in conversing with mankind.*
>
> *This kind of writing may be termed not improperly the comedy of romance, and is to be conducted nearly by the rules of comic poetry. Its province is to bring about natural events by easy means, and to keep up curiosity without the help of wonder: it is therefore precluded from the machines and expedients of the heroic romance, and can neither employ giants to snatch away a lady from the nuptial rites, nor knights to bring her back from captivity; it can neither bewilder its personages in desarts, nor lodge them in imaginary castles.*
>
> ...
>
> *The task of our present writers is very different; it requires, together with that learning which is to be gained from books, that experience which can never be attained by solitary diligence, but must arise from general converse, and accurate observation of the living world.*

This is what was seen to be new about the fictional narratives written by Defoe, Richardson and Fielding, whether or not these works were called novels. 'Life in its true state', 'accurate observation of the living world': these narratives have a relationship with _ordinary_ life, with the _detail_ of _contemporary_ experience, both social and individual, which sets them apart from the romance. Michael Seidel sums up these characteristics as follows: 'a concentration on daily life in particularized settings; a sense of information and immediacy; conventions of behaviour that would appear, at least to a reading audience, as part of its recognizable world' (Seidel 2000, 194).

It is true that fictions that deal with the other-worldly, with giants and castles and 'machines' and heroic expedients, have kept on being written since Johnson made his comment. As I have suggested, there is a line of descent that can be drawn from the romance through the gothic novel and science fiction and, in more recent times, to sub-genres such as the fantastic and cyberpunk. Nevertheless, as I shall argue below, this line of descent is generally recognized to be peripheral to what I have termed the mainstream novel.

Michael McKeon points out that 'even though Defoe, Richardson, and Fielding explicitly subvert the idea and ethos of romance, they nonetheless draw upon many of its stock situations and conventions', and he suggests that the 'general problem of romance in all three novelists is related to the particular problem of spirituality, equally antithetical to the secularizing premises of formal realism, in Defoe'. In addition, McKeon draws attention to the fact that the romance exhibits certain characteristics of formal realism, and that it continues to co-exist with the novel during the period of the latter's emergence (McKeon 1987, 2–3). J. Paul Hunter too has warned against drawing too absolute a distinction between the novel and the romance.

> _We do the novel – and not only the early novel – a disservice if we fail to notice, once we have defined the different world from romance that novels represent, how fully it engages the unusual, the uncertain, and the unexplainable. When we admit such concerns as part of the novel's territory, it also allows us to see more clearly where the novel came from, for the novel is only the most successful of a series of attempts to satisfy, in a context of scientific order, the itch for news and new things that are strange and surprising._
>
> _A closely related feature involves the novel's engagement with taboos. Operating from a position of semi-respectability from the start, the novel has always been self-conscious about appearing to be pornographic, erotic, or obscene. (Hunter 1990, 35)_

That contrast and tension between 'semi-respectability' and the 'pornographic, erotic, [and] obscene' is, if not a standard feature of the novel, certainly one of its recurrent features: the novel typically presents us not just with the ordinary but also with the extraordinary, the hidden and the repressed, which are to be found concealed in, or behind, the ordinary, the conventional and the everyday. Michael Seidel again has a useful comment, noting that, while it is true that paradigms of romance such as victimage, forbearance and rescue remain entrenched in the realist fiction that emerges in the form of the modern novel, 'what is removed are those generic parts of romance that define causality and circumstance by forces inapplicable to the world of conventional experience' (Seidel 2000, 196).

Before passing on, I would like draw your attention to a couple of terms used by Hunter: 'different world' and 'territory'. In the course of a discussion of fiction and the electronic media later on in this book I will consider the concepts of 'textual world' and 'simulated world' provided by two commentators on 'electronic fiction' (see p. 74). What readers seem always to require of a work of fiction is that it provide such a 'world', a *space* within which characters can move that is governed by a clear, coherent and consistent set of rules and conventions. In realistic fiction the world concerned is very much like the reader's, even though it may be removed in time, space or culture from his or hers. In fantasy, the ghost story, science fiction or cyberfiction, the world we encounter is very different from that of the reader – although the two may share certain important common elements. But however different, it must offer the reader a sense of inner consistency. Neil Cornwell provides a useful comment taken from T.E. Little's *The Fantasts*:

> *All writers of creative fiction are subcreators of Secondary Worlds. The secondary world of a non-fantastic writer will be as close to the Primary World as his talents and the needs of his art will allow. . . . A licence is granted to writers of 'normal' creative fiction to change the Primary World for the purpose of their art. Fantasy begins when an author's Secondary World goes beyond that license and becomes 'other'. . . . Such a creation should be called a* Tertiary World. *(Cornwell 1990, 16, quoting from Little 1984, 9–10)*

Cornwell himself notes that Mary Shelley's *Frankenstein* (1818) can be seen as a key text, because in it religion has been replaced by science as the basis of a reality different from the everyday, a suggestion worth thinking about when you read my later comments on the novel and secularism (p. 28). Cornwell also suggests that we should see fiction in terms of a continuum that can be split into two. The first half-continuum is 'mimesis dominated'. It moves from *non-fiction* to *faction* to *realism* to *uncanny realism* to the *fantastic–uncanny* and ends in the *pure fantastic*. The second half-continuum takes up from the *pure fantastic* and moves through the *fantastic–marvellous* to the *marvellous* and ends up in *mythology* (Cornwell 1990, 39). The proposed continuum is thought-provoking, but we should remember that many novels mix realistic and – say – supernatural elements. Think for example how many suggestions of the supernatural there are in Emily Brontë's *Wuthering Heights*, a novel that is also full of very specific references to a world of concrete objects and social realities.

The supernatural in Brontë's novel is often associated with dreams (Lockwood's and Cathy's) and superstition (the belief of the locals that Heathcliff 'walks' after his death, reported by Lockwood in the novel's closing pages). What is I think important is that nowhere in Brontë's text is there unambiguous evidence of the existence of the supernatural or the ghostly.

At this point I am conscious of the voice of an imaginary reader of this book, a student of literature who makes the following complaint. 'During my study of the novel and shorter fiction I have read Horace Walpole's *The Castle of Otranto* (1765), in which a key role is played by a ghost; Feodor Dostoyevsky's "The Double" (1846), in which the hero Golyadkin encounters his double, who takes over his life bit by bit and is treated as the "real" Golyadkin; Robert Louis Stevenson's *Dr Jekyll and Mr Hyde* (1886), in which the hero alternates between a good and a bad identity; Oscar Wilde's *The Picture of Dorian Gray* (1891), in which a man escapes the ageing process while his picture depicts a representation of an older and older man; Henry James's *The Turn of the Screw* (1898), in which the ghosts of two dead servants seduce two young children; Franz Kafka's "Metamorphosis" (1912), which opens with the hero discovering that he has turned into a giant insect; C.S. Lewis's *The Lion, The Witch and the Wardrobe* (1950), in which children go through their wardrobe into a magic world and meet a talking lion who is sacrificed but who returns to life; Philip K. Dick's "We Can Remember it for you Wholesale" (1966), which is set in a future world in which false memories can be purchased and implanted in the mind so that they are believed to be real; and Angela Carter's *The Bloody Chamber* (1979), which contains short stories that blend fairy-tale elements with real-world settings. How can you claim that the novel is to be distinguished from medieval romance because it presents us with our familiar, everyday world rather than impossible situations and enchanted worlds?'

I think that my response to this challenge would go something like this.

- Some of the works cited are generally categorized in a way that draws attention to their divergence from mainstream fiction – for example: 'the gothic novel', 'the ghost story', 'science fiction', 'magic realism' (see the Glossary for more on some of these terms). The very need so to categorize them suggests that we do not expect such elements in the mainstream novel.
- Many of the works referred to are short stories or novellas, and shorter fiction does seem more likely to contain fantastic or non-realistic elements (see p. 53 for a discussion of this).
- *The Lion, The Witch and the Wardrobe* is a story written for children, and romance and fantastic elements have survived in much stronger form in children's literature. Fairy stories, for example, are nowadays told mainly to children.
- In a number of the works named, the supernatural or fantastic occurrence is hinted at or presented as a possibility, but alternative, realistic explanations

are possible (Golyadkin is actually going mad and imagining his double, just as the governess imagines the ghosts in *The Turn of the Screw*; Dr. Jekyll's transformation is caused by science not magic; the implantation of memories *could* be possible in a future, technologically advanced world).

■ Finally, even where the events are fantastic, they may cause us to think about very this-worldly things. 'Metamorphosis' shows how people respond to chronic illness; 'We Can Remember it for you Wholesale' causes us to consider whether illusions can be as satisfying as reality; the stories in *The Bloody Chamber* remind us how many attitudes to gender are based on the highly stereotyped and discriminatory models found in the traditional fairy stories that are told to children. These stories thus still refer back to the everyday, rather than constituting an escape from the everyday in the manner of the medieval romance.

■ Life and pattern

In his excellent introductory book on the novel, the critic Arnold Kettle suggests that most novelists show a bias towards either 'life' or 'pattern' in their approach to writing: towards, in other words, either the aim to convey the vividness, the particularized sensations and experiences of living, or that of conveying some interpretation of the significance of life. According to Kettle, the novelist who starts with pattern often tries to 'inject' life into it, while the novelist who starts with life tries to make a pattern emerge out of it. He relates these two very general tendencies to, on the one hand, such sources and influences as the parables of the Bible, the morality plays of the Middle Ages, and the sermons which common people listened to every Sunday ('pattern'), and on the other hand, the seventeenth- and early eighteenth-century prose journalism and pamphleteering of such as Thomas Nashe and Daniel Defoe (who, we should remember, was a political journalist before he wrote prose fiction). As Kettle says of such writers, the germ of their books is never an idea, never an abstract concept; they are 'less consciously concerned with the moral significance of life than with its surface texture' (Kettle 1967, 20). Michael McKeon makes a similar point, arguing that in tracing the emergence of the early modern novel we detect a recurrent formal tension between 'what might be called the individual life and the overarching pattern' (McKeon 1987, 90).

In her essay 'Phases of Fiction', Virginia Woolf uses terms similar to those to be found in Kettle's later comments in explaining what she sees to be a fundamental tension within the genre of the novel:

> *For the most characteristic qualities of the novel – that it registers the slow growth and development of feeling, that it follows many lives and traces their unions and fortunes over a long stretch of time – are the very qualities that are most incompatible with design and order. It is the gift of style, arrangement, construction, to put us at a distance from the special life and*

to obliterate its features; while it is the gift of the novel to bring us into close touch with life. The two powers fight if they are brought into combination. The most complete novelist must be the novelist who can balance the two powers so that the one enhances the other. (Woolf 1966b, 101)

It is perhaps the mark of the greatest novels that with them it is most difficult to say whether or not the novelist has tried more to convey what Kettle calls 'life' and 'pattern' and Woolf calls 'design and order' and 'life', for both seem so consummately present.

■ The 'rise of the novel'

Let us return to the issue of that disputed birth date. In discussing 'the rise of the novel', to adopt the title of Ian Watt's influential study, there are two dangers involved which need to be confronted straight away. The first we can call the 'wisdom of hindsight' issue: the phrase conjures up a sort of hatching process in which an infant species emerges, small and weak perhaps, but with its whole future development laid out ahead of it. The second and related danger is that what we, retrospectively, see as an emergent species was actually many different things which are related only to the extent that they have all contributed to a later and more well-defined genre. Michael McKeon argues that 'the novel' is:

a deceptively monolithic category that encloses a complex historical process. It attains its modern, 'institutional' stability and coherence at this time because of its unrivaled power both to formulate, and to explain, a set of problems that are central to early modern experience. (McKeon 1987, 20)

These problems, according to McKeon, encompass both generic and social categories: questions about how to tell the truth in narrative ('questions of truth'), and questions about 'how the external social order is related to the internal, moral state of its members' ('questions of virtue'). McKeon sees a double process in the emergence of the novel: on the one hand, the change from what he calls 'romance idealism' or 'a dependence on received authorities and a priori traditions' to a 'naive empiricism' based upon a more empirical epistemology; on the other hand, the change from 'a relatively stratified social order supported by a reigning world view' that McKeon calls 'aristocratic ideology' to what he refers to as a more 'progressive ideology' which is itself later challenged by a 'conservative ideology' (1987, 21).

Most of those concerned to map and to explain the development of the modern novel are agreed in singling out certain factors crucial to this development. Of these the following are perhaps the most important.

Literacy

The novel emerged, and has developed, as a written form – unlike poetry, which existed for centuries prior to the development of writing and still flourishes in oral cultures today. There have been cases of illiterate people gathering to hear novels read; part of Dickens's audience was of this sort. It is also the case that many novels and short stories are presented as if they were written transpositions of oral deliveries, of spoken tellings. (See the discussion of the term *skaz* in the Glossary.) Nonetheless, the novel is typically *written* by one individual in private and *read silently* by another individual who has no personal relationship with the author. Michael McKeon points out that the development of literacy helps to encourage the growth of 'empirical attitudes' which in their turn encourage 'a more skeptical approach to the authenticity of saints' relics and a more rationalistic interpretation of the figurative status of the Eucharist' (1987, 35). Equally if not more important, I suspect, is the fact that silent reading is private and non-collective and thus helps the novel to mediate and express the new individualism of early capitalism while at the same time allowing easier access to the fantasy life.

It is surely not accidental that there was a rapid growth of literacy in the English-speaking world from 1600 to 1800, and that whereas in 1600 it is estimated that about 25 per cent of adult males in England and Wales could read, by 1800 the figure is probably between 60 and 70 per cent (Hunter 1990, 65–6). Although the figures for female literacy lag behind those for male literacy, more and more women too could read during this period.

Printing

The modern novel is the child of the printing press, which alone can produce the vast numbers of copies needed to satisfy a literate public at a price that it can afford. Michael McKeon points out that a number of different factors conspire to assist the development of printing – technological, social and legal:

> By the close of the seventeenth century England had become a major producer of paper, type, and various kinds of publication, a development that could not have occurred without the abolition of protectionist printing legislation. By the middle of the eighteenth, licensing laws had been replaced by copyright laws; the commodification of the book market as a mass-production industry had become organized around the mediating figure of the bookseller; and the idea that a writer should get paid for his work was gaining currency on the strength of the perception that there was a growing mass of consumers willing to foot the bill. On the other hand, these new consumers of print were also produced by print – most obviously by the early modern 'educational revolution', which received a great stimulus from the invention of the press and played the central role in raising the levels of literacy in England. (McKeon 1987, 51)

J. Paul Hunter sums up as follows: 'From the beginning, moreover, novels were artifacts of the world of print. They had been conceived that way, and they lent themselves readily to the physical, social, and psychological circumstances that affected potential readers of printed books' (Hunter 1990, 41). Later on in this book I shall consider the argument that it is the design of the physical book that imposes linear narrative on the novel, and that the growth of the electronic media is able to 'liberate' fiction from linear narrative (see p. 71).

One of the things that print brought with it was a change in the relationship between reader and writer: print allows for a more impersonal, even anonymous writing – but one that, paradoxically, by cutting the reader off from a known writer, allows him or her to feel that the reading of a novel is a personal, even intimate experience. As I have said, the novel is read *in private* by an individual. When we attend a play's performance it is hard to be unaware of how other members of the audience are reacting, and our reactions also have an effect on those around us. J. Paul Hunter has noted the novel's liking for the confessional and the exhibitionistic (Hunter 1990, 37); the problem pages of popular magazines will remind us that confession and self-exposure are often easier through the impersonal medium of print.

Print did not succeed oral delivery in one fell swoop; David Margolies points out that the manuscript circulation of written work represented a sort of in-between stage, and 'provided a model for the literary relationships of the early novelists' (Margolies 1985, 23). Margolies notes that writing for anonymous readers presented writers with a new set of problems, and he quotes from Austen Saker's *Narbonus* (1580):

> *and he must write well that shall please all minds: but he that planteth trees in a Forest, knoweth not how many shall taste the Fruit, and he that soweth in his garden divers Seeds, knoweth not who shall eat of his Sallets. He that planteth a Vine, knoweth not who shall taste his Wine: and he that putteth any thing in Print, must think that all will peruse it: If then amongst many blossoms, some prove blasts, no marvel if amongst many Readers, some prove Riders. (Margolies 1985, 24)*

Compare this to the opening words of Chapter 1 of Henry Fielding's *Tom Jones* (1749): 'An author ought to consider himself, not as a gentleman who gives a private or eleemosynary [i.e. charitable] treat, but rather as one who keeps a public ordinary [i.e. a public house], at which all persons are welcome for their money.' The relationship between the writer of a novel and its reader is, then, typically impersonal and commercial, rather than one based on personal acquaintance and friendship. This is such a familiar state of affairs for us today that we pay no attention to it: for us, it is a matter of note if we *do* know the author of a book we are reading. We should remember that this situation is historically new and is associated with the development of printing.

Novelists thus had to learn how to become adept at convincing their readers that they were in intimate contact with a narrator who was interested in them as individuals. As J. Paul Hunter argues:

> *[The novel's] rejection of familiar plots, conventional mythic settings, and recognizable character types represents a recognition that its future lies in developing a new kind of relationship with new combinations of readers.*
>
> . . .
>
> *One audience-related feature involves the novel's tendency both to probe and promote loneliness and solitariness, rather ironic in view of the novel's expressed design to portray people in their societal context. If the tendency to expose secrets of personal life points one way, the tendency to enclose the self, to treat the self as somehow inviolable and insistently separate in spite of the publication of secrets once thought too personal to articulate, points the other. (Hunter 1990, 39)*

Hunter makes the astute point that this may well be why the novel, although born in another time, is so well placed to represent some central experiences that first emerge in the twentieth century: a concern with subjectivity, isolation and loneliness (Hunter 1990, 41–2).

As David Margolies claims, writers did not necessarily learn the new ways of writing that we associate with print without difficulty; early printed works often show signs of a still-flourishing oral tradition, and J. Paul Hunter has argued that the first modern novels 'had their relevant contexts – ultimately even their origins – in a culture that was partly oral and partly written, where functions traditionally performed in communal and family rituals and by oral tradition more and more fell to the impersonal processes of print' (Hunter 1990, xvii). We should not look upon this as a disadvantage: the novel still owes much of its richness to the importation of techniques and perspectives from oral delivery. From its earliest days the novel has been able to make readers think that they are hearing a voice when they are actually reading print, and the gains of verisimilitude and dramatic immediacy that this has meant are considerable. One of the striking characteristics of many novels written in the twentieth and twenty-first centuries by writers from the working class of industrialized societies and by writers from newly independent ex-colonies is that oral rhythms and structures are taken from a rich heritage of non-literary traditions. Take the opening of Jack Common's semi-autobiographical novel, *Kiddar's Luck* (1951):

> *She was a fool, of course, my mother. Her mother said so: 'Bella is a fool, I'm afraid, a weak fool. Here she is marrying a common workman, one who drinks and is not a good Christian. She will never know happiness now.' You would think the old lady was great shakes herself to hear her. And she was in her way. Not that she had any money ever, but she made poverty respectable.*

The intimate relationship established here between writer and reader feeds off a living tradition of oral storytelling at the same time that it exploits the potentialities inherent in the privacy and anonymity central to the reader–writer relationship associated with the novel.

Market economy

The 'sociology of the novel' is based very much upon a market relationship between author and reader mediated through publishers. In contrast to earlier methods of financing publication or supporting authors such as _patronage_ (a rich patron would support a writer while a book was being written) or _subscription_ (rich potential readers would subscribe money to support a writer in order that a particular work might be written), a market economy increases the relative freedom and isolation of the writer and decreases his or her immediate dependence upon particular individuals, groups or interests (although, of course, it makes him or her _more_ dependent upon publishers and, especially, sales). The growth of a market economy is an integral aspect of the rise of capitalism – the socio-economic system which had displaced feudalism in Britain by the eighteenth century. In his book _The Rise of the Novel_ (1957), Ian Watt argued that there is a close relationship between the rise of the novel and the rise of the middle class – the class most involved in the triumph of capitalism in Britain. In different ways literacy, printing and a market economy can all be related to the growing dominance of capitalism in the period during which the novel emerges.

Michael McKeon draws attention to the debate in Cervantes's _Don Quixote_ between Don Quixote and Sancho Panza about whether the latter should receive 'favours' or 'wages', suggesting that the relationship between these two characters thus 'mediates the historical transition from feudalism to capitalism' (McKeon 1987, 283). J. Paul Hunter has gone further and has suggested that crucial to the development of the new genre in England is the confrontation between 'a Protestant, capitalistic, imperial, insecure, restless, bold, and self-conscious culture' and 'a constrictive, authoritarian, hierarchical, and too-neatly-sorted past' (Hunter 1990, 7).

Capitalism is of course founded on competition, and from its earliest days the novel is concerned with conflict. The novel's portrayal of confrontations between individuals very often has a representative quality, pointing in the direction of larger social, historical or cultural rivalries. This is significant in terms of not just the content of novels but also (and this of course is not a separate issue) their readership. Novels appealed to groups of individuals who were emerging into new prominence and increased power: women and young people, for example. Hunter points out that from its earliest days the novel has been particularly concerned with 'the crises of the decisive moments in adolescence and early adulthood' (Hunter 1990, 43). A novel such as Jane Rule's splendid _Memory Board_ (1987), which focuses on characters who are old and tackling senility, has few parallels before the twentieth century.

The novel and the individual

Ian Watt sees as typical of the novel that it includes 'individualization of ... characters and ... the detailed presentation of their environment'. Unlike

many of the narratives that precede it, the novel does not just present us with
'type' characters; we are interested in Tom Jones, David Copperfield, Maggie
Tulliver and Paul Morel as distinct individuals with personal qualities and
idiosyncrasies. As Ralph Fox puts it, somewhat tendentiously:

> *The novel deals with the individual, it is the epic of the struggle of the
> individual against society, against nature, and it could only develop in a
> society where the balance between man and society was lost, where man was
> at war with his fellows or with nature. Such a society is capitalist society.*
> *(Fox 1979, 44)*

Fox exemplifies his argument by contrasting the *Odyssey* with *Robinson Crusoe*
(1719), pointing out that, whereas Odysseus lives in a society without history
and knows that his fate is in the hands of the gods, Robinson Crusoe is
prepared to make his own history. Furthermore, whereas Odysseus's efforts
are directed towards returning *home*, for Crusoe it is the outward and not the
homeward trip that is important; he is 'the man who challenges nature and
wins'. Crusoe is thus, for Fox, representative of that spirit of expansionism,
self-reliance and experimentation that characterizes early capitalist man.

It certainly seems to be the case that the new spirit that accompanies the
early development of capitalism infuses the emerging novel. Along with a
stress on individualism goes, too, a growing concern with the inner self, the
private life, subjective experience. As the individual *feels* him- or herself an
individual rather than a member of a static feudal community with duties and
characteristics which are endowed at birth, then he or she starts more to think
in terms of having certain personal rather than shared communal interests.
This gives the individual something to *hide*. Without wishing to oversimplify
an extremely complex and far from uniform historical development, we can
say that in a certain sense the private life as we know it today is born with
capitalist society, and that the novel both responds and contributes to this
development.

It doubtless seems very odd to many readers to claim that people have not
always felt themselves to be individuals in the way that modern men and
women from developed societies do, and indeed this assertion has been
challenged by a number of recent writers, including Margaret Anne Doody
in her *The True Story of the Novel*. Other commentators have detected
Eurocentric and even racist attitudes behind the assumption that those from
non–literate cultures are not 'individuals' in the way that those from modern
developed cultures are.

Fictional works do nevertheless offer strong evidence to support the view
that people from non-literate cultures perceive themselves and their
individuality rather differently from the way in which those from literate
cultures do. (A classic case for this view is made by A.R. Luria in his book
Cognitive Development (1976).) In an important study, *Form, Individuality and
the Novel* (1990), Clemens Lugowski examines a number of much earlier
fictional works dating from the sixteenth and early seventeenth centuries,

including the anonymous *Eine schöne Historie von den vier Heymonskindern*, Georg Wickram's *Amadis*, the stories known as *Thyl Ulenspiegel*, and the novellas of the *Decameron*. He concludes that these works contain nothing that might be referred to as an 'individual'.

One of the things that the novel both reflects and helps to establish – in the form which it assumes from Defoe onwards – is a fundamental belief that what a person *is* goes beyond what that person *says or does*. We believe, today, that our identity exceeds what is observable to others. According to both Lugowski and Luria, not all human beings share or have shared this belief, and Lugowski argues that prior to the emergence of the modern novel, a view of fictional individuals as more 'components of a whole' than 'genuinely autonomous individuals' (what we might call types rather than real characters) means that fictional characters as we understand them did not exist (Lugowski 1990, 83). Lugowski's argument assumes that the ability to distinguish oneself from the world in which one lives is not universal, and that its gradual emergence encourages and takes support from the emergence of the novel in its modern form. He argues that 'when the autobiographer explicitly *wishes* to describe his own life, and yet then describes the world outside, then what this means is that his life really *is* the world' (Lugowski 1990, 155; compare Luria 1976, Chapter 7: 'Self-Analysis and Self-Awareness'). Moreover, Lugowski suggests that it is when human beings begin to question their 'position in and profound commitment to the world' that an individuality that involves seeing oneself as separate from the world can emerge (Lugowski 1990, 176).

Similarly, in his essay 'Forms of Time and of the Chronotope in the Novel', Mikhail Bakhtin says of the work of Rabelais (which he much admires), that in it 'life has absolutely no *individual* aspect. A human being is completely external.' He continues:

> For indeed, there is not a single instance in the entire expanse of Rabelais' huge novel where we are shown what a character is thinking, what he is experiencing, his internal dialogue. In this sense there is in Rabelais' novel no world of interiority. (Bakhtin 1981, 239)

Of all literary genres the novel most consummately unites an exploration of the subjective and the social, of the private and the collective. It is this combination of the broadest social and historical sweep with the most acute and penetrating visions of the hidden, private life, *and their interconnections*, that is characteristic of the novel and at the heart of its power and continuing life. Paradoxically, although the novel is both written and read in private, it relies upon a highly organized society and industry to produce and circulate it. Even in its sociology it combines the personal and the social, that combination that is at the heart of its aesthetic.

This is not to say that the novel is able critically and analytically to portray all human organizations and groups as well as it can represent and explore the individual. Brook Thomas has, indeed, suggested that 'the generic demands of the novel seem to guarantee that novelistic representations of corporations will lag behind the way in which other forms of discourse have been able to respond to the rise of corporations' (Thomas 1991, 150), implying that the novel is generically unfitted to portray and examine human beings in certain of their collectivities.

The novel and secularism

When we say that *secularism* is crucial to the development of the novel this is not to imply that a novel may not explore religious themes or be underpinned by a religious imperative. It does mean, though, that the modern novel emerges in a world in which people were more and more likely to try to find non-supernatural explanations for the problems which they faced, and that this cast of mind is reflected in the novel. Milan Kundera remarks: 'As God slowly departed from the seat whence he had directed the universe and its order of values, distinguished good from evil, and endowed each thing with meaning, Don Quixote set forth from his house into a world he could no longer recognize' (Kundera 1988, 6).

Even today, when a novelist wishes to make a religious point, he or she is typically encouraged by the conventions of the genre to set it in a context of secular explanation. Thus when a character in David Lodge's *Small World* (1984) prays for help when faced with the imminent task of delivering a conference paper which he has not yet written, his prayer is answered by a sudden outbreak of Legionnaires' Disease that requires that the conference be abandoned, and the reader is allowed to read this as either divine intervention or a fortunate coincidence. It is true that there are novels which encourage the reader to imagine supernatural occurrences and fantastic worlds different from our own (the gothic novel, science fiction, magic realism – see the definitions in the Glossary), but it is striking how consistently such novels hedge their bets by allowing for non-supernatural explanations or interpretations of what happens. It is for this reason, among others, that modern readers tend to find the novels of Ann Radcliffe more acceptable than they do her near-contemporary William Beckford's *Vathek* (1787), in which the supernatural interventions allow for no natural explanation.

In his book *Atlas of the European Novel 1800–1900* (1998), Franco Moretti repeats Robert Darnton's point that, as 'virtually all book historians agree', 'the publication of fiction developed, throughout Western Europe, at the expense of devotion'. He adds that this leaves a question: 'did the novel replace devotional literature because it was a *fundamentally secular form* – or because it was *religion under a new guise*?' (Moretti 1998, 169 n. 30). My own position is that the modern novel both reflects and responds to the increased secularism of life in Western Europe, while at the same time contributing to this process of secularization.

The novel and urban experience

The early association of the novel with town rather than country life is also sig-nificant. There are novels set in the country, of course, but from its earliest days the novel appears to have had a special relationship with town life, and in the eighteenth century both the readers and the writers of novels were more likely to be town–dwellers than country-dwellers. If we look at what has a fair claim to be one of the first modern novels – Daniel Defoe's *Moll Flanders* (1722) – we can see that the town and the novel form have much in common. Both involve large numbers of people leading interdependent lives, influencing and relying upon one another, but each possessing, nevertheless, a core of private thoughts and personal goals. Modern readers may need to be reminded that the growth of large towns and of urban life ushers in new forms of loneliness and privacy at the same time that, paradoxically, these large collectivities depend upon and bear witness to collective planning and human cooperation.

Consider the following three passages, each written in a different century. The first is from *Moll Flanders*, and it concludes the scene in which Moll robs a young child of a necklace:

> *Here, I say, the Devil put me upon killing the Child in the dark Alley, that it might not Cry; but the very thought frighted me so that I was ready to drop down, but I turn'd the Child about and bade it go back again, for that was not its way home; the Child said so she would, and I went thro' into* Bartholomew Close, *and then turn'd round to another Passage that goes into* Long-lane, *so away into* Charterhouse-Yard *and out into* St. John's-street, *then crossing into* Smithfield, *went down* Chick-lane *and into* Field-lane *to* Holbourne-bridge, *when mixing with the Crowd of People usually passing there, it was not possible to have been found out; and thus I enterpriz'd my second Sally into the World.*

The second is from Charles Dickens's *Oliver Twist* (1837–8), and describes Oliver's entry into London in the company of the Artful Dodger ('John Dawkins'):

> *As John Dawkins objected to their entering London before nightfall, it was nearly eleven o'clock when they reached the turnpike at Islington. They crossed from the Angel into St. John's Road; struck down the small street which terminates at Sadler's Wells Theatre; through Exmouth Street and Coppice Row; down the little court by the side of the workhouse; across the classic ground which once bore the name of Hockley-in-the-Hole; thence into Little Saffron Hill; and so into Saffron Hill the Great: along which the Dodger scudded at a rapid pace, directing Oliver to follow close at his heels.*

The third is from W.G. Sebald's *Austerlitz* (first published in German 2001).

> *For over a year, I think, said Austerlitz, I would leave my house as darkness fell, walking on and on, down the Mile End Road and Bow Road to Stratford, then to Chigwell and Romford, right across Bethnal Green and Canonbury, through Holloway and Kentish Town and thus to Hampstead Heath, or else south over the river to Peckham and Dulwich or westward to Richmond Park.*

How well the world of London – rendered 'real' by the detailing of actual streets – and the world we now associate with the novel fit! In all three passages we observe rapid mobility in a well-known world, that everyday world with which so many readers are familiar, alongside a sense of one's private self that, even in the place where so very many people live, is one's own alone (and the reader's). Privacy (even secrecy) and movement in a location crammed with other people: this mixture has remained central to the novel for nearly three centuries. (See also the discussion of travel on p. 32.)

Public world and private life

From its earliest days the novel seems often to split not just between novels where the author starts with 'life' and those in which the author starts with 'pattern' – to use Arnold Kettle's terms – but also between novels in which the author is more interested in the public world and novels in which the author is more interested in private life. Again, it is only the very greatest novels that seem to combine the two such that we feel no sense of subordination of either. Henry Fielding's *Tom Jones* (1749) and Samuel Richardson's *Clarissa* (1747–8) can be taken as representative here, with the former's greater interest in a masculine, public life of movement, action and life in the larger social world in sharp contrast to the latter's concentration upon a feminine, more inward life of feeling, personal relationships, and personal moral decision. This is not to deny that Fielding's novel includes a concern with feeling and moral duty and Richardson's with the larger social context of the inner world. Nonetheless there is a very significant difference between the two writers and their respective fictional works, and one of which their contemporaries were well aware. J.A. Downie has agreed that the creative dialogue between Richardson and Fielding was a significant factor in the growing popularity of 'the novel' (Downie 2000, 325), and in his *The Life of Samuel Johnson*, which was first published in 1791, James Boswell shows how attitudes towards these two writers could cause serious dissension. Talking to Johnson and Thomas Erskine, Boswell expressed surprise at Johnson's calling Fielding a 'blockhead' and 'a barren rascal', and continued:

> 'Will you not allow, Sir, that he draws very natural pictures of human life?' JOHNSON. 'Why, Sir, it is of very low life. Richardson used to say, that had he not known who Fielding was, he should have believed he was an ostler. Sir, there is more knowledge of the heart in one letter of Richardson's, than in all Tom Jones. … ERSKINE. 'Surely, Sir, Richardson is very tedious.' JOHNSON. 'Why, Sir, if you were to read Richardson for the story, your impatience would be so much fretted that you would hang yourself. But you must read him for the sentiment, and consider the story as only giving occasion to the sentiment.' (anecdote from 1772)

We do not need to accept Johnson's value judgements to feel the force of the distinction made here, between a primary interest in drawing very natural pictures of life – albeit low life – and in revealing knowledge of the human heart.

The female voice

I refer above to Fielding's interest in the masculine and Richardson's in the feminine sphere, and I should make it clear that this is a historical rather than a universal judgement; 'masculine' and 'feminine' are used as they were defined by eighteenth-century English society, in which men were able to live a public as well as a domestic life, a public life of travel, work, exploration and adventure. As I have already indicated, the relationship of women to the novel is a very important one. This importance is both as writers and as readers (and, of course, as characters). Towards the end of the eighteenth century in England, more and more women were writing novels, and even male novelists recognized the importance of female readers. The anonymous but probably male author of *The Amicable Quixote; or, The Enthusiasm of Friendship*, published in London in 1788, mentions in his preface 'the commendations of the ladies, *for whom works of this kind are generally written*'. Because of the market economy on which novel production depended, the increasing importance of female readers inevitably had an appreciable effect upon the sort of novels that were written, and there is evidence that some male authors experienced this as an unwelcome pressure. Here for example is a comment from the narrator of Richard Graves's *The Spiritual Quixote or The Summer's Ramble of Mr. Geoffry Wildgoose. A Comic Romance*, which was published in 1773:

> *Should any of my amiable country-women, I say, smit with the love of novelty, carry home this trifling volume from some Circulating-library; and throwing herself negligently upon her settee or sopha – or even on the feet of her truckle-bed – have patience to attend two such odd fellows thus far; she will probably be disgusted that she has not been entertained with a single love-tale, which are generally looked upon as essential to works of this kind; and not only make a principal part of every episode, but are usually interwoven with the body of the fable.*

This felt tension between what male authors wanted to write and what they perceived that female readers wanted to read clearly alters in important ways as more and more women themselves write novels. But even though, by the nineteenth century, women were a dominant force not just as readers but also as writers of the novel, this does not mean that within the world of the novel all the inequalities of the time miraculously disappear. Interestingly, it is often the experience of colonialism and imperialism that throws up issues of gender in sharp relief in the novel. I will return to this issue below.

It is arguable that the novel's success in exploring the private world, the subjective self, could never have been accomplished without the contribution to the genre of that introspective self-knowledge and sensitive perception of interpersonal relations that women's domestic imprisonment had trained them to be so expert in. No man could have written Jane Austen's novels. But no novel can totally escape the ideological bounds of its time.

The international life of the novel: form and culture

From its first appearance in the world, the novel is associated with movement and travel – with *mobility*, both geographical and social. In the passages I quote above from *Moll Flanders* and *Oliver Twist* we are reminded how important being able to move from place to place was for Moll and for Oliver, but we should remember, too, that for both characters *geographical* movement was closely linked to a desire for *social* movement or advance. (The case of Austerlitz is somewhat different.) It is certainly arguable that this stress upon mobility is one of the points at which the socio-historical conditions of the novel's emergence and the social tensions which contribute to its birth can be seen transposed into generic and formal features. The very name 'novel', of course, directs our attention to what is new, and we typically discover the new by changing our location and by seeing either new things or old and familiar things from an unusual perspective.

Peter Burke has suggested that travel is one of the factors which can help to explain the emergence of what he refers to as 'the autobiographical habit' in the sixteenth century. As he reminds us, this 'was the age not only of the rise of the autobiography or journal but also of fictional narratives in the first-person story, such as the picaresque novel in Spain or the sonnet-sequences of Sidney, Shakespeare and others', and he proposes three likely reasons for this development. First, the fact that this is the age in which print becomes a part of everyday life, which means that the diffusion of printed models can create a new or sharper sense of self. Second, urbanization, because the alternative styles of life offered by the city encourage a sense of individual choice. Third, travel, because travel 'encourages self-consciousness by cutting off the individual from his or her community' (Burke 1997, 22). While we remain in familiar surroundings we receive more regular confirmation of our identity from those who expect us to continue to be what we have been in the past, but in a strange situation, surrounded by people we do not know, we become aware that to a certain extent we are able to *choose* who we are.

Even that basic component of prose fiction – the linearity of narrative – models progression and movement for us. Some writers have attempted to 'de-linearize' the novel. Brian McHale (1987, 193) refers to two of the best-known examples – Julio Cortázar's *Hopscotch* (1963), which invites the reader to choose between two different routes through its text, and B.S. Johnson's *The Unfortunates* (1969), published in a box of twenty-seven stapled gatherings which can be read in any order. In both cases, one should note, any individual reading is still a linear progression from beginning to end through a finite text. (See also the later discussion of the impact of the electronic media on linear narrative in Chapter 5, which returns to the case of *The Unfortunates*.)

In the mainstream novel as the line of prose snakes its way ahead from page to page, pressing on in the direction our culture calls 'forward' and always moving away from its point of birth to that last line where it will stop for ever, it constantly reminds us not just of the individual human life journeying from birth to death but also of the typical fictional hero or heroine: progressing ever forward, continually encountering new blank pages untouched by the pen of experience. As Michael McKeon puts it, by arranging events in a certain linear order, that 'progressive narrative' which is integral to the emerging novel:

> *automatically invests personality with the distinct moral qualities that are implied in the condition of being either in decline or on the rise. These qualities imply, in turn, an explanatory rationale whose force is unmistakable. On one side are the extravagant and licentious older sons of nobility, sunk in decay and corruption; on the other, the industrious and virtuous younger sons or tradesmen, hard at work in their honest and quasi-Calvinist callings. (McKeon 1987, 220)*

McKeon's argument links a specific type of narrative with a particular sort of social mobility, but these two forms of directed movement are also and typically associated with geographical progression and movement in the novel. The stranger, the intruder, the traveller – whether the terrain crossed is geographical or social – are all familiar inhabitants of this 'novel' genre.

There is, then, a relationship of mutual dependency between the novel's concern with the new, its questioning of laws and conventions, its curiosity about the strange and unusual, and its stress on geographical mobility.

Imperialism and gender

'Geographical mobility' is a rather suspiciously abstract and bloodless term. When people move around the world they meet and interact with other people with whom they may have a range of different sorts of relationship: collaborative, subservient, antagonistic, competitive or exploitative. The travel experiences of a tourist are not those of a refugee; those of a soldier are not those of an ambassador. The modern novel emerged in a world in which relationships between peoples were certainly not of an exclusively collaborative or equal type; by the end of the seventeenth century, Europe was already some way into those processes of exploitation and repression which we know as colonialism and imperialism.

Firdous Azim has pointed out that from the moment of its birth the novel enjoyed an 'imperialist heritage', one which is visible both in its themes and also in the problematic nature of its status: '[t]he novel becomes a form dealing with adventures in far-off lands, Oroonoko and Robinson Crusoe on the one hand, and the sexual adventures of bold and courageous women at home – Zara, Rivella, Moll Flanders and Roxana, on the other' (Azim 1993, 21). (We might add that Moll Flanders' adventures are not just 'at home': she also travels to America, where a significant portion of Defoe's novel takes place.)

'Imperialist heritage' may sound somewhat tendentious, but it is nevertheless a fact that the modern novel emerges in Western Europe at a time when this part of the world is in the early stages of a long process of imposing its will and influence – by both peaceful and non-peaceful means – on other peoples. Thus the master–slave relationship in, for example, *Robinson Crusoe* has to be seen as more than just an interesting part of the story, an element in the work's content. Defoe's hero explores his own individuality in a number of ways, but one that is of defining importance to this novel, as well as to the experience of its author and his or her fellow citizens, is the imposition of one's individual and collective will on the inhabitants of other lands. Crusoe discovers who he is – *makes* his identity – in part by establishing Friday's subordination to himself.

One of the most interesting chapters in Judie Newman's book *The Ballistic Bard: Postcolonial Fictions* (1995) looks at a range of recent novels that have attempted to confront, expose or reject the novel's perceived 'imperialist heritage'. Newman focuses on Jean Rhys's novel *Wide Sargasso Sea* (1966) and its attempted settling of accounts with Charlotte Brontë's *Jane Eyre* (1847), and in so doing shows how closely imperialism is related to issues of gender in the novel. Brontë's novel has served as a mine of hidden or repressed cultural information for feminists: the very influential study, *The Madwoman in the Attic* (Gilbert and Gubar, 1979), takes its title from the situation of Rochester's concealed and incarcerated first wife, and the book presents her situation as in many ways emblematic of a much wider repression and denial of female oppression – and not just in Brontë's culture.

Jean Rhys's interest in the West Indian aspect of Brontë's novel was doubtless related to her own problematic upbringing in Dominica and even more problematic travel to England, but her taking what has generally been experienced as a marginal or peripheral element in Brontë's novel and making it a central issue in her own intertextual reworking of *Jane Eyre* has had the effect of allowing modern readers to approach the earlier work from a revealingly different perspective.

Newman points out that Charlotte Brontë's portrayal of Bertha is designed to obliterate all sympathy for her:

> *[Bertha] is described ... in terms which appeal to both racial and sexual prejudices. Her hereditary madness, which is supposedly accelerated by sexual excess, clearly reflects Victorian syphilophobia. (The nineteenth century had shifted the point of origin of syphilis to Africa.) Brontë's Bertha has 'a discoloured face', 'a savage face' with 'fearful blackened inflation' of the features: 'the lips were swelled and dark'. Successively described as a demon, a witch, a vampire, a beast, a hyena, and even an Indian Messalina, Bertha unites in one person all the available pejorative stereotypes.*

Newman draws attention to the description by (Brontë's) Rochester of Jamaica as 'hell', its sounds and scenery those of 'the bottomless pit'. She also notes that when Rochester contemplates suicide he is saved by a 'wind fresh from Europe', and she reminds us that 'Penny Boumelha has observed that in *Jane Eyre* all the money comes from colonial exploitation' and that 'Jane herself gains her financial independence as a result of a legacy from an uncle in Madeira who is connected to the same firm which Mr. Mason, Bertha's brother, represents in Jamaica'. Finally, Newman quotes again from Penny Boumelha, and provides us with a phrase very similar to one already taken from Firdous Azim. For Boumelha, Rhys's vindication of Brontë's 'madwoman' serves to display and to criticize 'the legacy of imperialism concealed in the heart of every English gentleman's castle' (Newman 1995, 14; for Penny Boumelha's comments, see Boumelha 1988, 111–22). It also serves to demonstrate that inequalities associated with imperialism and colonialism are intertwined with inequalities of gender.

Cultural imperialism and the novel

There is another, rather different, way in which the novel can be seen as an 'imperialist' genre. William B. Warner has noted that, as the producer of the greatest number and variety of fictions, 'France of the seventeenth and early eighteenth centuries is positioned as something of a "Hollywood" for romances and novels'. Europeans, Africans and Asians are today generally much more familiar with parts of the culture of the United States than Americans are familiar with European, African or Asian culture. In like manner, as the novel conquered European culture in the late eighteenth and nineteenth centuries, so too did ideas, attitudes – ideologies – associated not now solely with France but with England too, succeed in influencing and even dominating the cultures of Europe. Moretti puts it thus:

> [I]n the crucial century between 1750 and 1850 the consequence of centralization is that in most European countries the majority of novels are, quite simply, foreign books. Hungarian, Italian, Danish, Greek readers familiarize themselves with the new form through French and English novels: and so, inevitably, French and English novels become models to be imitated. (Moretti 1998, 187)

In his *Atlas of the European Novel 1800–1900* (1998), Franco Moretti provides powerful evidence in support of the thesis that by the nineteenth century the novel had consolidated a cultural dominance that was based in the centres of political and economic power in Europe – France and Britain. Not only does the novel come to dominate the bookshelf both in the private house and the public library from the late eighteenth century onwards (to the dismay, as Moretti reports, of nineteenth-century library committees), but novels set in and emanating from the powerful urban centres of major European powers – especially France and England – tend to dominate that increasingly large amount of shelving set aside for fiction. Moretti comments:

> Be it mid eighteenth-century Britain ... or mid nineteenth-century Italy ... the message is the same: the novel is the most centralized of all literary genres. And its centralization increases with the passage of time ...

> *Because, first, the novel closes European literature to all external influences: it strengthens, and perhaps it even establishes its* Europeanness. *But then this most European of forms proceeds to deprive most of Europe of all creative autonomy: two cities, London and Paris, rule the entire continent for over a century, publishing half (if not more) of all European novels. It's a ruthless, unprecedented* centralization *of European literature. (Moretti 1998, 165, 186)*

We must conclude that if the novel is significantly the *product* of social change on the national level and cultural influence on the international one, at the same time it becomes one of the most important and powerful *tools* of cultural influence both nationally and internationally.

■ For whom does the novel speak today?

Although I will consider the impact of the electronic media on fiction later in this book, most works of fiction are still read in printed form, and even if this situation changes, many of the points following apply as much to electronic as to printed texts. Indeed, access to books presents far fewer problems to the very poor than does access to electronic texts. Printing involves not just the technical and economic means to produce and circulate books but also a universal or at least widespread literacy that comes from a highly developed system of public education. Generally speaking, where literacy is not universal in a culture, more men than women are taught how to read and write. In those countries which have recently emerged from colonial rule not only may education be closed to many, but much of the publishing business is controlled by foreign, often multinational, companies. Even when high levels of literacy are established in post-colonial countries, education systems have frequently been built up by colonial or imperialist powers and modelled upon European or North American lines. It is not so very long ago that little of the literature read by the student of English in many newly independent African countries was actually written by Africans.

Issues such as these have led a number of commentators to ask not just whether the novel as a genre is non-collective, 'Western', and masculinist, but whether the novel is or has been used as a weapon of ideological propaganda or control by those cultures within which it emerged and from which it allegedly took its defining characteristics. These questions – or accusations – are of course linked: the implication is clearly that the novel can be used as an ideological or political weapon precisely because those characteristics which distinguish it reflect and even celebrate a pattern of human relationships first identified and acclaimed in the late seventeenth and early eighteenth centuries in Western Europe.

What force does this challenge to the novel have? It seems to me that it is quite wrong to treat a novel written today in Africa or India as just no more than a European import. As a starting point, consider the following words by the Indian novelist Mulk Raj Anand. They compose part of his introduction to a collection of Indian fairy tales:

> *The stories contained in this volume were told me by my mother and my aunts during my childhood. The primary inspiration to retell them, therefore, came from the nostalgic memories of the hour when 'once upon a time' began and when one's eyes closed long before the story had ended.*
>
> *But I also had in mind the fact that in the old stories of our country lay the only links with our broken tradition. I fancied that only by going back to the form of these stories, told by mother to son, and son to son, could we evolve a new pattern for the contemporary short story. Of course, the modern short story is a highly developed folk tale if it is a folk tale at all. But a revival of the short story form . . . seemed a fit occasion to relate it to its more primitive antecedents which, surprisingly enough, seem to lie in the sources of the sheaf of tales which I have gleaned. At any rate, I must confess that although I have taken in much new psychology into my own writing of the short story, I have always tried to approximate to the technique of the folk tale, and the influence of these fairy stories has always been very deep on my own fiction.*
>
> *These fairy stories can, therefore, be read not only by children, but by those adults who have not forgotten the child in them. And, however foreign they may seem to non-Indians, in their atmosphere and effect, I offer them here, not as something completely alien to the Western peoples, but as familiar and well known themes to set beside the fairy tales which they have read in their childhoods, because there has been much international traffic in folk lore between India and the West through traders, travellers, gypsies, craftsmen and crusaders, and many of the stories current abroad have their source in the same springs in which these stories have their origin. (Anand 1946, 7–8)*

The comments are interesting for a number of reasons. First, because they remind us that, just as a tradition of fictional tales emerged and established itself in Europe before literacy became widespread, so too can comparable traditions be found in those cultures and societies which were on the receiving end of colonialism and imperialism. Second, because, as Anand points out, the stories with which he is concerned strike non-Indian readers as both 'foreign' and familiar. Oral prose fiction traditions may all share some common or familial features, but they are also possessed of that which is culture-specific, and thus, to the extent that such traditions inform a new tradition of novel writing and reading, this new tradition will also have something that is its alone, something native to its own culture. Third, because, as Anand also points out, 'there has been much international traffic in folk lore', and although the emerging novel may reflect the inequalities and injustices of its mother-culture, it is also the resting place for many perspectives which are critical of that mother-culture and its dominant values. Indeed, as the phrase 'dominant values' may remind us, the societies from which the early novel emerged were by no means monolithic; they contained minority views, 'faultlines', oppositions and contradictions.

Anand's collection of fairy tales was published in 1946, in the dying years of British India. (Indian readers of the collection were probably more immediately aware of what the discreet term 'broken tradition' referred to than are present-day European readers.) Anand knew as well as anyone what imperialism and colonialism were capable of, but he also knew that in addition to the crusaders and the traders there were also travellers, gypsies and craftsmen moving from country to country, and that the commerce was not all one way. The gypsies came originally from India, and were certainly part of Western European culture by the eighteenth century, although of course neither a dominant nor a privileged part.

In short, not only can a novelist writing in newly independent lands incorporate powerful elements of native storytelling tradition into his or her work, but the European tradition of the novel is itself not exclusively European.

Where does this leave us in our quest to determine the extent to which the genre of the novel is or is not value-neutral? It seems to me to be arguable that the novel *is* probably less well suited to the expression of collective or communal experiences and beliefs than are some other forms such as orally delivered poetry or drama. Not only do such performance arts involve a direct contact between artist-performer and audience, thus allowing both for collective response and also collective feedback from audience to creator, but the drama also allows for the dramatized presentation of distinctive voices – often simultaneously. Now the skilled novelist can resist the individualistic and monologic tendencies of the genre, and indeed I have already referred to Mikhail Bakhtin's belief that the novel is naturally dialogic (see p. 13). In my comments on the narrative technique used by Lewis Grassic Gibbon in his *A Scots Quair* (see p. 131), I suggest that this technique is designed to help us to experience a working-class collectivity and that it largely succeeds. Nevertheless, it is arguable that the representation of such collectivity is more difficult for the novelist than it is for the dramatist. What is more, a culture whose vital life is more closely associated with oral expression and an oral tradition than with written expression and a written tradition may find more natural expression in the drama or poetic recital than in the printed pages of a book.

Having said all this it seems to me that, if we are asking the crude question 'Is the novel essentially a bourgeois, individualist and "Western" (or imperialist) genre?', it is perhaps more productive to look at issues of tradition and economic control than of innate generic identity – in other words, to focus more upon differences of culture and on socio-economic issues than on the inherent formal or technical qualities of the genre. Indeed, so far as the latter are concerned I should repeat that although the novel does seem to be generically predisposed in the direction of representing individual experience, especially when that experience is that of a socially and geographically mobile individual, it is also the case that the novel is a genre which seems to survive by permanently revolutionizing itself, in the light of which fact it is dangerous to talk of what the novel cannot do because of its innate generic identity.

Snatching the pen

If we turn to the issues of tradition and economic control we do I think see how particular values and perspectives may be associated with the genre. To explore this issue I would like to take two novels by the Kenyan novelist Ngũgĩ Wa Thiong'o: his first published novel, *Weep Not, Child*, which appeared in 1964, and *Devil on the Cross*, which was published first in Gĩkũyũ in 1980 and then in the author's own English translation in 1982. In fact, when *Weep Not, Child* was first published, its author's name was given as 'James Ngugi'. Both books were published by Heinemann, now a part of the Reed Elsevier conglomerate.

Weep Not, Child is a wonderful first novel and was welcomed as such on its initial publication. Re-read today from the perspective of Ngũgĩ's later work, the novel nonetheless gives the sense of a writer having to adapt to the requirements of a tradition and a publishing situation which are partly alien to him and which restrict his freedom of movement. Take the following short passage from the opening pages of the novel:

> *There was only one road that ran right across the land. It was long and broad and shone with black tar, and when you travelled along it on hot days you saw little lakes ahead of you. But when you went near, the lakes vanished, to appear again a little farther ahead. Some people called them the devil's waters because they deceived you and made you more thirsty if your throat was already dry. And the road which ran across the land and was long and broad had no beginning and no end. At least, few people knew of its origin. Only if you followed it it would take you to the big city and leave you there while it went beyond to the unknown, perhaps joining the sea. Who made the road? Rumour had that it came with the white men and some said that it was rebuilt by the Italian prisoners during the Big War that was fought away from here. (Ngugi 1972, 5–6)*

It seems clear that this passage attempts to present the reader both with the consciousness of Njoroge, the main character of the novel, and also with a sense of the, as it were, collective consciousness of Njoroge's people, as well as of the immediate history of his land and culture. Such multiple perspectives are not uncommon in the novel, especially in novels which deal with 'suppressed' or oppressed groups whose lives and experiences are sharply different from those of the writer's intended or expected readers. (Again, my comments on Lewis Grassic Gibbon's narrative technique on p. 131 are relevant to the present discussion, not least with regard to both writers' use of the collective 'you' to affirm and represent shared and communal knowledge.) What the passage gives us is a statement of what, because it is shared cultural knowledge, is actually unlikely ever to be stated unless an outsider asks the right questions, and so putting it in Njoroge's unspoken but verbalized thoughts is slightly jarring.

Who is the 'implied reader' (see the Glossary)? Ngũgĩ seems very conscious of the fact that many of the first readers of this novel would know nothing about Kenya or Kenyans, nothing about the history or culture of this part of Africa. Passages such as the one which I have quoted seem in part designed to impart knowledge to such individuals. Writing a novel, in English, for an international publisher, Ngũgĩ must have felt the pressure of his potential readers' ignorance in a way in which a middle-class European of his age and generation would not have done. This may help to explain a stiffness at certain points of the narrative of *Weep Not, Child*.

> *Ngotho often wondered if he had really done well by his sons. If he and his generation had failed, he was ready to suffer for it. ... But whatever Ngotho had been prepared to do to redeem himself in the eyes of his children, he would not be ordered by a son to take an oath. Not that he objected to it in principle. After all, oath-taking as a means of binding a person to a promise was a normal feature of tribal life. But to be given by a son! That would have violated against his standing as a father. (Ngugi 1972, 83–4)*

In this passage it seems to me that the sentence 'After all, oath-taking as a means of binding a person to a promise was a normal feature of tribal life' also jars somewhat: it is sandwiched by sentences which are in Free Indirect Discourse, specifically in represented thought (see p. 98), but it cannot itself be read in this way. This is an authorial interpolation, an explanatory detail provided for the benefit of the reader who is not familiar with the 'tribal life' in question. Writing about that part of Charles Dickens's *Bleak House* which is narrated by Esther Summerson, E.M. Forster comments in his *Aspects of the Novel* (first published in 1927), that even when Esther is ostensibly telling the story Dickens may snatch the pen from her and take notes himself (Forster 1962, 86). I have a sense of something similar happening in Ngũgĩ's first novel.

By the time of Ngũgĩ's *Devil on the Cross* we feel that this writer is possessed of much greater self-confidence. It is neither accidental nor irrelevant to the argument in hand that this is a novel that is thematically very much concerned with the issues of cultural independence and cultural subservience. In the author's own English translation, words which appeared in English in the original Gĩkũyũ version of the novel are italicized, so that the text of the novel gives a sense of cultural struggle, as the author's very language is invaded by English words and phrases. One of the characters – Gatuĩria – actually finds it hard to speak in Gĩkũyũ without peppering his speech with English words: ironically enough he is a 'junior research fellow in African culture', and to double the irony he uses English in order to describe his post.

This is a novel in which we feel that the novelist's technical assurance is directly related to his sense of who he is writing for and why. Where culture-specific details have to be provided for European readers they are given in footnotes rather than being smuggled into the thoughts or speech of the characters. The novel speaks freely from within a culture to those sharing the culture: its dedication 'To all Kenyans struggling against the neo-colonial stage of imperialism' provides convincing evidence concerning the readers for whom Ngũgĩ intended the work. The whole theme of cultural imperialism is foregrounded in the novel, and this allows Ngũgĩ the freedom to use the resources of his own culture without self-consciousness or a concern that this might not be proper or understood. For all that he is presented as a victim of cultural imperialism, Gatuĩria is aware of the process that is oppressing him and he bemoans the loss of an indigenous cultural tradition: 'Our stories, our riddles, our songs, our customs, our traditions, everything about our national heritage has been lost to us' (Ngũgĩ 1982, 59).

Devil on the Cross does not just propose such a case in abstract terms: by incorporating the force and vitality of such indigenous cultural and narrative traditions into its own telling, the novel also enacts a process of cultural self-assertion and revolt. It is very difficult to illustrate this by means of selective quotation, because the shifts between more traditional realism and the fantastic, which are mediated through a range of narrative techniques including 'standard' third-person narrative, riddles and sayings, dance-songs and verses, and other forms unfamiliar to European readers such as that of the 'verse-chanting competition', have a cumulative effect which is lost in brief extracts. The result is to revolutionize the genre within which Ngũgĩ is working and to open the novel to traditions which are certainly 'un-Western', collective rather than individualistic, holistic rather than fragmented. What the novel is today it is partly because of its enrichment by writers such as Ngũgĩ. This is not to deny that literary forms such as that of the novel are involved in international processes of economic, political and cultural conflict, repression and domination, nor that the novel may be better suited to the representation of the individual than the collective consciousness, and to processes of linear development than to complexities of simultaneity and reciprocal interaction. Nor is it to deny that a print-based genre is better adapted to the expressive needs of a literate culture than it is to those of an oral one. But the example of a magnificent novel such as *Devil on the Cross* goes to show that the novel can adapt to and incorporate the strengths of rich oral and communal traditions – whether these are those of Kenya or of the Scottish peasantry and industrial working class about whom Lewis Grassic Gibbon writes.

Topics for discussion

■ If the novel rises with the middle class, is it a middle-class genre?
■ To what extent do romance traditions survive in the novel?
■ Must the novelist choose between 'life' and 'pattern'?
■ How does silent, private consumption condition novel-reading?
■ Is the novel one of the first examples of cultural imperialism?

3
Shorter fiction

Preview

This chapter deals with:
- the short story and the novella as recent categories
- the taint of commercialism and 'definition by length'
- the 'anecdotal' and the 'epiphanic' short story
- compression, suggestiveness and the short story
- the distinctiveness of the novella

I have already suggested that our familiar tripartite division of prose fiction into the novel, the short story and the novella is one that simplifies a more complex and varied reality, and it is as well to start this chapter with a warning against allowing a use of these categories (more popular perhaps with academics than with writers or the common reader) to obscure the variety of forms open to the writer of prose fiction – both today and in the past. It is also the case that the terms 'short story' and 'novella' are by no means as widely used or as unambiguous as is the term 'novel'. Although the term 'novella', from which the English 'novel' descends, can be traced back to the Italian, use of this term today to designate a prose fiction that is shorter than a novel but longer than a short story descends from nineteenth-century German usage. The term is little used outside schools and universities. The term 'short story' is more widely understood, but it too is problematic in ways that – for all of the issues of definition that I have discussed in the previous chapter – the term 'novel' is not. Graham Good provides a useful summary of these terminological problems:

> Short fiction terminology is extremely varied and often inconsistent. The word 'novella' is gradually gaining acceptance in English among publishers, writers, and latterly critics, to denote a fictional prose narrative of 'medium' length. This usage is supplementing rather than supplanting 'short story,' which has been firmly established since the turn of the century. The older terms 'tale' and simply 'story' were still employed by writers like [Henry] James and [Joseph] Conrad to refer to any narrative shorter than a novel, from about five to a hundred or more pages. (Good 1994, 148)

In fact, Conrad used the term 'tale' rather more promiscuously than this suggests: his longest novel, *Nostromo*, is sub-titled 'A Tale of the Seaboard'. One of the reasons why the terms 'short story' and 'novella' were pressed into use by writers and critics from (especially) the early days of the twentieth century is almost certainly because alternative terms such as 'tale' were just too elastic.

Behind the search for terms is a sense that length does make a difference, and that although the cake of fiction could be cut into slices of varying sizes, a tripartite division best accords with our experience of reading fictional works varying from (say) the 1,824 words of James Joyce's 'Eveline' through the 42,700 words of Henry James's *The Turn of the Screw* to the 168,000 words of *Nostromo* (and there are many novels that are longer by far than *Nostromo*). Although not all commentators are happy with these terms or the categories they propose, I will use them in what follows to structure my comments since the general acceptance of the tripartite division between novel, novella and short story is indicative of a certain utility and convenience. To take a random but not unrepresentative example, Hortense Calisher's *Extreme Magic: A Novella and Other Stories* (1964) consists of six stories ranging from 12 to 25 pages, and the title story 'Extreme Magic' which is 83 pages long.

What it is important to remember is that certainly so far as fiction is concerned, most if not all of the novels written since 1800 that you are asked to study will have been written by authors who had a clear sense of what a novel was. But the same cannot be said of the short story or, especially, the novella. I suggest later on that it can be helpful to think of works such as D.H. Lawrence's *The Fox* and Joseph Conrad's *Heart of Darkness* as novellas, but to the best of my knowledge neither of these writers actually used the term 'novella', certainly not to describe these works. Mary Doyle Springer has suggested that '[t]he kinds of works which are now recognized as novellas began to arise in the nineteenth century' (1975, 8), but the application of the term 'novella' to these works only becomes common in English-speaking cultures in the 1970s.

A letter written on 7 January 1902 by Conrad to his publisher illustrates some of these terminological issues. In the letter Conrad outlines a plan for a new piece and comments: 'Of course it shall be "fiction" in the same sense that *Youth* is fiction. Some critics, at the time, called it a short story!' (Karl and Davies 1986, 368). 'Youth' is only about 13,400 words long, and my guess is that when it is included on a school or university reading list today it is categorized unproblematically as a short story. Conrad clearly views this term with disdain, and his shorter works are given a range of other sub-headings: 'a tale', 'a story', 'a narrative', 'a sketch', 'a memory', 'an episode' – but never 'a short story'. It is very likely that Conrad liked the term 'tale' because it linked works of shorter fiction with a tradition of oral narrative (many of his works are presented as oral tellings), and that he disliked the term 'short story' because of its association with the commercial and the popular.

■ The short story
Commercialism and size

Two spectres haunt the short story. The first of these involves a reaction against what the critic Norman Friedman, in an article entitled 'What Makes a Short Story Short?' (first published in 1958), has called the taint of commercialism – the belief that the short story is a debased form to which writers descended only in order to earn money (Friedman 1976, 131). (Short works of fiction published in magazines in the late nineteenth and early twentieth centuries generally earned far more per word for their authors than did long novels.) The second involves the fear that perhaps all that distinguishes the short story from longer works of prose fiction is its shortness, rather than any more aesthetically interesting characteristic. Both of these spectres have made serious writers and serious critics – those who share an interest in raising the status and the dignity of short fiction – suspicious of the term.

There is a strong tradition of usage that links the short story with more unambiguously commercial works of the sort associated with the American writer O. Henry, works that appealed to a popular market and that were characterized by, among other things, unexpected endings of an ironic or whimsical variety. One recent commentator – William O'Rourke – has commented on the revealing fact that 'as fewer commercial magazines publish it and the general public continues to avoid it, the short story rises in critical favor, not only among professors but among literary reviewers' (O'Rourke 1989, 199).

Then there is shortness. Norman Friedman has stated the problem bluntly, referring to 'the only observable commonality which all short stories share and which does indeed separate them from novellas and novels – their shortness' (Friedman 1989, 24). Discussing the 'very basic problems of terminology involving terms like "sketch", "tale" and "novella"', Valerie Shaw has noted that, in the case of literature written in English, 'it is especially difficult to fix an aesthetic borderline between short story and nouvelle [the latter term here used as a synonym of novella]: Henry James, for example, used the terms "tale", "story" and "nouvelle" quite unsystematically for any fiction where concision and rigorous selection were operative principles' (Shaw 1983, 20). Many theorists of shorter fiction have disagreed, and have tried to find a more respectable basis in terms of which the short story and the novella can be set aside from their prose-fiction siblings. I would like now to turn to some of the more interesting of these attempts.

Oral or written? Traditional or modern?

Arguments as to whether the short story is the product of a long tradition of oral storytelling or a modern form associated with magazine publication are clearly intertwined with arguments about whether it is a very old or a very modern genre.

If, as I have claimed, the novel is very much the child of print, one might assume that at least superficial resemblances between the short story and oral narratives – tales, anecdotes, and so on – might suggest that the short story has much older parents, which is in part what Mulk Raj Anand implies (see p. 37). It is certainly the case that the length of the typical short story makes it possible to associate it with a single oral telling, and there is no doubt that many writers have seized upon this possibility. In an essay entitled 'A Theory of the Short Story' that was first published in 1917, James Cooper Lawrence confidently asserts that '[t]he more we look into the matter the more evident it becomes that the limits and distinguishing characteristics of the short story as we know it today are the limits and distinguishing characteristics of the spoken story as it has existed from the beginning of time' (Lawrence 1976, 61). Certainly the man or woman talking to a group of listeners, the individual reminiscing to friends, the *speaker* rather than the *writer*, the tale as heard rather than the tale as read – all of these admittedly fictional narrative elements have appealed to writers wishing to conceal or qualify the situation of the lonely writer reaching out through the mediation of print to a similarly lonely reader. The ostensibly spoken narrative allows the writer access to colloquial speech, to those hesitations and unwilling disclosures that writing conceals, to the collectivity of a listening group, and to exchanges between teller and (fictional) listeners (see the discussion of *skaz* in the Glossary). Longer novels can be presented as spoken rather than written, but the conventions start to creak as the pages mount up. Joseph Conrad reacted to criticism of the impossibility of most of *Lord Jim* being delivered as one continuous oral account, but his protestations are not wholly convincing.

Many recent commentators have however argued that the short story is a modern form rather than one with a venerable history. Introducing *The Faber Book of Modern Short Stories* in 1936, Elizabeth Bowen – herself a writer of novels and short stories – states bluntly that the short story 'is a young art: as we know it, it is the child of this century. Poetic tautness and clarity are so essential to it that it may be said to stand at the edge of prose; in its use of action it is nearer to drama than to the novel' (Bowen 1976, 152). Frank O'Connor, one of the most influential theorists of the short story, also resists associating the short story with the centuries-long tradition of the spoken tale. He argues that the short story, like the novel, 'is a modern art form; that is to say, it represents, better than poetry or drama, our own attitude to life'.

This is not to say that O'Connor believes the short story to be merely a truncated novel: 'even from its beginnings, the short story has functioned in a quite different way from the novel' (O'Connor 1963, 13). In his attempt to describe the nature of this difference, O'Connor is thought-provoking if, on occasions, eccentric. He suggests that, unlike the novel, the short story does not encourage identification between the reader and a character.

> In discussions of the modern novel we have come to talk of it as the novel without a hero. In fact, the short story has never had a hero.
>
> What it has instead is a submerged population group – a bad phrase which I have had to use for want of a better.
>
> . . .
>
> Always in the short story there is this sense of outlawed figures wandering about the fringes of society, superimposed sometimes on symbolic figures whom they caricature and echo – Christ, Socrates, Moses. ... As a result there is in the short story at its most characteristic something we do not often find in the novel – an intense awareness of human loneliness. Indeed, it

might be truer to say that while we often read a familiar novel again for
companionship, we approach the short story in a very different mood.
(1963, 17–18, 19)

This argument implicitly extends the claim that the short story is a modern
form, as the outlaw figure and a concentration on human loneliness are both
very much part of the modernist movement (about which I will talk more in
the next chapter).

Fragments and wholes

Another Irish critic, Sean O'Faolain, has argued in a book on the short story
first published in 1948 that there can be no development of character in the
short story – a point of which Henry James was, O'Faolain argues, unaware
(O'Faolain 1972, 221). Of course, characters in a short story may undergo
shocking experiences and they may experience dramatic illuminations, but
these are, nonetheless, different from that gradual development of character
that we can observe in a full-length novel. For O'Faolain, at the heart of the
short story has to reside the writer's ability to make fragments of experience
speak for the whole of life (185). The suggestion is an interesting one, and it
again associates the short story with the development of literary modernism,
from let us say around the start of the twentieth century. Valerie Shaw links
'the rise of the short story in England' with 'the emergence of the
characteristic figure of the modern artist, and with anti-Victorianism in its
widest sense' (Shaw 1983, 4), while Suzanne Ferguson, in an article entitled
'The Rise of the Short Story in the Hierarchy of Genres', argues that 'the
preeminence of the short story as a modernist genre grew out of the modern,
highbrow audience's acceptance of fragmentation as an accurate model of the
world, with a concomitant focus on "being" – as in Woolf's "moments of
being" – rather than the "becoming" that characterizes the plot of the
Romantic and the Victorian novel' (Ferguson 1989, 191). For a writer such
as James Joyce, for example, the depiction of an 'epiphany' – a moment of
sudden and climactic illumination that grants revelatory insight into extensive
truths – can be as effectively achieved in one of the short stories collected in
Dubliners (1914) as in the over 700 pages of *Ulysses*. The economy of the
epiphany inevitably makes it attractive to the writer with limited space at his
or her disposal.

The 'anecdotal' and the 'epiphanic' short story

In an essay entitled 'The Debunking Rhythm of the American Short Story',
Thomas M. Leitch reports that short-story theorists have continued to
distinguish between two different kinds of – or structures for – the short story,
which he terms the 'anecdotal' and the 'epiphanic':

The anecdotal story, typified by Hawthorne's 'The Birthmark,' Poe's 'The
Gold-Bug,' and the Sherlock Holmes stories of Arthur Conan Doyle,
presents an Aristotelian action with a beginning, middle and end; the

epiphanic story, represented by Chekhov's 'The Lady with the Dog,'
Joyce's 'Ivy Day in the Committee Room,' and Crane's Civil War stories,
adumbrates a fictional world not by developing a plot involving purposive
agents but by unfolding particular sensations or emotions and proceeding to
a climactic revelation that does not necessarily take the form of a complete
overt action. (Leitch 1989, 130–31)

The terms are thought–provoking, but I suspect that they are more useful in isolating aspects of different short stories than in categorizing short stories either as one or the other type.

The short-story cycle

Not all short stories are published in magazines – or at least, not only in magazines. Some of the most important examples of the short story owe part of their force to publication in single-volume collections. The title of James Joyce's *Dubliners* (1914), for example, clearly signals that the different stories contained in the volume have something in common, and that the volume as a whole says something about a city and its inhabitants. As many commentators have pointed out, the first paragraph in 'The Sisters', the first story of *Dubliners*, has the youthful first-person narrator musing over three words that prepare the reader for themes that recur throughout the collection as a whole. All of the stories in Angela Carter's *The Bloody Chamber* (1979) offer disturbing blendings of traditional fairy tales and modern settings and issues. The cycle or collection allows the short-story writer to obtain that sense of an extended investigation into a particular issue or topic that the novelist can achieve in the course of a single work, and authors often plan individual short works as component parts of a larger whole. In a letter written in 1900, Conrad admitted that *Lord Jim* 'has not been planned to stand alone', that '*H[eart] of D[arkness]* was meant in my mind as a foil, and *Youth* was supposed to give the note' (Karl and Davies 1986, 271). Critics and theorists may have invented the word 'intertextuality', but the idea behind the term, that works draw part of their strength from being read with their connections to other works in mind, is one that many authors have held. The component stories in a collection or cycle can thus be possessed of a cumulative force, even while maintaining an autonomy that exceeds that of the single chapter in a novel.

Telling and suggesting

If the modernist short-story writer is interested in making a fragment or epiphany imply or display a larger whole, the writer must become adept at replacing *direct telling* by *suggesting*:

Telling by means of suggestion or implication is one of the most important
of all the modern short-story's shorthand conventions. It means that a short-
story writer does not directly tell us things so much as let us guess or know
them by implying them. The technical advantage is obvious. It takes a long

time to tell anything directly and explicitly, it is a rather heavy-handed way
of conveying information, and it does not arrest our imagination or hold our
attention so firmly as when we get a subtle hint. Telling never dilates the
mind with suggestion as implication does. (O'Faolain 1972, 177)

To make his point, O'Faolain presents his readers with a splendid analysis of
the opening sentence of Anton Chekhov's short story 'The Lady with the
Little Dog' (in his account granted a slightly different title in English
translation from that used by Thomas M. Leitch). O'Faolain concentrates
upon this opening sentence because he believes that the openings of short
stories in particular demand of the author that he or she be adept at
influencing the reader by means of suggestion and implication. The sentence
in question reads as follows: 'It was reported that a new face had been seen
on the quay; a lady with a little dog.' Here is O'Faolain's commentary:

The amount of information conveyed in that sentence is an interesting
example of the shorthand of the modern short-story. What do we gather
from it? ... We gather, altogether by implication, that the scene is laid in
a port. We gather that this port is a seaside resort, for ladies with little dogs
do not perambulate on commercial docks. We gather that the season is fine
weather – probably summer or autumn. We gather that this seaside resort
is a sleepy, unfrequented little place: for one does not observe new faces at
big, crowded places like Brighton or Deauville. Furthermore, the phrase 'it
was reported' implies that gossip circulates in a friendly way at this sleepy
resort. We gather still more. We gather that somebody has been bored and
wakes up at this bit of gossip; and that we shall presently hear about him.
I say 'him', because one again guesses, when it is a question of a lady, that
the person most likely to be interested is a man. (O'Faolain 1972, 177–8)

As he adds (perhaps redundantly, in view of the contrast between the length
of his commentary and the length of the sentence in question!), 'we may
imagine how much time it would take, and how boring it would be, to have
all that told at length'.

The short story is normally read at one sitting – Edgar Allan Poe in fact
suggested that this was a necessary feature of the short story. Because of this,
the reading of a short story tends to be less reflective and more concentrated
an experience; we rarely stop several times for prolonged thought in the
middle of reading a short story. The plot of a short story typically limits itself
to a brief span of time, and, as O'Faolain argues, rather than showing its
characters developing and maturing, will often show them at some revealing
moment of crisis – whether internal or external. Short stories rarely have
complex plots; again the focus is more upon a particular episode or situation
rather than on a chain of interlinked events.

Much of the skill of the short-story writer has to be devoted to making characters appear three-dimensional in spite of the fact that we see them for only a
very short period of time. In addition, care has to be taken to render atmos-

phere and situation convincingly. Very often the short-story writer will use something akin to shock tactics to make the reader think and respond: an unexpected ending, a dramatic unveiling, a surprising twist of plot. Many consider these to be artistically inferior techniques, less sophisticated than other means of creating depth and body in the short story. What are these means?

We have already mentioned *suggestion*, and clearly there are a number of techniques whereby we get people's imaginations racing. We should probably remember that there are two sorts of suggestion: the first when we know exactly what it is that we want the target person to think (as Iago gets Othello to imagine that Desdemona has been unfaithful without actually stating as much), and the second when a person's imagination is stimulated to be innovative and to think of things that the suggester him- or herself may never have intended. A much-quoted example of this second sort is to be found in Henry James's comment in his 'New York' Preface to a collection of tales including *The Turn of the Screw*:

> *Only make the reader's general vision of evil intense enough, I said to myself – and that already is a charming job – and his own experience, his own imagination, his own sympathy (with the children) and horror (of their false friends) will supply him quite sufficiently with all the particulars. Make him* think *the evil, make him think it for himself, and you are released from weak specifications.*

There seems little doubt that the second of these alternatives is potentially richer and more aesthetically rewarding, as it gives the reader's imagination a genuinely *creative* function. For me a classic example of such suggestiveness used to full aesthetic effect is to be found at the end of James Joyce's 'The Dead' (started 1907, published 1914), the final story in his *Dubliners*. At this point of the story, the character Gabriel, in a hotel room with his sleeping wife after the annual dance held by Gabriel's aunts, is sinking into sleep. The final lines of the story read:

> *A few light taps against the pane made him turn to the window. It had begun to snow again. He watched sleepily the flakes, silver and dark, falling obliquely against the lamplight. The time had come for him to set out on his journey westward. Yes, the newspapers were right: snow was general all over Ireland. It was falling on every part of the dark central plain, on the treeless hills, falling softly upon the Bog of Allen and, farther westward, softly falling into the dark mutinous Shannon waves. It was falling, too, upon every part of the lonely churchyard on the hill where Michael Furey lay buried. It lay thickly drifted on the crooked crosses and headstones, on the spears of the little gate, on the barren thorns. His soul swooned slowly as he heard the snow falling faintly through the universe and faintly falling, like the descent of their last end, upon all the living and the dead.*

The suggestiveness of this very rich passage is partly a matter of inexplicitness: what for example does 'The time had come for him to set out on his journey westward' mean? We have earlier learned that Gabriel does not want to accompany his wife on a visit to the west of Ireland. Has he changed his mind, or is the reader supposed to recall that the idiom 'to go west' means to die, and to associate this with sleep as proleptic of death? This is my second sort of suggestiveness, one that is creative and open-ended rather than closed and with a single, fixed objective.

Those who have read 'The Dead' will recognize that in this final paragraph a shift to what we can call a different mode takes place; the language becomes more poetic, and the more literal meanings of certain statements are hard to determine, while at the same time there is uncertainty as to who is making them. The ending makes extremely difficult demands on the reader, and is suggestive in a number of different ways (to take a simple example, the mention of 'crosses', 'spears' and 'barren thorns' inevitably calls the Passion of Christ to mind, a very different passion from the one experienced by Michael Furey, although one which also ended in death and which thus fixes a certain association between passion and death that has already been implied).

In addition to being suggestive, the ending is also evocative. It calls up particular states of mind and forms of experience, very often in their concrete particularity. Having said this, it is less easy to say exactly what it is that is evoked. There is a general movement in the paragraph towards a greater and greater universality, fixed in the actual mention of the word 'universe' in the last sentence. It is as if we leave Gabriel (whose consciousness we depart from as the vision becomes more and more general), and take more and more in our view. As this shift coincides with Gabriel's falling asleep, one of the experiences evoked is precisely that of falling asleep, leaving more rational, specific topics of thought and entering into a dream-state that deals with more general and universal topics. Note that what I have written about this passage is necessarily tentative. Necessarily, because if one is dealing with suggestion then certainty is no longer possible.

The last paragraph of 'The Dead' illustrates other important techniques. The use of poetic devices such as repetition and chiasmus (reversal involving the pattern 'ab ba', as in the opposition of 'falling faintly' and 'faintly falling'), symbolism (see the discussion of symbol and image starting on p. 123, which pays particular attention to the repeated references to snow in 'The Dead'), and other techniques are not limited to the short story, but they very often have to carry a heavier weight in this genre to compensate for the limitations that a restriction of length places on the development of plot and character.

■ The novella

The novella has had less theoretical attention devoted to it than has the short story, and this is especially so in its modern and its Anglo-Saxon manifestations. In my first chapter I suggested that the novella was typically between about forty or fifty and a hundred pages long, and Mary Doyle Springer proposes a word-count between 15,000 and 50,000 (Springer 1975, 8).

Its use in Britain and the United States is, as I have said, relatively recent; during three years of undergraduate study of English in the early 1960s I never encountered the term at all. When I studied D.H. Lawrence's *The Fox* (1923), it was described by my lecturer as a 'short novel'.

The Fox is just over 27,000 words long – 62 printed pages in the standard edition of Lawrence's *Collected Stories*. It offers us a good test-case for the need for a third generic term in addition to 'novel' and 'short story'. A 62-page work of fiction seems too short to be dubbed a novel, and of those characteristics that we associate with the short story – a lack of character development, a focus on epiphanic enlightenment or revelation rather than slow change, coverage of a very limited time-span – only the moment of epiphany is to be found in *The Fox*. There is restriction: there are essentially only three characters involved in Lawrence's story, and their interaction takes place exclusively in one place. But to call *The Fox* a short story seems as misleading as to call it a novel.

Theories of the novella are often constructed with particular reference to the German novella tradition as the novella has enjoyed a greater prominence in Germany than it has elsewhere in Europe, and as a result one needs to guard against making large generalizations on the basis of a limited sample of novellas. However, it does seem to be the case that the novella often has a dominant symbol or complex of symbols at its heart, and that it is these rather than the complexity of its plot that give the novella its depth and significance. It is not hard to see why this should be. Symbols function in an extremely economical way: they are like capsules of concentrated meaning that expand in the mind of the reader.

In *The Fox* we meet two women in their late twenties – Banford and March – who are trying to make a success of running a farm in the years immediately following the First World War. They are not well equipped for this task, and the farm is going badly.

> *One evil there was greater than any other. Bailey Farm was a little homestead, with ancient wooden barn and low-gabled farm-house, lying just one field removed from the edge of the wood. Since the war the fox was a demon. He carried off the hens under the very noses of March and Banford. Banford would start and stare through her big spectacles with all her eyes, as another squawk and flutter took place at her heels. Too late! Another white Leghorn gone. It was disheartening.*

Early on in the work, March, who we have been told in the second paragraph of the tale 'would be the man about the place', goes out with a gun and falls into a sort of musing trance.

> *The trees on the wood-edge were a darkish, brownish green in the full light – for it was the end of August. Beyond, the naked, copper-like shafts and limbs of the pine trees shone in the air. Nearer the rough grass, with its long, brownish stalks all agleam, was full of light. The fowls were round about –*

the ducks were still swimming on the pond under the pine trees. March looked at it all, saw it all, and did not see it. She heard Banford speaking to the fowls in the distance – and she did not hear. What was she thinking about? Heaven knows. Her consciousness was, as it were, held back.

She lowered her eyes, and suddenly saw the fox. He was looking up at her. Her chin was pressed down, and his eyes were looking up. They met her eyes. And he knew her. She was spellbound – she knew he knew her. So he looked into her eyes, and her soul failed her. He knew her, he was not daunted.

She struggled, confusedly she came to herself, and saw him making off, with slow leaps over some fallen boughs, slow, impudent jumps. Then he glanced over his shoulder, and ran smoothly away. She saw his brush held smooth like a feather, she saw his white buttocks twinkle. And he was gone, softly, soft as the wind.

Soon after this epiphanic, revelatory episode occurs, a young man – Henry Grenfel – chances upon the farm and ends up staying to work for the women. As soon as she encounters him, March sees him in a particular way.

The youth stared at them without changing colour or expression. If he had any expression, besides a slight baffled look of wonder, it was one of sharp curiosity concerning the two girls; sharp, impersonal curiosity, the curiosity of that round young head.

But to March he was the fox. Whether it was the thrusting forward of his head, or the glisten of fine whitish hairs on the ruddy cheek-bones, or the bright, keen eyes, that can never be said: but the boy was to her the fox, and she could not see him otherwise.

As this identification is strengthened, so too is another one: 'Meanwhile he was talking softly and smoothly to Banford, who loved nothing so much as gossip, and who was full of perky interest, like a bird.'

I will stop at this point, and suggest that if my account has whetted your appetite then you get hold of Lawrence's tale and read it. The desire to read on is aroused less by what any of the characters has said or done overtly than by the sense Lawrence's narrative creates of a parallel plot taking place below the surface of the work's realistic detail. Our impression of a mystical or supernatural identification of human characters with animals – fox, bird – creates a sense of profundity, as if the realistic plot detail is but the visible part of the iceberg. And in this way, if I can extend my spatial metaphor, the very limited *length* of the work is supplemented by a sense of greater *depth*.

Thus although the typical novella is more limited in its concerns than the novel, often restricting itself to a single state of affairs, set of relationships or setting, it characteristically compensates for this limitation by means of a greater reliance on implied or suggested secondary meanings. Hence it has some of the concentrated power of the short story, but without the frequent one-dimensionality that characterizes many short stories.

Probably the most-studied work of short fiction in English is Joseph Conrad's *Heart of Darkness*, at just under 39,000 words somewhat longer than *The Fox*. It is hard to imagine many short stories that could have generated the enormous body of interpretative responses that *Heart of Darkness* has done, and its force has once again something to do with its symbolic richness. I have warned that generalizations are dangerous, however, and the attentive reader will spot that what I have just said is difficult to reconcile with my earlier comments about the suggestiveness of the short story and my comments on the ending of Joyce's 'The Dead'. I would venture, however, that 'The Dead' probably *is* unusual among short stories in terms of the richness and intensity of its symbolism, and it will also be noted that it is relatively long for a short story (about 15,600 words). Mary Doyle Springer treats it as a novella rather than a short story in her *Forms of the Modern Novella* (1975, 4), and it is clearly near the borderline between the two forms. Furthermore, although a short story may be suggestive in O'Faolain's sense, and this may lead to a rich reading experience, it does not necessarily involve the same potentiality for interpretative complexity that we find in a major novella such as Joseph Conrad's *Heart of Darkness*.

The actual events of *Heart of Darkness*, like those of *The Fox*, could be summarized in a few lines; whatever we read this work for it is not primarily for complexity of plot development. It is true that in his *The Deceptive Text: An Introduction to Covert Plots* (1984), Cedric Watts argues that *Heart of Darkness* has a dual plot structure consisting of both an overt and a covert plot. But the covert plot is implied or suggested only by means of the occasional hint and comment. Equally important are such things as Conrad's use of symbol and image in the work, the complexities of narrative technique (the 'tale within a tale' and the interplay between the frame and framed narrative, each of which has its own narrator), and the texture of the prose.

The novella is dominated by Marlow (narrator of the framed narrative), and his fascination with, and search for, the mysterious figure of Kurtz. Early on in the story Marlow comes across a painting that Kurtz has executed:

> *Then I noticed a small sketch in oils, on a panel, representing a woman, draped and blindfolded, carrying a lighted torch. The background was sombre — almost black. The movement of the woman was stately, and the effect of the torch-light on the face was sinister.*

We see here, I think, how a relatively short work can be given a complex unity by means other than those involving the intricacies of plot development. The picture is one of a number of symbolic 'moments' in the work which draw various threads together in a masterly way. We note a relationship between the blindfolded woman carrying a lighted torch and those Europeans (including Kurtz) who have claimed that they are bringing light to Africa but who are actually 'going at it blind', either self-deceived or dishonestly plundering. We are reminded of Kurtz's fiancée, 'the Intended', whom we meet at the end of the tale and who is as blind metaphorically as the painted woman is literally. (As Marlow's account makes clear, European women have to be left in the dark about what their men are doing in Africa at this time – including what they are doing with African women such as Kurtz's mistress.) The references to light and blackness link up with a repetitive pattern of black–white images in the work which have an intricate relationship to sets of moral judgements indicated by Conrad in indirect ways.

Writers of short stories and novellas do not just produce truncated novels. These different fictional genres require a different use of the resources of prose, and they should not be read or judged in the way that we read or judge a 500-page novel.

Topics for discussion

- Should we accept that the short story is just that – a story that is short?
- Imagine what a favourite short story would be like extended to novel length – or a novel compressed into a short story. What are the gains and losses? Does the novel have all the advantages?
- How significant is it that we can read a whole short story in one session?
- Try to list what you enjoy (or dislike) about reading short stories as opposed to novels.
- 'Neither one thing nor another.' Is the novella more than a failed novel or too long a short story?

4

Realism, modernism, postmodernism

Preview

This chapter deals with: ■ the problems of defining realism, modernism and postmodernism
- realism as content or realism as effect on the reader
- modernism and postmodernism as periodizations and as generic classifiers
- modernism and the inner self
- fragmentation and 'realities' in modernism and postmodernism
- postmodernism and the celebration of disunity

The three terms mentioned in the title of this chapter occur so frequently in discussion of the novel that they merit separate consideration at this point. All three terms are used not just in relation to literature or fiction, but in order to isolate important cultural tendencies of (primarily) the past three centuries. Realism in particular is especially associated with consideration of the birth and growth of the modern novel, and of prose fiction in general.

All three terms are further complicated by the fact that each can be used both to refer to *historical periods of literature* and also to trans-historical *types of literature* (although the term 'modernism' is not normally applied to literature written before the final years of the nineteenth century). In this respect the problems associated with the use of these terms are not dissimilar to those attached to the use of the term 'romanticism', another word that can also be used to denote both a tightly delimited period of literature and a more general variety of literature or set of cultural attitudes.

Just as not all literature written during the romantic period is necessarily romantic, so too not all modern fiction is modernist, and indeed much fiction written today is neither modernist nor postmodernist. Moreover, just as there are arguments about what does or does not characterize romanticism, so too there is by no means any universal agreement as to what constitutes realism, modernism or postmodernism in the novel.

Given all these complications it might be thought wise merely to avoid using any of these terms. This simple solution is not, alas, a viable one. The history of the novel is so intimately bound up with the issue of realism that we can hardly talk about the novel without addressing it. Moreover, that there is a family of new characteristics to be found in much modern art and literature can scarcely be disputed, and the term 'modernism' helps us to isolate these characteristics and to distinguish between radically different lines of development in the art and literature of the twentieth and twenty-first centuries. Finally, although theories of the postmodern have come into major prominence only during the last three decades, they are so central to discussion not just of recent experimental fiction but also of many much older works that they need to be considered.

■ Realism

We saw in our earlier discussion of the emergence and development of the novel that the genre is distinguished by what we can call its 'formal realism': it is stocked with people and places that *seem real* or *evoke the real* even if they are imagined, whereas genres such as the romance or the epic were peopled with people and places that seem (and were meant to seem) unreal and that do not turn our attention to everyday reality. We can note, furthermore, that 'realism' is a term which a large number of novelists have felt the need to use in connection with their work.

On a simple level it can be said that something – a character, an event, a setting – is 'realistic' if it resembles a model in everyday life. The matter becomes more complex, however, when we remember that a novelist can make us think seriously and critically about the real world by creating characters, events and settings that in many ways diverge from what we would expect in everyday life – in 'reality'. Peter Lamarque has noted that a 'fiction is realistic if it describes characters with combinations of properties that would not be strange or out of place if exemplified in individuals in the real world', but he goes on to discuss the problems raised by a novel such as George Orwell's *Animal Farm* (1945) which, in spite of the fact that it contains farmyard animals which speak, think and reason exactly like human beings, also strikes us as 'realistic' or 'true to life'. He suggests that what we need to explain this apparent contradiction 'is an appeal to levels of interpretation or understanding' (Lamarque 1996, 38). In other words, it is difficult to arrive at a concept of realism which is not trivial unless one goes beyond a concern with simple resemblance and proceeds to consider not just *what is in*, say, a novel but also *how a reader responds* to this content and its presentation.

This is a shift of emphasis that opens up a set of new problems. William B. Warner, for example, has argued that, because what he calls 'the realist effect' can be provoked by a given novel at one time and not at another, the whole association of the novel with realism is thus rendered suspect: 'Because history undermines the naturalness and self-evidence of received modes of representing the real, it has proved difficult to sustain any "realist claim" made by or for a novel' (1998, 35). This I feel casts the baby out with the bathwater, for even though readers may find the same novel more or less 'realistic' at different periods of history, as conventions become stale and apparent rather than invisible, such changes seem to me to involve relative rather than absolute shifts of response. We still find Dickens's novels more realistic than *Vathek*, even though we are perhaps more conscious of many conventional elements in them than were Dickens's first readers.

Warner's point does serve to remind us that a novel seems realistic to readers even when it charts events and describes characters that are far from typical or everyday: think how many unusual coincidences and extraordinary events there are in those novels which are normally described as highly realistic. (George Eliot's *Middlemarch* (1871–2) is a good example.)

Lamarque's mention of *Animal Farm* should also draw our attention to the issues raised by parody and satire, both of which can be used by the novelist to make us think about the real world we inhabit. A parody is often very unrealistic in one sense, depending upon such extremes of exaggeration and such pointed selection that it cannot be said to give us anything that can be compared to our everyday world *in terms of direct, one-to-one resemblance*. Even so, parodies and satires clearly *do* cause us to see our everyday world very differently. The paradox, then, is that sometimes that which distorts what the real world is like may actually lead us to see the real world more accurately.

Brecht, Lukács and the realism debate

One of the most influential debates about the nature of realism in the twentieth century involved a critic very much associated with the novel – the Hungarian Georg Lukács. For Lukács, who saw realism as the contemporary artist's necessary, even ultimate, aim, the artist was required to represent the totality of reality at any given point in history, to penetrate between surface appearances, and to reveal processes of change. This sounds a tall order, and of course Lukács accepted that 'the totality of reality' could only be displayed by the writer through representative selection. For Lukács, the artist's task was similar to that set for himself by Marx: to understand world history as a complex and dynamic totality through the uncovering of certain underlying laws. In practice this led Lukács to place a supreme value upon certain works of classical realism in the novel – the names of Tolstoy, Balzac and Thomas Mann are frequently on his lips or at the tip of his pen – and to wage an unceasing campaign against different aspects of what he classified as modernism (see below). At the end of his *The Historical Novel* (written 1936–7), Lukács referred to the 'misunderstanding' of his position as one entailing 'a formal revival, an artistic imitation of the classical historical novel' (Lukács 1969, 422), but in spite of this disclaimer many commentators have seen his opposition to modernism as so all-embracing that this is actually what would have been required in order to satisfy his requirement that a literary work be realistic. Lukács's views are important for us to know about, because whatever his intention (and this is still a matter for debate), his arguments tended to encourage a view of the 'classic realist novel' of the nineteenth century as the pinnacle of artistic achievement of the novel, from which point on a decline took place as novelists abandoned that which the genre demanded of them. As this shift from realism to modernism coincides with the 'serious' novel's loss of its unambiguously popular status, the common reader has been dragged into discussions about the proper role and form for the novel.

Thus when the German dramatist Bertolt Brecht, writing about the concept of realism, stated that we 'must not derive realism as such from particular existing works' (Brecht 1977, 81), the unstated target was clearly Lukács (especially as he goes on to refer to Balzac and Tolstoy). Brecht's argument is, in a nutshell, an anti-essentialist one. In other words, realism for him is not intrinsic to a literary work, born with it like a genetic code and remaining unchanged through all its vicissitudes, but a function of the role the work plays or can play – the effect it has on a reader's (and not necessarily *all* readers') view of the world. Brecht's realism focuses on questions not of form or content, but of function. The important point to bear in mind is that, when a critic discusses whether or not a novel is realistic, he or she can be referring either to what it contains or to what it does. Now very often critics and lecturers use the term in a loose sense and restrict it to the question of verisimilitude, but we should remember that a novel can be unrealistic in the former sense but realistic in the latter – or vice versa.

Think of it this way: if what we read in a novel seems just like the world we experience every day, it may be unlikely to encourage us to examine that world critically, to see it in a new light, to ask whether its appearance is deceptive. In contrast, if a novel presents us with a world that seems extremely unusual, it *may* encourage us to ask to what extent our familiar world is really like this, in ways we have not previously considered. Novels that are most like our everyday reality are not always the ones that lead us to think most critically about that reality. Travel broadens the mind, and that includes travel to imagined worlds different from our own.

One other, related point: most present-day commentators agree that James Joyce's *Ulysses* (1914–22) manages to get closer to how human beings actually experience the world than did the works of most of his novel-writing contemporaries. Yet many (but not all) of those who read this novel upon its first publication did not see it this way: they thought that it presented an idiosyncratic, even perverted set of consciousnesses. What can we learn from this? Perhaps that one of the achievements of major art is to get us to recognize our world and our experiences as strange and unfamiliar rather than as we comfortably view them in our everyday lives. If this is so, then we must confront the paradox already mentioned in connection with William B. Warner's argument on p. 57: very often that which is later accepted as realistic will at first appear unrealistic. Conversely, Roman Jakobson pointed out in a classic essay that predates Warner's argument by many years that art which appears realistic to one generation may appear artificial to a subsequent one (Jakobson 1971, 38–46). (See also the discussion of realism in Chapter 6, p. 92.)

The term 'realism' very often implies that the artist (and not just the literary artist) has tried to include a wider and more representative coverage of social life in his or her work, and in particular that he or she has extended the coverage of the work to include 'low life' and the experiences of those deemed unworthy of artistic portrayal by other artists. The apparent realism of the early novel was intimately related in the public mind to the fact that it often concerned itself with the lives of the sort of human being who would not only never have been portrayed by the romance but whose depiction was clearly out of bounds too for the genteel eighteenth-century poet. Fielding's *Joseph Andrews*, Defoe's *Moll Flanders*, Smollett's *Humphry Clinker* – none of these characters or their real-life equivalents could have entered into the polite world of Alexander Pope except in certain forms of satire or burlesque. This is one of the reasons why *Joseph Andrews* (1742), *Moll Flanders* (1722) and *Humphry Clinker* (1771) are generally taken to be more realistic works than *The Rape of the Lock* (1711).

'Realism' also has a specific reference to a particular literary movement which started in France in the early nineteenth century, and flourished in the latter part of the century. The names of the novelists most associated with this movement are those of Balzac, Stendhal and Flaubert. These writers made enormous efforts to ensure that 'factual details' in their works were 'correct' – that is to say, capable of being checked against an external reality by empirical investigations. They achieved this accuracy by lengthy and painstaking research. 'Realism' in connection with these writers is thus both a term denoting a group of novelists and also a term referring to a particular *method* of composition. (See also the comments on 'naturalism' in the Glossary.)

The British heirs of the French realists included Arnold Bennett and George Moore – the former attacked by Virginia Woolf in essays such as 'Mr Bennett and Mrs Brown' for being a 'materialist' who was more interested in external details than in that inner life which, according to her, 'escapes' from his works.

One conclusion that can be drawn from the foregoing is that the term 'realistic' should be used only with extreme care in connection with a novel; it is a problematic rather than a self-obvious term and raises complex questions about what 'reality' is (our fantasies are after all real in the sense that they really exist and are related to our experiences in the real world), and about the means whereby a novelist explores the real. Having said all this it remains important to be able to distinguish between novels that – in however complex and indirect a way – cause us to think about reality critically and those which encourage us not to try but rather to escape from reality into a world of illusory imaginings.

One more important point needs to be reiterated at this juncture. It will be seen that Brecht's views, to which I referred above, also suggest that a particular set of novelistic conventions can be productive of a realistic work at one point of time, but, because they become familiar and present the reader with no new perspective on the world, can lose that power at a later stage. Thus we should not, today, make the mistake of dismissing naturalist (or other) theories and methods as unsound merely because in our own time we believe them to be insufficient as a basis for producing fiction that will encourage readers to see the world in a new manner. We should try, rather, to find out what their force was at the time that they were formulated, and remember that the way we see the world may owe something to the effect that they had on readers in the past. We should, in other words, learn to read novels historically.

Although the fiction of the last hundred years is often divided in very broad terms into 'realist', 'modernist' and 'postmodernist' fiction, this should not be taken to imply that fiction that is neither modernist nor postmodernist is somehow old-fashioned and unmodern. Moreover, the survival of realist conventions (a plot based upon cause-and-effect, well-defined characters, a general assumption that the world is knowable and susceptible to rational enquiry) in much popular fiction gives food for thought. One can posit either that the common reader is old-fashioned in his or her tastes and wishes to be presented with a world that is seen in ways that are familiar and thus undemanding, or alternatively that those writers and readers who produce and consume modernist fiction have another view of reality – a different world-view – from the mass of people who read detective stories, science fiction and popular romance.

■ Modernism

Modernism is a term which has come into more general use only since the Second World War, although (as with the term postmodernism) those texts to which we now apply the term predate the term itself. It refers to those art works (or the principles behind their creation) produced since the end of the nineteenth century which decisively reject the artistic conventions of the previous age. Foremost among such rejected conventions are those associated with realism in its more straightforward sense. In particular, modernist works tend to be *self-conscious* in ways that vary according to the genre or art form in question; they deliberately remind the reader or observer that they *are* art works, rather than seeking to serve as 'windows on reality'. Whereas one may forget that one is reading a novel when immersed in, say, *War and Peace* (1865–8) – responding to characters and events as if they were 'real' – this is not a reading position invited by a modernist work such as Virginia Woolf's *The Waves* (1931). Thus Picasso's rejection of representational art and of the conventions of perspective in his early paintings can be compared with the rejection of the 'tyranny of plot' by novelists such as Joyce, Woolf and Marcel Proust. This shift in attitudes from realism to modernism can be witnessed in the work of Joseph Conrad. In 1898 Conrad wrote to his friend Cunninghame Graham, 'You must have a *plot*! If you haven't, every fool reviewer will kick you because there can't be literature without plot' (Karl and Davies 1986, 5). Four years later, in 1902, he wrote to Arnold Bennett (one of Woolf's 'materialists' and thus far from what we now call modernism), 'You just stop short of being absolutely real because you are faithful to your dogmas of realism. Now realism in art will never approach reality' (Karl and Davies 1986, 390). What we see here is a writer beginning to question 'dogmas of realism' and to search for alternatives to the well-made plot, the rounded and lifelike character, the knowable world wholly accessible to reasoned and rational enquiry.

Modernism and the inner self

The modernist novel typically focuses proportionally greater attention on the states and processes *inside* the consciousness of the main character(s) than on public events in the outside world. If the twentieth century was the century of Freud and Marx then we can say that the modernist novel has much more in common with the former than the latter (which explains, incidentally, why an orthodox Marxist critic such as Georg Lukács argued so bitterly for realism and against modernism during his long life). Moreover, as I will go on to argue in greater detail in Chapter 6, modernism has a profound effect on novelists' conception of *character*. Michael Levenson opens his book *Modernism and the Fate of Individuality* as follows:

> *This thing we name the individual, this piece of matter, this length of memory, this bearer of a proper name, this block in space, this whisper in time, this self-delighting, self-condemning oddity – what is it? who made it? Ours may be the age of narcissism, but it is also the century in which ego suffered unprecedented attacks upon its great pretensions, to be self-transparent and self-authorized. (Levenson 1991, xi)*

For the great modernist novelists (Levenson pays particular attention to Conrad, James, Forster, Ford Madox Ford, Wyndham Lewis, Lawrence and Woolf), character can no longer be taken to be self-transparent – more than one character in a modernist novel asks 'Who am I?' without receiving a clear answer. Nor is the self any longer its own source of authority – which does not necessarily mean that any alternative source of authority is readily available.

   This focusing upon the problems of the self and of the inner life has encouraged the development of new *methods* of fictional expression. If modernism can be defined negatively in terms of its rejection of realist conventions and assumptions, its positive side can be seen in its remarkable development of techniques such as *stream of consciousness* and *internal monologue*, its challenging of traditional conceptions of story and plot, its markedly greater emphasis upon what Joyce calls 'epiphanies' and Virginia Woolf 'moments' – points in time when reality seems to stand revealed and to speak itself – and its revolutionary use of various forms of what we can call 'poetic expression' in the novel. (Witness my earlier discussion of the final paragraph of Joyce's 'The Dead'.) Such techniques will be discussed in Chapter 6.

A brief comment should be added concerning the philosophical underpinnings of modernism. These are very often implicit rather than overt, but frequently we find that modernist novels are pessimistic in tone, unsure about the sense or logic of the world, and look on human beings as isolated and alienated. The philosophical corollary of the rejection of perspective in art, and of an omniscient view of a knowable world obeying certain laws in fiction, seems to be a view of reality as lacking any unifying logic, to the extent that one should perhaps talk rather of 'realities' than of reality. (Again risking a generalization, we can say that modernists have a monist view of reality but accept that complete knowledge of this reality is impossible, while postmodernists adhere to a pluralist view and deny that it makes any sense to talk of a single reality.) Thus, for the modernist, different perspectives have to be combined because although what they reveal may appear contradictory, there is no 'super-perspective' by means of which to rank their validity.

■ Postmodernism

With the term 'postmodernism' we move on to other terminological problems. One perhaps inevitable confusion has arisen from the fact that, although one commentator has traced this term back to the mid-1930s (Hassan 1985, 119–31), it has only really come into more common use in Europe and the United States in the last three or four decades. Thus works which before this time were categorized as either 'experimental' or 'modernist' have in some cases received a new, often disputed, categorization as postmodernist. As Andreas Huyssen puts it, 'one critic's postmodernism is another critic's modernism' (Huyssen 1988, 59). A sharper critique comes from John Frow who, in a chapter of his book *Time and Commodity Culture: Essays in Cultural Theory and Postmodernity* (1997) entitled 'What Was Postmodernism?', argues that the concept of postmodernism is incoherent. He gives two reasons to back up this claim. First, those who use the term either give no examples of what or who falls into the category, or alternatively one person's examples are quite different from another's. Second, there is no agreement concerning the period associated with the term (Frow 1997, 26–8).

Other commentators have also argued that the term does not really isolate any significant characteristics (in art, literature or culture) that cannot be covered by the term 'modernism'. Such individuals frequently make what amounts to a political gesture by pointedly referring to 'late modernism' rather than 'postmodernism': behind the debate is the issue of whether we now inhabit a new sort of reality – the 'postmodern world' – which is fundamentally different from the world, or social systems, that produced the great modernist art. This political edge to the debate is worth noting, as the term 'postmodernism' is typically used in a rather wider sense than is 'modernism', referring to a general human condition, or society at large, as much as to art or culture (a usage which was encouraged by Jean-François Lyotard's book *The Postmodern Condition: A Report on Knowledge*, the English translation of which was published in 1984). Not surprisingly, traditional Marxists, who believe we live within the same old capitalist system, are suspicious of the implications of the term 'postmodernism'.

Postmodernism, then, can be used today in a number of different ways: (i) to refer to the non-realist and non-traditional literature and art of the post-Second World War period; (ii) to refer to literature and art which take certain modernist characteristics to an extreme stage; and (iii) to refer to aspects of a more general human condition in what is tendentiously referred to as the 'late capitalist' world of the post-1950s which have an all-embracing effect on life, culture, ideology and art, as well as (in some but not all usages) to a generally welcoming, celebratory attitude towards these aspects.

Those modernist characteristics which may produce postmodernism when taken to their most extreme forms include the rejection of representation in favour of self-reference – especially of a 'playful' and non-serious, non-constructive sort; the willing, even relieved, rejection of artistic 'aura' (sense of 'holiness') and of a view of the work of art as organic whole; the substitution of confrontation and teasing of the reader for collaboration with him or her; the rejection of 'character' and 'plot' as meaningful or artistically defensible concepts or conventions; even the rejection of meaning itself along with the belief that it is worth trying to understand the world (or that there is a world to understand).

As Christopher Butler has suggested, many postmodern texts are baffling to those who (like critics!) wish to find or impose coherence by means of 'coherence-conferring strategies'. He continues:

> *In reading a story like Donald Barthelme's 'The Indian Uprising', we cannot say 'who' the Indians are, what they 'symbolize', why the narrator makes tables out of hollow-cored doors while living with various women, why Jane is beaten up by a dwarf in a bar in Tenerife, as notified to the narrator by International Distress Coupon, and so on. And even if we could explain these elements separately in symbolic terms, there seems little chance that such explanations would be compatible with one another. (Butler 1984, 131; for Barthelme's story see* Unspeakable Practices, Unnatural Acts *(1976))*

Postmodernism takes the subjective idealism of modernism to the point of solipsism, but rejects the tragic and pessimistic elements in modernism in the apparent conclusion that if one cannot prevent Rome burning then one might as well enjoy the fiddling while it burns. A list of characteristics such as this has led some commentators to claim that certain much earlier works are postmodernist: the fiction of Franz Kafka, Knut Hamsun's *Hunger*, even Laurence Sterne's *Tristram Shandy*. I am unhappy with such claims, as they obscure what I see as crucial differences between modernism and postmodernism. It is also possible to argue that there are affinities between postmodernism and the philosophical positions to be found in the work of various post-structuralist and deconstructive critics such as Jacques Derrida, Michel Foucault and Jacques Lacan (see Chapter 9).

Postmodernism is characterized in many accounts by a more welcoming, celebratory attitude towards the modern world. That this world is one of increasing fragmentation, of the dominance of commercial pressures, and of human powerlessness in the face of a blind technology, is not a point of dispute with modernism. Even so, whereas the major modernists reacted with horror or despair to their perception of these facts, in one view of the issue it is typical of postmodernism to react in a far more accepting manner to them. The extent to which postmodernism is mimetic of recent and new social, economic and political practices in the societies in which it appears is a matter of some debate. Some have argued that the different but uncommunicating worlds with which many a postmodern novel faces the reader reflect the fact that more and more people in the modern world live in self-contained ghettoes about which outsiders know little or nothing. David Harvey's *The Condition of Postmodernity* (1989) initiated much discussion around such issues, and subsequent debates between (among others) Terry Eagleton and Fredric Jameson further helped to create a wider awareness of the issues involved. It should be added that those suspicious of the term (often on the political left) have argued that postmodernist views reflect not so much a changed world but more the contemporary isolation of certain artists and intellectuals, who then generalize their experiences and try to impose them on the rest of the world in their art.

In our third possible usage of the term there is also a perception that the world has changed since the early years of the twentieth century. In the developed ('late capitalist') countries the advances of the communications and electronics industries have (it is argued) revolutionized human society. Instead of reacting to these changes in what is characterized as a Luddite manner, the postmodernist may instead counsel celebration of the present: enjoyment of that loss of artistic aura or 'holiness' which follows what Walter Benjamin (one of the most important theorists of modernism and to a certain extent also a prophet of postmodernism) called 'mechanical reproduction'. In common with some much earlier avant-gardists, many postmodernists are fascinated with rather than repelled by technology, do not reject 'the popular' or the commercial as beneath them, and are very much concerned with the immediate effect of their works: publication is for them (allegedly) more a strategic act than a bid for immortality.

The following writers and their works have been categorized as postmodernist: John Barth, Richard Brautigan, Angela Carter, Thomas Pynchon, Donald Barthelme, William Burroughs, Walter Abish, Alain Robbe-Grillet, Salman Rushdie, Ronald Sukenick, and Jorge Luis Borges.

Finally, just to complicate matters even further, the Glossary entry for the term *magic realism* should be consulted.

Topics for discussion

- Do you like novels to be 'true to life'? Explain why (or why not).
- Why do governments often fear 'unrealistic' parodies and satires?
- What is the most realistic novel or short story you have read? List what makes it realistic.
- Is modernism 'the realism of the age of Freud'?
- Is postmodernism just modernism taken to an extreme degree?
- What technical innovations are associated with modernism and postmodernism? Why are they needed?

5
Fiction and the electronic media

Preview

This chapter deals with: ■ new technology and traditional forms in 'electronic fiction'
■ electronic texts: the end of the linear narrative?
■ technology and artistic value

■ A new sort of fiction?

According to an online newspaper article accessed on 3 August 2004, up to four million players world-wide regularly visit make-believe lands to fight, hunt for treasure or just chat (Meek 2004, 1). All of these individuals are participants in online fantasy games known by the acronym MMORPG ('Massively multiplayer online role-playing games'). Each player adopts an online identity and, using this identity, is able to enter virtual worlds and to interact with other players (who also, of course, have entered the game by means of other adopted identities). Here there is no single plot, no shared beginning and – the companies who earn vast amounts of money from these games earnestly wish – no ending. MMORPGs represent only one of the new fictional experiences currently on offer to those with a personal computer and (ideally but not essentially) an internet connection.

What has this to do with the study of fictional works such as *Wuthering Heights* and 'Fanny and Annie'? In immediate terms, not much, perhaps. The very nature of such online games with their multiple plots and character-lists that make a novel by Charles Dickens look underpopulated do not lend themselves to academic study. But the history of prose fiction is the history of a succession of low-status popular forms that are eventually accorded academic respectability (compare Bakhtin's comments on the 'heterogeneous' ancestors of the novel, quoted on p. 13), and it would be rash to suggest that none of the new fictional forms associated with the electronic media will ever produce anything worthy of serious attention. That however is a matter for history to rule on; so far as the present is concerned, these new fictional forms deserve some comment for a number of reasons. The first is that many of them are heavily parasitic on certain traditional fictional genres and sub-genres, ranging from the folk tale to fantasy and science fiction, and this survival of such popular and often highly formulaic fictional modes prompts us to ask whether these often despised modes answer some essential need in human beings.

The second reason for devoting some brief attention to new forms of fiction associated with the electronic media is that those who have analysed them have often found some of the tools developed by literary critics and, especially, narratologists extremely useful, and this too may tell us something about underlying continuities in the narratives we read and enjoy.

The third reason is the one I find most important. Some of the new possibilities brought to fiction by the electronic media such as reader/player-text interaction, (permanently) postponed closure and multiple, non-linear plots, frequently appear to be counter-productive in terms of artistic quality, however much they may increase reader/player enjoyment on a short-term basis. This may suggest some link between the high artistic achievements of traditional prose fiction and certain of its conventional formal elements. Another way of putting this is to suggest that although it is possible for the writer of fiction to do things in a text that is published electronically that are not possible with traditional book publication, this increased freedom may cut away some of the constraints that have helped to produce novels and short stories of great artistic merit. Greater technical possibility is by no means a guarantee of greater artistic accomplishment: the advent first of sound, and then of colour, did not immediately result in the production of better films. It is in particular the *fixity* of the printed text and the *linearity* of the printed narrative that seem to have been instrumental in establishing a set of artistically productive limits for the novel. The reason why there is no universally acknowledged great work of electronic fiction may not merely be that the 'text' followed in various electronic fictional forms is ephemeral and thus hard to subject to collective scrutiny, but also that the loss of the fixed linear narrative may also entail a loss of artistic worth.

In what follows, then, I want to look briefly at some of these new fictional forms, searching them for evidence of new potentialities in fiction while also using them to explore some of the sources of the artistic importance of more traditional forms such as the novel, the novella and the short story. Paying some attention to the typical computer game or to interactive fiction can be productive in much the same way that looking at a film adaptation of a novel can be: it may show what the traditional novel is incapable of achieving, but it may also show what the traditional novel can do that is beyond the reach of film or interactive fiction.

Let us start by reminding ourselves of certain things about traditional fictional forms such as the novel. When we pick up a novel we know that we are expected to start reading at the beginning and read sequentially through to the end, following the single track of what is known as a '(uni)linear narrative' (a telling that follows a single line of written text). Note that even if the narrative is telling us about two or more separate threads in the plot, the actual *telling* still has this quality of 'one thing at a time' – in contrast to a film which can (and generally must) depict a number of things going on at the same time. The 'conventional generic requirements' that I have mentioned sanction pauses to contemplate what we have read, and the reader is also permitted to flick back to pages that have already been read so as to review their content. A reader can also choose his or her own speed of reading, and can vary this from chapter to chapter or paragraph to paragraph. Note that this gives the individual reader a control over his or her own reading experience that the members of the audience of a play or a publicly shown film do not enjoy. Peering at a novel's conclusion before we have read all the pages that precede it, omitting chapters or even deciding to ignore the final chapter printed in the book and writing our own conclusion – such behaviour is in contrast *not* sanctioned by the unstated but universally agreed conventions of novel-reading; it breaks the established and understood codes that all novel readers have to a greater or lesser extent internalized. Moreover, the fact that a novel is contained in a physical object – a book – means that we have a very clear sense of how much more there is to read as the right-hand collection of pages gets thinner and thinner.

We expect, furthermore, that excepting a few rare and unrepresentative cases, what we read will be the responsibility of a single author, however much he or she may have been influenced by others. (Interestingly, in a number of cases of joint authorship the writers conceal their plurality behind a single pseudonym.) We also assume that this single person is ultimately both author and authority: he or she alone can decide what happens in the world of the novel. We do not expect to open a newspaper and to read a headline that states: 'Readers Reject Conclusion of New Harry Potter Novel: Publisher Sacks Author and Starts Search for a Replacement'. (If that seems a merely silly example, we should remember that this sort of thing actually happens all the time in the world of television soaps and comedies – usually without millions of viewers knowing that it has happened. The high status, visibility and legal authority possessed by the writers of novels is not enjoyed by all writers of fiction.)

It is often assumed that such conventions were faithfully and uncomplainingly adhered to until suddenly the possibilities offered by the new electronic media presented writers and readers with the chance to subvert or ignore them. But in *The Anthology and the Rise of the Novel: From Richardson to George Eliot*, Leah Price shows that subversions were there from the start, and sometimes encouraged by the authors themselves. Thus Samuel Richardson himself published an anthology of 'sentiments, cautions, aphorisms, reflections and observations' taken from his 1747 novel *Clarissa* (and published only three years after the novel) and arranged in alphabetical order. By 1760 Richardson was responsible for a 'set of entertaining Cards, neatly engraved on Copper-Plates, Consisting of moral and diverting Sentiments, extracted wholly from the much admired Histories of PAMELA, CLARISSA, and SIR CHARLES GRANDISON' (Price 2000, 17). So much for the subversion of linear narrative! But Price also reports that Lady Bradshaigh

> accepted Richardson's invitation for friends to write a sequel to Grandison which he himself would merely edit, so 'that every one of my Correspondents, at his or her own Choice, assume one of the surviving Characters in the Story, and write in it; and that … I shall pick and choose, alter, connect, and accommodate, till I have completed from [the contributions], the requested Volume'. (38)

So much too, then, for the view that interactive fiction was born in and with the necessary help of the electronic age – although it is noticeable here that

Richardson does retain for himself the power to decide what to include and what to alter or omit. While these 'subversions' are interesting, what I find more telling is the fact that today we still read *Clarissa* but the entertaining cards and the anthology of sentiments are to be found only in dusty library vaults.

Within a few years of this example, Chapter 20 of the first book of Laurence Sterne's *Tristram Shandy* (1759–67) shows an author attempting to create at least the illusion of interaction with a particular reader. The chapter opens with the following much-quoted lines.

> – *How could you, Madam, be so inattentive in reading the last chapter? I told you in it, That my mother was not a papist. – Papist! You told me no such thing, Sir. – Madam, I beg leave to repeat it over again, that I told you as plain, at least, as words, by direct inference, could tell you such a thing. – Then, Sir, I must have miss'd a page. – No, Madam, you have not miss'd a word. – Then I was asleep, Sir. – My pride, Madam, cannot allow you that refuge. – Then, I declare, I know nothing at all about the matter. – That, Madam, is the very fault I lay to your charge; and as a punishment for it, I do insist upon it, that you immediately turn back, that is as soon as you get to the next full stop, and read the whole chapter over again. I have imposed this penance upon the lady, neither out of wantonness nor cruelty; but from the best of motives; and therefore shall make her no apology for it when she returns back: – 'Tis to rebuke a vicious taste, which has crept into thousands besides herself, – of reading straight forwards, more in quest of the adventures, than of the deep erudition and knowledge which a book of this cast, if read over as it should be, would infallibly impart with them . . . .*

This is a joke, of course: Sterne is pretending that the author can communicate personally about his or her text with each individual reader. But in making the joke, Sterne is also exposing the limits and limitations of print-based fiction and, moreover, making a distinction between two sorts of reading that can be compared both to Samuel Johnson's comment on the two possible ways of reading Richardson's fiction (to which I refer on p. 30) and also to very recent attempts to produce non-linear narratives.

From the start of the modern novel, then, there have been sporadic if not widespread attempts to subvert, expose or submit to pressure some of the most established of fictional conventions: linearity and fixed sequential progression through the text of the novel (which does not, of course, entail a fixed chronological progression through the events of the story; see the discussion of story and plot on p. 111), a fixed text determined by a single author who cannot be interacted with directly by the reader, and a coherent and unitary story-world within which certain laws of irreversibility generally apply. ('Generally', because genres such as fantasy and science fiction do complicate this last element somewhat.) Granted that such precedents can be found, however, it is certainly the case that the electronic media have opened up new possibilities for such subversion – or, to avoid prejudgement, let us say for rewriting the ground-rules of fiction. What possibilities in particular do the electronic media offer? Let us consider the most important ones.

Fixity

A book or story once printed cannot be significantly altered. Misprints and mistakes can be indicated in an 'erratum' slip, and new editions can always be produced, but there is a very powerful tendency in print culture to consider printed texts as complete, unalterable and sacrosanct. The dramatist Joe Orton ended up in prison after being caught defacing library books, and even if this is an extreme example, it does show how alterations to written texts have tended to be seen not as creative additions but as violations. In the days of hot-metal typesetting (which only really disappeared in the book trade in the 1970s), publishers used to send out instructions to authors along with proofs warning them that the addition of a single comma could necessitate the re-setting of several pages of print, at very great cost. Today an electronic typesetter is able to make such an adjustment in a fraction of a second, and everyone knows how very easy it is to alter electronic text. But even with electronic typesetting, once a book has been printed it cannot be changed in the way that an electronic text on a computer screen (or an electronic book display unit) can. It is thus hard to treat an electronic text as 'finished', as complete and unalterable, in the way that a book appears to us to be. Even a text written by someone else can be imported and changed on a computer. One result of this fixity is that whereas traditional books have beginnings and ends, the beginnings and ends of electronic texts tend to have a much more provisional quality to them. When the final page of a book is read, there is no more. With an electronic text, what is the final word today may be followed by additional text tomorrow.

Linearity

According to Milan Kundera, 'since its very beginnings, the novel has tried to escape the unilinear, to open rifts in the continuous narration of a story', and he notes that although Cervantes' Don Quixote travels on a linear journey, he meets other characters who tell their own stories and thus the reader is able to step outside the novel's linear framework (Kundera 1988, 74). But the reader has to follow Cervantes' line of prose wherever it takes him or her, even if the line of Quixote's journey may be interrupted.

No one who has surfed the net can be unaware that by clicking on a succession of links one can take a path through a variety of texts that may well be unique to oneself. It is typical of the reading experiences offered by the electronic media that they do not conform to a strict linear pattern. It does seem to me that this may represent a fundamental shift in reading habits. Of course, we can always say that the person who read a novel and who stopped every now and then to look up a word in a dictionary, or to consult an entry in an encyclopaedia, or even to check what happened in another novel by the same author, was exploring 'links' in just the same way as a person who clicks on a link on a computer screen. However, although there is arguably a parallel here, it is a weak and a very restricted one, and cannot obscure the fact that while linear progression characterized most reading experiences – and especially the reading of fiction – from the eighteenth century to about 1990, the growth of the World Wide Web means that nowadays this is no longer the case. We have even coined a new verb to reflect this: 'to surf'. Readers in the past could skim or skip or browse or 'dip into' books, but surfing is arguably different from all of these slightly shameful ways of dealing with printed texts.

Interaction and collective authorship

Generally speaking, although the reader can tell an author what he or she thinks of a novel after having read it, actually influencing how it is written *while* it is being written has until recently been possible only for a few intimate friends of the author. We have two endings for Charles Dickens's *Great Expectations* because Edward Bulwer-Lytton, who read the novel in proof, persuaded Dickens to write a happier ending. And to remain with Dickens: the special circumstances of serial publication meant that readers could plead with him concerning the fate of favoured characters. However, this example is perhaps as well known as it is precisely because it is so unusual and atypical. The resources of the electronic media have enabled the creation of so-called interactive fiction, or IF, based on programs that require 'readers' to make choices that resemble the choices a map-reader makes in working his or her way across a town. The program allows for a number of possible 'routes', but a single reading will involve only one such route. Other web-based writing resources allow for more genuinely democratic interaction, where participants are free to submit text that may be voted in to form a part of a constantly evolving collective fiction.

These new resources of the electronic media have been exploited by those claiming to offer revolutionary new forms of fiction. Among these are the following.

The computer game

It may seem odd to introduce discussion of the computer game in a book on the novel. However, in his book *More Than a Game: The Computer Game as Fictional Form*, Barry Atkins argues that 'computer game-fiction is a form of popular fiction' (Atkins 2003, 9). For Atkins, many of the most popular computer games available today can be linked directly to forms of traditional narrative. Discussing one of these games – *Tomb Raider* – he argues that in many ways it 'conforms to the generic conventions of the folk tale, and particularly the quest narrative, and wears many of its folk tale credentials on its sleeve' (42). He explains:

> As in Tomb Raider *there are few extraneous or irrelevant encounters within the folk tale quest narrative: anyone or anything encountered will*

prove to be either an adversary or a helper. Overcoming adversaries through violence is virtually mandatory and, as in Tomb Raider *or any amount of contemporary* Ramboesque *versions of the quest narrative, there is no ethical or moral problem with such violence.*

. . .

The occasional riddle must be solved. Often an object must be retrieved. (43)

Of course, the riddles to be solved differ in nature from those in the traditional folk tale, and the player of the game must solve problems correctly before being allowed to proceed through the narrative, but the parallels between the computer game and, say, the picaresque novel (see the Glossary) are striking. One important difference, however, is that although the reader of a picaresque novel is able to empathize with the picaro, some of the experiences of the *hero* in the earlier form become the experiences of the *reader/player* in the new one. I should add that many computer games do allow players to shift their point of view – to experience events at one moment through an active 'hero' or 'heroine' and at another moment from a more detached and contemplative perspective.

As Atkins points out, the computer game is only 'interactive' in a very limited way: one cannot stray too far from the 'correct', and circumscribed, path and generally one can only perform actions that have been predicted or allowed for by the game-fiction's designers (41). But then much the same can be said of the experiences offered by different varieties of popular fiction to which the label 'formulaic' has been attached – the folk tale, the picaresque novel, the detective novel and the romance, for example. However formulaic and restricted the choices offered by the computer game may be, they do show how very traditional elements from narrative fiction can be married to the resources of the electronic media in ways that will inevitably become more sophisticated (and perhaps, although not necessarily, more aesthetically productive) as time goes by.

Interactive fiction

It is not a long jump from computer games to what is known as interactive fiction, or IF. Indeed, deciding where the frontier between the two forms is to be drawn is by no means a straightforward matter. According to Nick Montfort, 'IF works are often, among other things, games, with an optimal outcome that the interactor, acting as a player, tries to attain' (Montfort 2003, 13). Like Barry Atkins, Montfort also notes that the narratives generated by IF 'are often more trivial and repetitive than even the bluntest folktale' (14). Montfort explains that a work of IF is not itself a narrative: 'it is an interactive computer program' that can, when 'played', generate narratives (25). When we start such a program our initial experience is that we are much more active than we are when we read the printed text of a traditional novel. We have to respond, to make decisions, to *interact* with the program. Should we take this route or that route, should we do this or do that? My choice of words is deliberate here, because IF programs typically present us with a finite – indeed a small – number of pre-decided options to choose from rather than asking us to come up with a totally new and original plot movement. The experience of IF is thus closer to the experience of finding our way through a maze than to sitting down and reading a novel from scratch – something strongly suggested by the title of Montfort's book: *Twisty Little Passages: An Approach to Interactive Fiction.* This is why I wrote that *our initial experience* is that we are much more active than we are when we read the printed text of a traditional novel – because the sort of activity in which we engage when we play a computer game is actually rather less sophisticated, and less artistically satisfying, that the sort of mental activity generated in us when we read a major novel. When we read *Bleak House* or *The Waves* we do not interact with the text by deciding how the plot will unfold – by choosing between or amongst proffered plot alternatives. But if we search back into our reading experiences we will find, I think, that they are by no means purely passive, and this is one of the reasons why no two readings of an important novel, whether by the same reader or by two different readers, are identical. This is an important point and I would like to suggest that the reader pause here and consider the sorts of 'interaction' that take place when we read a challenging novel. Isn't one of the dangers of establishing a sub-genre known as 'interactive fiction' that this may imply that the reader of a traditional novel does not interact with it?

As is the case with the computer game, the artistic or aesthetic worth of such generated narratives is not generally deemed to be high, but interactive fiction is worth commenting on for a couple of reasons. The first is that it is striking how useful the conceptual tools of modern narratology have been found in describing elements in the IF world. Thus for example Montfort distinguishes between the *commands* keyed in by the IF 'reader' – which are 'diegetic' and refer to an action in the IF world – and *directives*, which are keyed in instructions 'such as those that save, restore, quit, restart, change the level of detail in the room descriptions, or address some entity that is not part of the IF world – for instance, to ask for hints' (26), and which are by implication 'extradiegetic'. Why is this significant? Because for fiction to work it seems that we need fictional worlds that are to a certain extent enclosed and insulated from direct contact with our everyday world. In her excellent study *Narrative as Virtual Reality: Immersion and Interactivity in Literature and Electronic Media* (2001), Marie-Laure Ryan discusses the tension and the interplay between 'immersion' and 'interactivity' in the reading of fiction. Her discussion has points of contact with my contention in this book that both when reading and when studying the novel we have to alternate between treating the characters and events as in some way real, and treating them as creations of the writer's craft (see for example p. 146). Ryan suggests, correctly I think, that 'immersion' in a fictional work of any sort is only possible by means of 'an imaginative relationship to a *textual world*' (Ryan 2001, 14), and she suggests that our concept of a textual world assumes four features: 'connected set of objects and individuals; habitable environment; reasonably intelligible totality for external observers; field of activity for its members' (91). The word 'external' is important here: it only makes sense to talk about *immersing* ourselves in the world of a fiction if that world is in some way fenced off from our own world. One further important point argued by Ryan is that when we assess the viability of a work of fiction 'as a document of real-world events', we are no longer reading it as fiction but as non-fiction (105). In other words, immersion in a fictional world necessitates some sort of abandonment of our own 'real world'.

This very sharp distinction between the extrafictional world within which the 'reader' lives, and the realized world of the fiction that can only be entered imaginatively and interacted with by him or her if the rules of this realized world are adhered to, is one that is familiar to readers of conventional fiction, although once again it is important to underline that we are talking about two very different sorts of interaction here. Nothing that goes on in my head while I am reading *Wuthering Heights*, or after I have finished reading it, will change the text of that work, although – and this is an important point – it *will* change my perception of that text. Nevertheless, one of the things that traditional print-based novels from *Moll Flanders* to *The Hours* have in common with various modes of electronic fiction is that they offer what Montfort calls 'simulated worlds' that are possessed of an internal coherence and logic that may mimic the coherence and logic of the extrafictional world but that are nevertheless distinct. The second reason why IF is worthy of consideration, then, is precisely because it reminds us that a fiction is only of interest to the extent that it offers the reader some *resistance*. A generated IF fiction in which the reader-player can change the rules of the fictional world at will is merely boring; however much we may want certain things to happen when we are reading a novel, a fiction that allows us to realize and enact any desired outcome is neither stimulating not satisfying. Imagine reading a work of fiction on the screen of an electronic book, and coming across the following message:

> Final chapter: press 1 for happy ending, 2 for tragic ending, 3 for ambiguous ending (advanced users only) ■

It is quite clear that the technological capacity to offer readers such options is already present – and electronic texts offering a succession of such choice-points may soon be on offer (if they are not already). But one of the aspects of the extrafictional world that is simulated by fiction is that reality is not something that we can mould at will and to our will. Marie-Laure Ryan expresses the matter with telling economy:

> *If the reader or spectator can choose whether Jack will be a hero or a coward, this means that Jack's behavior, and by extension the fate of the entire*

fictional world, is determined not by any kind of internal necessity but by the decisions of an omnipotent creator located in the real world. Yet the loss of the sense of the autonomy of the fictional world that occurs at every decision point is not compensated by a gain of creative power, because the choices are all prescribed paths. (2001, 283)

If then the fictional world is one into which we can enter, which we can observe, and to which we can emotionally respond, but which we cannot act within or change, does not this turn the reader into a sort of voyeur? Ryan would not be dismayed by the question: 'Whether or not we like to admit it, voyeurism has a lot to do with the pleasures we take in narrative fiction: where else but in a novel can we penetrate into the most guarded and the most fascinating of realms, the inner workings of a foreign consciousness?' (149).

Modes such as the computer game and IF may thus teach us a negative lesson: the fixity of print-based fiction, the unalterability of a novel published in book form, may actually be necessary to artistic force. Our ability to change the physical and social world is significantly limited; perhaps the unchangeability of the printed text mirrors and models this aspect of our experience of the world. Is not our interaction with a major novel very often of the type: 'What would I have done in this situation?' And is not this a more productive form of interaction than that involved in choosing one of a number of predetermined plot paths or story-lines? One of the easy assumptions into which we can fall is that indulging our fantasy in fiction is pleasant because nothing nasty ever happens and we can control everything. As Ryan puts it, if we feel that things happen in a created fictional world not as a result of 'internal necessity but by the decisions of an omnipotent creator located in the real world' – whether that omnipotent creator is the designer of a computer program or an author who keeps speaking in his or her own voice and reminding us of his or her power – then does not this undermine the crucial ability of fiction to model the problems and experiences of the world in which we live?

Hypertext fiction

Nick Montfort, whose book *Twisty Little Passages* I have referred to above, provides a neat definition of hypertext fiction:

A hypertext fiction (as it is most commonly defined and discussed) is a system of fictional interconnected texts traversed using links. An interconnected text is referred to by George Landow (1992) and others as a lexia, a term borrowed from Barthes (1974), who applied it differently as a block of signification or unit of reading that was empirically determined, during a reading. [. . .] There is, however, nothing in the nature of the lexia or the link, those fundamental elements of hypertext, that allows the reader to type and contribute text or provides the computer with the means to parse or understand natural language. (2003, 12)

The definition does not state whether these varied 'lexia' are written by the same person or by a number of individuals, or whether the 'fiction' is produced with all of its lexia available from the start, or whether it can be added to as time goes on. These are presumably details that vary from fiction to fiction.

Marie-Laure Ryan notes that for some commentators

> *Hypertext thus becomes a metaphor for a Lyotardian 'postmodern condition' in which grand narratives have been replaced by 'little stories,' or perhaps by no stories at all — just by a discourse reveling in the Derridanean performance of an endless deferral of signification. (2001, 7)*

This short comment needs some unpacking. One of the characteristics attributed to our 'postmodern condition' by the French theorist Jean-François Lyotard is the replacement of 'grand narratives' by 'little narratives' (see p. 63 and the Glossary p. 195 for discussion of postmodernism). These 'narratives' are not those that constitute works of literary fiction, but explanatory 'stories' by means of which we make sense of our lives. 'Grand narratives' are ideological systems of belief such as Marxism or religious beliefs such as Christianity, and for Lyotard the postmodern world is characterized by the loss of such all-embracing and comprehensive stories that provide meaning. Instead, we live in a world and at a time when sense and meaning have only a local purchase. Ryan's reference to the French philosopher Jacques Derrida deals especially with Derrida's concept of 'différance', a term that in French combines the meanings 'to differ' and 'to defer'. The concept is part of a much more complex argument on Derrida's part, but the important point for our purposes is that it builds upon a vision that also rejects some of the formal characteristics of the traditional narratives that we use to make sense of our lives, especially fixity of meaning, cause-and-effect, and completion (what is often referred to as 'closure').

This somewhat wordy excursion into theory is necessary to explain why for some commentators the technical possibilities displayed by hypertext do no more than actualize already existing elements in the postmodern world: a loss of totalizing systems of meaning, a concern with local, self-contained explanations rather than final answers, and an individually chosen and potentially never-ending route through a maze of possibilities rather than a walk along a broad single highway of meaning in the company of everyone else, until the end of the road is reached. Ryan calls such modes of organization 'rhizomic', picking up on ideas taken from another French theorist, Gilles Deleuze. The potato plant exemplifies such a connective system, with each potato (in botanic terms a rhizome) connected to other potatoes not in one long linear string, but in a network of interconnections. As Ryan puts it:

> *In a rhizomic organization, in opposition to the hierarchical tree structures of rhetorical argumentation, the imagination is not constrained by the need*

to prove a point or to progress toward a goal, and the writer never needs to sacrifice those bursts of inspiration that cannot be integrated into a linear argument. (2001, 8)

Ryan also provides a useful distinction between *multilinear* texts, which are those that offer the reader a choice among many well-charted sequences, and *nonlinear* texts, which are those 'that allow the reader to break her own trail' (209).

From such a perspective the traditional novel with its linear narrative, single fictional world, story-line linked by laws of cause and effect, and an overall meaning relating to a plot with a beginning, middle and end, is based upon assumptions that no longer match our experience of, or beliefs about, the world. In contrast, the infant mode of hypertext fiction reflects more accurately the world in which we live, and the ways in which we live in the world.

In very broad terms such a view can be said to be sociological in essence. It argues a broad similarity between the dominant characteristics of an age (both how the age 'works' and how people living at that time perceive reality) and the dominant characteristics of fiction. The argument goes something like this. In the nineteenth century the fiction produced in developed countries was realist because it reflected the way people made sense of the world (a shared sense of what was real, explanatory narratives based on strict rules of cause and effect, unitary characters with an understanding of themselves and their identities, and a commitment to 'grand narratives' that were 'teleological', that is, that were moving towards a predetermined and meaning-conferring goal). In the modern age (that is, for the first three-quarters of the twentieth century), in contrast, people yearned to live in this same world but could not, and thus modernist fiction contrasts the tragic gap between the need for a comprehensive system of belief that explained the individual's place in the world, and the recognition that actual experience is meaningless, personality is fragmented, and communication between human beings is at best partial. Finally, in the postmodern world of today, an acceptance that meaning can be at best local, and that the movement from experience to experience is largely or completely random and fortuitous, finds expression in postmodernist fiction. And postmodernist fiction is able to be most completely itself when granted the resources of the electronic media, resources that finally allow it to shrug off the fetters of the single linear plot, the fixed text, and the passive reader.

It should be clear that although I find such arguments interesting, I strongly suspect that they are at best half truths (among other things, the proposed periodization strikes me as crude and simplistic). But I will allow myself just two final comments that reiterate points that I have made earlier in this discussion. The first is that when one considers the ways in which fictional composition and reading habits have been adapted to the electronic media, one cannot but be struck by the blending of the very old and the very new.

Modes such as the computer game and IF, as a succession of commentators have pointed out, wed advanced computer technology to some of the most traditional (and among the lowest-status) narrative and fictional conventions.

The second (and perhaps related) comment is that even sympathetic commentators on the various modes of electronic fiction generally concede that, so far, the great work of electronic fiction remains unwritten. This may of course be because the modes I have been considering do not produce single texts. But it may also be, as Marie-Laure Ryan concludes, that there is something about linear narrative that makes it indispensable to Western culture and, arguably, to culture in general (2001, 270). A name that frequently comes into discussion of twentieth-century attempts to subvert or supersede the limitations of the linear narrative of printed prose fiction is one that I have mentioned earlier in this book: the novelist B.S. Johnson. As critic Frank Kermode points out in a review article discussing Johnson's work, the most striking instances of such subversion or supersession are to be found in his novel *Albert Angelo* – which has a hole cut in a page so that readers can read a sentence that comes some pages later – and another novel, *The Unfortunates*, which was published in 'a box containing a bundle of unbound gatherings to be read in random order' (Kermode 2004, 11). We can be forgiven the wistful thought that Johnson, who took his own life in 1973 at the age of 40, was one to whom the cliché 'born before his time' was thoroughly appropriate. Was he not a would-be electronic writer imprisoned in print? Born thirty or forty years later, could he not have produced fictional works not with just a hole in one page, but hypertext links every other line?

Kermode is sympathetic but sceptical, noting that *The Unfortunates* 'is interesting and well written, but it has never been the primary topic of conversation, the sensationally loose gatherings in the box having pre-empted that position' (2004, 11). He further suggests somewhat laconically that resonances between remote parts of a story 'can be achieved without cutting holes in pages' (12). The moral, it seems to me, is, first, that the non-linear narrative of traditional prose fiction does not exclude subtle and artistically productive effects, and second, that technical innovation does not always lead to greater artistic achievement.

Topics for discussion

- Do any of the new electronic fictional texts have any artistic merit?
- Is the escape from linear narrative a liberation or a curse?
- Would you like to be able to decide what happens in the novels you read?

6
Analysing fiction

Preview

This chapter deals with:
- the different ways in which a novel or short story can be narrated
- different sorts of narrator; different relationships between narrator and story
- stream of consciousness, interior monologue, Free Indirect Discourse
- types of character and methods of characterization
- story and plot; setting and theme
- symbol and image
- representing speech and dialogue in the novel

■ Prose fiction and formal analysis

The association of the novel with realism has meant that there has always been a strong temptation to discuss it as one would discuss reality – however defined – and ignore the art (especially the verbal art) that is a necessary part of its existence. Poetry typically calls attention to its verbal art and formal techniques, while performance arts such as drama require the discussion of verbal detail as a part of the planning of performance. There are venerable traditions of theoretical discussion of the art of the dramatist and the poet, starting with Aristotle, that have bequeathed a vocabulary and a set of principles to the critic. Moreover, the very popularity of the novel – something, as we have seen, that has been found regrettable by various guardians of culture – has meant that it has seemed inappropriate or unnecessary to devote the same analytical attention to novels as has been paid to plays and poems.

I do not want to suggest that detailed analytical concern with prose fiction (as against a scholarly interest in its texts and its history) cannot be found in the eighteenth or nineteenth centuries. However, it is the case that such a concern emerged in its recognizably contemporary form in the late nineteenth century and developed via a number of routes. First, early modernists such as Henry James, Joseph Conrad, Virginia Woolf and James Joyce – and their contemporaries writing in languages other than English – took their art seriously and often wrote about it, and by frustrating the expectations of the reader, drew attention to the changing conventions on which it was based. Second, the academy began to provide for the study of literatures other than those of Classical antiquity. Third, particular schools of criticism such as the Russian and Czech Formalists and the New Critics (see Chapter 7) significantly extended our understanding of the art of the novelist by means of detailed analysis. Fourth, the application of structuralist ideas and approaches to narrative technique helped to build up a far more precise vocabulary and conceptual basis for the analysis of narratives in general and prose fiction in particular.

Much of what follows in this chapter is indebted to these sources. This chapter focuses not on the novel's history and its historical identity but rather on those techniques and skills – the craft of the novelist – that can be found in novels and shorter works of prose fiction from various cultures and historical periods. The reader should remember that this craft has its own history, and different techniques emerge at different times in response to changes in the way people live and think – although they typically outlive the circumstances of their birth and the forces behind their creation. The founder of structuralism, Ferdinand de Saussure, wrote of the study of language that '[i]f time is left out, the linguistic facts are incomplete' (1974, 78). The same is true of the study of prose fiction.

■ Narrative technique

In my opening chapter I drew attention to the fact that everything we read in a novel comes to us via some sort of 'telling'. We are told what happens in a novel; no matter how successful the novelist is in making a scene seem dramatic it is never dramatic in the way that a play or a film is. We may feel that we 'see', but we see as a result of what we visualize in response to a telling, not an enactment. Even in those relatively rare cases in which a novelist makes extended use of the present tense, a technique which gives an added sense of immediacy to the narrative, we are still *told* what is happening rather than witnessing it directly as we can with a play or a film. The fact that when reading a novel we know that we can flip forward a page or a chapter, or look at the last page, is thus worth thinking about: it explains that sense we have that in reading a novel we are going through what *has already happened*, that which is being *re*counted to us. Whereas the last page of a novel is already printed and waiting there for us, the final scene in a play has not yet been performed as we watch the first scene, even if it has been written.

In one respect however the writing of a novel is comparable to the making of a film. When we watch a film we seem to be seeing 'things as they are' – 'reality'. We need to remember that a director has *chosen how* we see these things, this reality; he or she has decided whether the camera will be placed high or low, whether or not there will be rapid cuts from one camera angle to another, whether a camera will follow one character as he or she walks along a street – and so on. One scene in a film could be shot in innumerable ways, and each of these ways would produce a different effect upon the audience. Even with a simple conversation between two characters the audience's attitude towards each character can be affected by different camera angles, cutting, and so forth.

The novelist has a far greater range of choices open to him or her than does the film director, and we conventionally refer to that particular selection which he or she makes as the *narrative technique* of a particular work. Narrative technique includes such matters as the choice of narrator and narrative situation, the creation of a *plot*, selection and variation of perspective and voice (or 'point of view'), implied narrative *medium*, linguistic register (for example, the choice between colloquial or formal language), and techniques such as Free Indirect Discourse. All of these I will discuss below. The Glossary can also be consulted for definitions of many of these terms.

Narrators: impersonal or personified

Let us start with narrators, with the individuals or voices who (or which!) *tell us* the story. Perhaps most obviously, an author can have the story told through the mediation of a *personified narrator*, a 'teller' recognized by the reader as a distinct person with well-defined individual human characteristics. Alternatively, the narrative source can seem so undefined as to make it doubtful whether or not we are dealing with an individualized human source which comes between the author and the reader. (There is no ideal term to describe such a narrator: *authorial*, *impersonal* and *third-person* all have their drawbacks. The first suggests identification with the real-life author, the second suggests a lack of intimacy which may be misleading, and the third excludes those first-person narrators on whom we are unhappy to bestow 'personhood'.)

Consider the narrator of Sterne's *Tristram Shandy*, whose distinct personality is thrust at us in the opening words of the novel: 'I wish either my father or my mother, or indeed both of them, as they were in duty both equally bound to it, had minded what they were about when they begot me'. The opening of D.H. Lawrence's *Sons and Lovers* (1913), in contrast, strikes us as far more impersonal; whereas the opening of Sterne's novel focuses our attention on the narrator, who is talking about himself, the narrative of *Sons and Lovers* focuses our attention on what is told rather than who tells or how: '"The Bottoms" succeeded to "Hell Row". Hell Row was a block of thatched, bulging cottages that stood by the brookside on Greenhill Lane. There lived the colliers who worked in the little gin–pits two fields away.' Some narrators may even have names and detailed personal histories, as does Nick Carraway, the narrator of F. Scott Fitzgerald's *The Great Gatsby* (1925). Other narrators merely indicate to us that they are persons – perhaps by the occasional use of 'I' in their narrative – but tell us no more about themselves than this. We thus have a continuum of possibility: (i) personified, named, and with a full human identity; (ii) human but anonymous; (iii) not corresponding to any normal human perspective.

Narrators: inside or outside the story

One obvious distinction between the narrative of *Tristram Shandy* and that of *Sons and Lovers* is that the first of these novels is narrated in the first person, while the second is what is often referred to as a third-person narrative – it is a narrative told from a source external to the world of the novel by a narrator who is not one of the characters in the novel. Two different issues are thus involved here: (i) Is the narrator personified? (ii) Is the narrator presented as an individual who lives in the same world as the characters? While it is the case that there is a conventional association of personified narrators with life inside the world of the novel, and of third-person narrators with omniscience or a perspective on characters and events from outside the world of the novel, there are exceptions. The narrator of Henry Fielding's *Tom Jones*, for example, is personified and makes first-person comments but he appears to be omniscient with regard to the world of Tom and the other characters and is able to comment upon their fictionality. He is thus outside of this world even though he can see into it.

The standard technical terms now used to specify whether the something (including the narrator) is part of, or outside of, the world of the story are 'intradiegetic' (in the world of the story) and 'extradiegetic' (outside the world of the story): see the entry for *diegesis and mimesis* in the Glossary.

'Omniscient' means 'all-knowing', and the word implies that the narrator knows everything in the work. There have been criticisms of this term recently (see the entry for *omniscience* in the Glossary), but these objections are unlikely to get rid of the term. As human beings are not generally all-knowing it is conventional for omniscient narrators to be unpersonified, although this convention is sometimes broken. The term 'omniscient' is often used in a loose way to indicate any work in which the narrative has access to that which – like a character's secret thoughts – is normally concealed to observers in the real world. Thus a so-called omniscient narrator may not, actually, be completely all-knowing. The first sentence of Joseph Conrad's *Lord Jim* reads: 'He was an inch, perhaps two, under six feet, powerfully built, and he advanced straight at you with a slight stoop of the shoulders, head forward, and a fixed from-under stare which made you think of a charging bull.' The word 'perhaps' reveals that, however much this narrator may appear to 'see all', it is not quite all that is seen – perhaps because Conrad wants the reader to respond to the narrator more as a personified individual than as an omniscient source of information at this stage of the novel.

It should be remembered that, just as novelists may decide to give a narrator more knowledge than is possessed by an ordinary human being, so too they may decide to restrict this knowledge when it suits them. Complete omniscience is not only unfamiliar to human beings; it may work against the creation of that tension and uncertainty that exercise the reader's mind in a creative fashion.

Thus my earlier comments should not be taken to suggest that if in the course of a long novel the narrative lapses into the first person on one or more occasions then the reader is justified in assuming that the whole novel is told to him or her by the 'person' who lies behind the use of 'I' or 'me'. A novelist may wish to attribute his or her narrative to a single, personified source at one point in its unfolding, while creating the impression at other such points that it emanates from a more diffuse, less specific or human source. In his study of Conrad's narrative technique, Jakob Lothe (1989) has discussed two such examples of the sudden intrusion of the first person into a previously unpersonified narrative, in *The Secret Agent* and *Nostromo*. One of the things at which the student of the novel has to become adept is recognizing when such a shift of overt or implied narrative source takes place in a work of fiction. Such shifts can be either marked or unmarked; that is to say the author may or may not draw attention to them.

Framed narratives

One classic way of effecting such a shift is by means of a 'framed narrative'. Examples of this technique can be found in both Henry James's *The Turn of the Screw* and Joseph Conrad's *Heart of Darkness*. Both of these works start with a group of people talking, and then one of the conversationalists starts to deliver the 'framed' narrative, the main telling contained in the work. In both cases the 'outer' narrator is unnamed, while in Conrad's novella the inner narrator is named. I shall have more to say about the narrative of *The Turn of the Screw* in Chapter 8 when I discuss film adaptations of works of fiction.

It is interesting to note that many readers and critics assume that the outer narrator (or 'frame narrator') of *The Turn of the Screw* is a man – perhaps because 'he' makes many dismissive remarks about the ladies present – but there is no direct evidence that this is the case, and indeed in 1965, A.W. Thomson argued that James's frame narrator was 'fairly obviously a woman' (Thomson 1965, 35). In her book *A Rhetoric of the Unreal*, Christine Brooke-Rose (1981) takes many critics of *The Turn of the Screw* to task for reading details into the work that are not there, but she herself refers to the outer narrator as 'he'. The example shows how *active* the reader inevitably is in creating an image of a narrator on the basis of hints and suggestions in the text. A skilled author will, of course, make use of this fact – sometimes relying upon it, and sometimes challenging and undermining it. We assume, for example, that a personified narrator will belong to one of two genders and will not change sex, but an author can frustrate this assumption if he or she decides that this will be productive.

I find it revealing that in these two works both James and Conrad feel the need for a combination of named and unnamed narrators. The granting of a name conventionally intensifies the degree of personification, the extent to which we think of a narrative source as human and individual, although some unnamed narrators (Jane Austen's, for example) can appear to the reader as highly individual and possessed of a well-defined personality. (Or is it, rather, that we have a detailed knowledge of the values and attitudes relating to Austen's narratives, without necessarily individualizing or personifying them? Or do we rather attribute them to the person of the author herself?)

Intimacy and involvement

If we turn to Charles Dickens's novel *Bleak House* (1852–3), and focus upon those parts of it which are not told by the personified narrator Esther Summerson, we see something very different. Chapter 20 opens thus:

The long vacation saunters on towards term-time, like an idle river very leisurely strolling down a flat country to the sea. Mr Guppy saunters along with it congenially. He has blunted the blade of his pen-knife, and broken the point off, by sticking that instrument into his desk in every direction. Not that he bears the desk any ill will, but he must do something.

This narrative seems human perhaps in its gentle irony, but its viewpoint corresponds to no possible human viewpoint in ordinary life. The narrator is uninvolved dramatically in the scene, but he (is it he?) knows what is going on in Mr Guppy's head perhaps better than does Mr Guppy. Yet at other points in this narrative the narrator betrays an ignorance of things that we have learned from Esther Summerson's narrative. (So the narrator certainly cannot be Charles Dickens himself!)

Dickens uses the present tense in this extract; his anonymous narrator in *Bleak House* makes recurrent use of this tense, and it has a very definite effect on the way the reader responds to the narrative. We often use the present tense to tell stories or jokes, and so one effect of Dickens's use of it here is to make the narrative seem more familiar, intimate, colloquial. At the same time, the use of the present tense gives the scene more *dramatic* force: we feel that we are actually watching Mr Guppy as he is doing something, although without losing a sense of the guiding presence of the narrator. The main point I want to make here, however, is that, although there are situations outside of literature in which we deliver present-tense narratives, the extract I have quoted could be nothing other than literary. If we suddenly turned the radio on and heard these words being read, or if we discovered them on a scrap of paper somewhere, we would still know that they had to come from a piece of fiction, for in no other situation would this content and this narrative style be found in such combination.

In Joseph Conrad's *Heart of Darkness*, for instance, his narrator Marlow tells a story in which he personally has been involved. The 'outer', unnamed narrator in this same novella is also in a sense involved in the outer action (the 'frame') of the story, but clearly this narrator's relationship to events in the work is very different from Marlow's. In Charles Dickens's *Great Expectations* (1860–1), the narrator Pip tells us his life story, but the great difference of age and maturity between the narrating and the narrated Pip means that the narrator can be either very involved or relatively uninvolved in the story at different times. Indeed, when we are talking about fictional narratives such as this it is a good idea to shake off the habit of treating the mature narrating person and the youthful narrated person as the same, and to see them *in narrative terms* as essentially two separate people (compare the comment I quote from Javier Marías on p. 7).

In *Wuthering Heights*, Mr Lockwood is in a sense involved in present-time events in the novel (and the novel's time-sequence is complicated enough to give us a number of different 'present times'), but he is really an observer of the key events in the work which are narrated by Nelly Dean to him, although an observer *from the perspective of the same world in which these other characters live.*

Some theorists use the term 'homodiegetic' to refer to a narrator such as Lockwood who is a narrator of a novel's main story but (and this is the key point) who also participates in the story as a narratee (he listens to Nelly Dean's narrative, which is directed at him). A further term you may encounter is 'autodiegetic': an autodiegetic narrator is him- or herself the main character in the story he or she tells (thus, in her own narrative, the governess in *The Turn of the Screw* plays an autodiegetic role). See the entry for *diegesis and mimesis* in the Glossary.

Narrative medium and language

In addition to choosing a narrator or narrative source, the novelist can (but need not) select a stated or implied *medium* for his or her narrative. Now of course all novels consist of written, normally printed, words in a literal sense, but a novel may well be presented to the reader as if it were spoken or thought rather than written, or it may even be presented in such a way as to suggest that it is a sort of medium-less narrative – something impossible outside the realms of literature.

Thus, to take two very different examples, Agatha Christie's *The Murder of Roger Ackroyd* (1926) and Fyodor Dostoyevsky's *Notes from Underground* (1864) are both presented to the reader as *written* documents. We learn this only towards the end of Christie's story, when the narrator explains how he came to write his account (and that should make us pause for thought: think of the oddness of reading a story and not knowing until the end of the story whether it is a written document we are reading: that is because the written text *we* see stands for another text, about the precise nature of which we can be left in the dark by the novelist). In Dostoyevsky's story we find the following interpolated comment on the first page:

> *(A poor witticism; but I won't cross it out. When I wrote that down, I thought it would seem very pointed: now, when I see that I was simply trying to be clever and cynical, I shall leave it in on purpose.)*

We may well ask: why should one author want to reveal the implied narrative medium of the story on the first page, and another only towards the end? What difference does it make to the reader's response to the story? (Compare Philip Roth's *Portnoy's Complaint* (1969), in which the fact that the narrative is a spoken one is revealed on the last page along with the precise context of its delivery.)

Where a novelist does not state his or her implied narrative medium, all sorts of variations are possible. Emily Brontë's *Wuthering Heights* opens as if it might be some sort of diary entry: '1801. – I have just returned from a visit to my landlord – the solitary neighbour that I shall be troubled with. This is certainly a beautiful country!' Other parts of the novel, told by Mr Lockwood, as is this opening passage, read more like thought processes than writing. This is the third paragraph of Chapter 10:

This is quite an easy interval. I am too weak to read, yet I feel as if I could enjoy something interesting. Why not have up Mrs Dean to finish her tale? I can recollect its chief incidents, as far as she had gone. Yes, I remember her hero had run off, and never been heard of for three years: and the heroine was married: I'll ring; she'll be delighted to find me capable of talking cheerfully.

Mrs Dean came.

There is, I think, a slight clumsiness here. Novelists following Brontë perfected techniques for making such transitions between narrative viewpoints and media less obtrusive.

Closely related to the foregoing issues is the matter of *linguistic register.* (By 'register' is meant a particular sort of language-use that is appropriate to a given circumstance.) Whether a narrative is formal or colloquial, for example, depends a lot upon whether it is told by a personified or unpersonified narrator, and upon whether we are to assume that it is spoken, written, or thought. (Conversely, of course, the degree of informality of a novel's language may lead us to infer that a narrative is, for example, a spoken tale by a personified narrator.) Language in one sense is the medium of a novel as paint is the medium of a painting, but this is a poor comparison as painters do not generally represent paint whereas novelists often represent language: *Heart of Darkness*, for example, is not just *in* language, it *represents* language – the language uttered by Marlow and used by the novella's frame narrator. Thus in one sense the *actual* medium of this novel – language – is also its *implied* medium (although of course the implied medium of *Heart of Darkness* is spoken, not written, language).

While a novel's actual medium is written language its implied medium need not be, and indeed as I have already pointed out, a novel need have no implied medium at all, and the text of a novel need not even represent language – it could represent a state of mind, a sequence of events and experiences that have not necessarily been verbalized by anyone but which are translated into words for the reader by the novelist, and so on. A novel may well have no stated narrative medium: Joseph Conrad's *The Shadow-Line* (1916–17) can be read as if written, spoken or thought in origin. (Interestingly, as a result of gout in his hand Conrad actually dictated rather than wrote a significant section of this work.)

Narrative and representation

The previous comment may seem to contradict what I said earlier about all narrative being a telling: does not a telling necessarily require a medium by means of which the telling takes place? It should be said that this touches upon a number of very complex disputes within the theory of narrative. Some theorists prefer to distinguish between representation and telling, and claim that the novelist can represent – say – a character's consciousness in such a way as gives the reader knowledge of this consciousness without any sense of this information being told or transmitted – something that is, of course, impossible outside the realms of written narrative. Thus the narrative theorist Ann Banfield has argued that representation is, as the name suggests, a 're-presentation' which makes 'present' what is either absent or past, and which is thus unlike narration, having only a single point of reference with respect to time and place (Banfield 1982, 268). (A narration has two: the time and place of the narrated events, and the time and place of their narrating.) Banfield thus argues that, so far as certain examples of representation are concerned, to enquire into the process of 'telling' bespeaks only the critic's lack of comprehension of what representation involves – hence the title of the book in which she argues this case: *Unspeakable Sentences*. In Banfield's view, the novelist may give us sentences which are not and cannot be spoken by anyone; their function is that of representation, not telling or narrating.

Ways of telling

Let us pause for a moment and ask why all this is important. What difference does it make? Well, in everyday life *who* tells us a story, and *how,* make a very big difference. A proposal of marriage uttered directly, in emotional speech, strikes the recipient rather differently from one formally written and received by post. Source and medium affect the *selection*, the *authority* and the *attitude towards what is recounted* of the narrative – and thus, of course, the effect on the reader or listener. (One of the problems involved in Banfield's view of representation is, it seems to me, that even such representation involves selection, and the act of selection implies some form of mediation.)

The same is true with the novel: different narrators, different narrative media *change* a story; they affect not just how we are told something but what we are told, and what attitude we take towards what we are told. Nobody knows this better than novelists themselves, and different novelists have given us some revealing accounts of the problematic processes that deciding upon a narrative technique involves. There is, for example, a fascinating entry in Virginia Woolf's diary dated 25 September 1929, outlining her plans for her novel *The Waves*, which at this stage of her work on it she had provisionally entitled *The Moths*. She writes:

> *Yesterday morning I made another start on* The Moths, *but that won't be its title; and several problems cry out at once to be solved. Who thinks it? And am I outside the thinker? One wants some device which is not a trick.* (Leonard Woolf 1972, 146)

Note how the choosing of a particular perspective, a particular centre of perception for the telling, presents itself as a *problem* right at the start of Woolf's work on this novel. Note too her distinction between 'I' and 'the thinker' – in other words, between the creative-moral centre of authority and the perceiving-observing-telling situation, in the novel. It is very important to recognize the fact that these two are not necessarily identical, either in *The Waves* or in any other novel or short story. Finally, that comment that she 'wants some device which is not a trick' also underlines the fact that this sort of choice is not a purely technical one, but has aesthetic and moral implications which demand careful consideration.

A succession of fascinating letters written by Jean Rhys provides relevant evidence concerning her choice of a way of telling her novel *Wide Sargasso Sea* – a novel with complex intertextual links with Charlotte Brontë's *Jane Eyre* (see my comments concerning the links between these two works in Chapter 2, p. 34). 'Way of telling' is a formulation I use which includes both 'perspective' and 'voice' (see the discussion of this distinction on p. 95 and in the Glossary). What Rhys is concerned about here is, strictly speaking, the choice of a particular voice, although this has implications for narrative perspective. To her daughter, in 1959, Jean Rhys writes about the forthcoming novel:

> *It can be done 3 ways. (1) Straight. Childhood, Marriage, Finale told in 1st person. Or it can be done (2) Man's point of view (3) Woman's ditto both 1st person. Or it can be told in the third person with the writer as the Almighty. Well that is hard for me. I prefer direct thoughts and actions.*
> *I am doing (2).*

Later on in the same year she writes to Francis Wyndham admitting that the novel has already been written three times, first told by the heroine in the first person, second told by the housekeeper Mrs Poole as the 'I', and now using two 'I's: 'Mr Rochester and his first wife'. According to Rhys it was unsatisfactory to have the heroine tell all the story herself because the result was obscure and 'all on one note', and it was also unsatisfactory to have the housekeeper Grace Poole tell the whole story because although technically this was the best solution, the character 'wouldn't come to life' (Wyndham and Melly 1984, 162). Before we leave this example, you should think a bit about the phrase 'Man's point of view'. This has both a technical and an ideological or 'sexual political' meaning: a writer's choice of 'point of view' is rarely just a technical matter.

Other considerations can also be important. Christopher Isherwood's autobiography *Christopher and his Kind* contains an enthralling account of his problems in fixing the narrative voice for his novel *Mr Norris Changes Trains* (1935). He felt that he wanted the reader to experience Arthur Norris personally, and believed that this could only be done by writing in the first person, subjectively, and having the narrator meet Norris. The problem was that the narrator could not be Christopher Isherwood because Isherwood was not prepared to reveal his own homosexuality publicly by having the narrator an avowed homosexual, although he scorned to have the narrator heterosexual. Thus the narrator of the work ended up with no explicit sex experiences in the story, and was dubbed a 'sexless nitwit' by one reviewer. An additional aspect of the problem is mentioned by Isherwood. He wanted the reader's attention to be concentrated upon Norris and not on the narrator, and if the narrator had been made a homosexual he would have become so 'odd' and interesting that he would have thrown the novel out of balance by attracting too much of the reader's attention.

Isherwood makes a further point. If a narrator is given no personal qualities then when something happens to him the reader will assume that his responses are not likely to be unusual; the reader can thus identify with the narrator and experience with and through him. A narrator who is somehow 'odd', on the other hand, will prevent the reader from identifying with him even if the reader is sympathetic to him (Isherwood 1977, 141–2).

Let us return to the issue of choosing a way of telling in the light of our understanding of the crucial importance of such decisions by the novelist. Many critics have found it useful to distinguish between *reliable* and *unreliable* narrators, a distinction that touches upon some of the points raised by Isherwood. We can also note that, reliability apart, we associate some narrative choices more with the views and position of actual authors, and some not at all (or far less) with their creators. In general we can say that a single, consistent, unpersonified voice is more likely to be associated with authorial beliefs than is a personified narrator in a novel with many narrators, although of course in both cases this depends upon the attitudes expressed in and revealed by the narrative.

Thus it is easier to assume that the opinions expressed by the anonymous narrator of Conrad's *The Secret Agent* (1907) are close to those of Conrad himself than it is in the case of his personified narrator Marlow, who appears in a number of his works. Moreover, even if Marlow is a generally reliable narrator, we do not take everything he says on quite the same trust as we do what the narrator of *The Secret Agent* tells us, simply because we see Marlow from the outside and treat him as another person, whereas we adopt the perspective of the narrator of *The Secret Agent* and, as we read, think ourselves fully into his position from the inside.

Consistency is a crucial issue here. An inconsistent narrator cannot, logically, be wholly reliable, although we may recognize in fiction as in life that inconsistency may be the result of a continued and painful attempt to be truthful and accurate. The fact that Gulliver in Swift's *Gulliver's Travels* seems to vary from book to book, being alternatively percipient and obtuse, blindly patriotic and unchauvinistically humanistic, warns us that we cannot relax into unguarded acceptance of his statements or opinions. On the other hand, although few if any readers of *Wuthering Heights* can identify totally with Mr Lockwood, he is consistently portrayed, and so we feel more and more confident in assessing his opinions in the light of our view of his personality and character.

In addition to choosing a narrator and (perhaps) an implied narrative medium, the novelist has to select a *form of address* for his narrator. In so doing, he or she normally helps to define what has been termed a *narratee*: the person to whom the narrative is addressed (see the Glossary). Note that the narratee may be the actual reader, but is not necessarily so. The narrative can, for instance, be directly addressed to the 'Dear Reader', or it can be spoken or written to another intradiegetic (or 'intra-fictional') target or destination, or it can be projected into a void. In *Tom Jones,* Henry Fielding uses 'interchapters' in which the reader is addressed directly, while the remainder of the novel is less overtly pointed at any reader or listener.

What, for example, do we make of the opening lines of Albert Camus' *The Outsider* (1942)? 'Mother died today. Or, maybe, yesterday; I can't be sure. The telegram from the Home says: *Your mother passed away. Funeral tomorrow. Deep sympathy.* Which leaves the matter doubtful: it could have been yesterday.' In a previous edition of this book I wrote of this passage: 'Clearly this could be addressed to someone (would there be any sense in saying it to oneself?), but the narrative might represent a state of mind and a sequence of events which the reader is not meant to think are actually aimed at any recipient in particular.' A correspondent has suggested that this could indeed be Meursault talking or thinking to himself. I had assumed that the passage gives the reader the *expression* of Meursault's thoughts or state of mind, whereas I concede that it can equally well be read as the *depiction* of these. A general problem here is that because our mental statements or questions to ourselves are not necessarily verbalized, or at least not rendered in formally correct sentences, when such processes are depicted in fiction the writer has the choice either to help the reader and use formally correct sentences (thus making the processes appear unrealistic), or to try to capture the nature of non-linguistic or semi-linguistic thoughts in unconventional language (thus risking losing the reader). My correspondent also pointed out that the importance of existentialist ideas to Camus needs to be taken into account, and it is certainly true that Camus may well be trying to capture Meursault's state of 'being in the world', and focusing on the tension between the unchangeable facts of the world and his own more fluid reactions to these facts.

As this suggests, the same fictional character can be both narrator and narratee. In the final section of James Joyce's *Ulysses*, Molly Bloom is both narrator and narratee. Part of the narrative complexity of *The Turn of the Screw* comes from the fact that there are different narratees for different levels of narrative (see the discussion on p. 165).

Complicity and intrusion

Narratives can also involve such elements as *complicity, intrusion* and *intimacy* – all of which are normally instantly recognized by readers while remaining tricky to analyse.

Take for example the following brief extract from Chapter 3 of E.M. Forster's *Howards End* (1910), in which Mrs Munt is talking at cross purposes to Charles Wilcox, believing him to be engaged to her niece Helen:

> *'This is very good of you,' said Mrs Munt, as she settled into a luxurious cavern of red leather, and suffered her person to be padded with rugs and shawls. She was more civil than she had intended, but really this young*

> *man was very kind. Moreover, she was a little afraid of him: his self-possession was extraordinary. 'Very good indeed,' she repeated, adding: 'It is just what I should have wished.'*
>
> *'Very good of you to say so,' he replied, with a slight look of surprise, which, like most slight looks, escaped Mrs Munt's attention.*

That final narrative comment is the culminating stroke in a process whereby the reader is sucked into complicity with the narrator. We are amused with the narrator at Mrs Munt's obtuseness and self-importance, and as a result of such passages we are likely to be far more malleable in the hands of the narrator, far more willing to accept his value-judgements and assessments of characters. It should perhaps be added that at this and other points many readers feel that it is the author himself with whom we become complicit, and although this view has become unfashionable in recent decades, it should not be dismissed. (It is perhaps for this reason that it seems natural to refer to this narrator as 'he'.)

If we think of Jane Austen's intimate address to the reader in her novels, and Henry Fielding's intrusive interpolation of interchapters in *Tom Jones*, we can see that the narrator has a wide variety of relationships with the narrated events and characters, and with the reader, at his or her disposal. Choosing the right relationships is essential to success for the writer of fiction. For many readers, the last paragraph of Thomas Hardy's *Tess of the d'Urbervilles* (1891) starts with an annoyingly intrusive and heavy-handed comment from the narrator, a comment which such readers feel detracts from the power of the scene depicted at this point of the novel: 'Justice was done, and the President of the Immortals, in Aeschylean phrase, had ended his sport with Tess.' In contrast, at the end of the first chapter of Jane Austen's *Mansfield Park* (1814), we find this concluding sentence about Mrs Price (Fanny's mother): 'Poor woman! she probably thought change of air might agree with many of her children.' Although technically intrusive, this seems less to break in upon an established tone or perspective than does Hardy's comment, and so seems to have offended fewer readers than has that final paragraph of *Tess of the d'Urbervilles*.

It will be understood that the word 'intrusion' suggests that the fictional world is to a certain extent closed off from the real world of the author or even of his or her narrator. My earlier comments on modernism and post-modernism in Chapter 4 have I hope suggested that much fiction that can be classified as modernist or postmodernist does not present the reader with a separate, enclosed, fictional world. Instead, it is characterized by a breaking down of that firm distinction between the fictional and the real that we associate with classical realism. One of the paradoxes about classical realism is that it rarely admits to its own fictionality – something to which modernist and postmodernist fiction confesses most frequently. This is paradoxical because it means that the classical realist novel wants to portray everything in the world as it is – with the exception of itself! Thus it is no accident that I have chosen to exemplify narrative intrusion by reference to novels by Jane Austen and E.M. Forster – both writers of works which, albeit in very different ways, are more satisfactorily classified as realist than as modernist or postmodernist. Interjections from the real or implied author in much modernist and post-modernist fiction are so frequent as hardly to be experienced as intrusion.

A narrative can be either *recollective* or *dramatic*. Of course, *any* narrative involves recollection; to be told a story is to be informed of something which has already happened, something which is being *re*membered, *re*counted. We should probably except those rare examples of future narrative, although even here, because we are given the impression that the narrative *knows* what events are to happen, in a sense they exist already in completed form – have already taken place and are being recollected. In Margaret Atwood's short story 'Weight' (1991), for example, the present-tense, first-person narrative gives way in the four final paragraphs to the future tense. In these paragraphs the speaker is thinking about what she will do the next day and what will happen then, and so the emphasis is still on the present thinking rather than the future happening.

Present-tense narrative is more problematic, but it can be argued that this technique at least implies a gap between the happening and the recounting, although in English the use of the present continuous can give a sense of immediacy. Thus on the penultimate page of Atwood's 'Weight' we can read the following paragraph:

> *Charles is walking me to the door, past white tablecloth after white tablecloth, each held in place by at least four pin-striped elbows. It's like the* Titanic *just before the iceberg: power and influence disporting themselves, not a care in the world. What do they know about the serfs in steerage? Piss all, and pass the port.*

There is no doubt that the reader is given a sense of being present as things happen here, although I think that probably this is the female narrator's retrospective imagining-what-it-was-like-when-it-took-place: the things that have happened unfold in her head as she remembers the events in the restaurant. What is narrated is the retrospective unfolding in the head rather than the actual events.

Such subtleties and marginal cases should not obscure what every sensitive reader of fiction knows: some ways of telling a story can have far more dramatic effect than others (as is clear from Samuel Richardson's comment on his epistolary technique, quoted on p. 188). Note how in the following passage Jean Rhys changes tense in order to create dramatic immediacy in her novel *Good Morning, Midnight* (1939):

> *The lavatory at the station – that was the next time I cried. I had just been sick. I was so afraid I might be going to have a baby. ...*
>
> *Although I have been so sick, I don't feel any better. I lean up against the wall, icy cold and sweating. Someone tries the door, and I pull myself together, stop crying and powder my face. (ellipsis in original)*

Compare a passage from a much-quoted scene in Chapter 4 of Charles Dickens's *Great Expectations*. The young Pip has robbed the pantry of food which he has given to the escaped convict, and is eating Christmas dinner with his family in fear and trembling:

> *Among this good company I should have felt myself, even if I hadn't robbed the pantry, in a false position. Not because I was squeezed in at an acute angle of the table-cloth, with the table in my chest, and the Pumblechookian elbow in my eye, nor because I was not allowed to speak (I didn't want to speak), nor because I was regaled with the scaly tips of the drumsticks of the fowls, and with those obscure corners of pork of which the pig, when living, had had the least reason to be vain. No; I should not have minded that, if they would only have left me alone. But they wouldn't leave me alone.*

Here the author does all in his power to reduce immediacy and to *distance* the reader from Pip's experiences. In reality a young child in Pip's situation would have suffered torments, and would certainly not have found anything amusing in the situation. The reader is not encouraged to experience with the young Pip: rather we look at him from the outside, experiencing rather with the older, narrating Pip and sharing his humorous view of the events from his childhood. Such narrative distancing does not necessarily prevent the reader from experiencing with a character; it can sometimes involve deliberate understatement which allows the reader to imagine for him- or herself what the experience involved must have been like. A novelist can control the extent to which a reader empathizes with a character by means of the manipulation of narrative distance. The more 'here and now' the narrative is – both spatially and temporally – the more likely the reader is to enter into the character's experiences.

Note that first-person 'autobiographical' narrative has the effect of dividing the character of the teller into two, a point made by the first-person narrator of the Spanish novelist Javier Marías' novel *All Souls* (published in Spanish in 1989):

> *But in order to speak of them, [three people the narrator met in Oxford] I must speak of myself and of my time in the city of Oxford, even though the person speaking is not the same person who was there. He seems to be, but he is not. If I call myself 'I', or use a name which has accompanied me since birth and by which some will remember me, if I detail facts that coincide with facts others would attribute to my life, or if I use the term 'my house' for the house inhabited by others before and after me but where I lived for two years, it is simply because I prefer to speak in the first person and not because I believe that the faculty of memory alone is any guarantee that a person remains the same in different times and different places. The person recounting here and now what he saw and what happened to him then is not the same person who saw those things and to whom those things happened; neither is he a prolongation of that person, his shadow, his heir or his usurper. (Marías 1995, 3)*

A useful question to pose is: 'What does the narrative know?' Literary critics have traditionally used the technical term *point of view* to pinpoint this particular issue. The term has the disadvantage that different critics have used it in slightly different ways, to mean either the *narrator*'s relation to the story told or the *writer*'s attitude to his or her work. This distinction should be borne in mind, but one should also remember of course that an author conveys something about his or her attitude towards the work by choosing a particular relationship to the story told for his or her chosen narrator. Thus, in the passage from *Great Expectations* discussed above, the narrating Pip's distance from his youthful self's Christmas dinner agonies suggests that Dickens was not at this point too concerned to explore these agonies in detail.

Perspective and voice

Another disadvantage with the term 'point of view' is that it obscures what recent theorists have identified as an extremely important distinction, that between *perspective* and *voice*. We can sum up what these terms cover in two questions: 'Who speaks?' and 'Who sees?' In Katherine Mansfield's short story 'The Voyage' (1922), for instance, the voice is essentially that of a third-person narrator who is semi-omniscient and extradiegetic or 'outside the story'. The reader is, nevertheless, encouraged to see everything through the eyes of the main character of the story, the little girl Fenella. We experience through her senses, even though what we know of these experiences comes to us via a third-person narrative. Hers is the only consciousness we enter (it is always worth asking to whose thoughts we are made privy in a novel or a short story, as the answer gives us significant information about the author's focus of concern). In 'The Voyage', then, the *voice* is that of a semi-omniscient third-person narrator, but the *perspective* is Fenella's.

We should also get used to asking whether the view of characters and events which is given by the narrative is a recognizably human one. In other words, does it resemble that which a real human being might actually have experienced; were the characters and events real? In the case of Conrad's Marlow, Defoe's Moll Flanders, Dickens's Pip or Jean Rhys's Sasha Jansen, we can say that a real human being might share such a relationship to the events depicted as they have (which is not to say that such a real human being would *tell* his or her story as they do – or even at all). In contrast, no human being in real life would know what the narrator of George Eliot's *Middlemarch* knows about the characters and events that are depicted in that work. (Compare the point I quote from Dorrit Cohn on p. 3 that only in fiction can a narrative enter into a consciousness other than that of the narrator.)

What difference does this make? Well, a good way to demonstrate this is by means of what we can call the *transposition test*: transposing a novel (in one's imagination) from one 'camera angle' to another. Imagine *Middlemarch* told in the first person by Dorothea, or by Dorothea and Lydgate in successive sections. What would *Wuthering Heights* be like as an epistolary novel, with Isabella's letter about her marriage to Heathcliff as only one of a whole sequence of letters describing the events and developments of the work? Or told exclusively through Heathcliff's eyes? It can be an extremely revealing exercise to take a brief passage from a novel and to rewrite it in this manner.

Thus it is interesting to know that Franz Kafka started his novel *The Castle* (1926) in the first person, and that the manuscript of the novel has 'I', crossed out and replaced by 'K', throughout the early part of the work. If you have read this work you will appreciate how very differently it reads with 'I' rather than 'K'; the reader's whole relationship with the main character is quite different. Kafka clearly found the right voice and perspective for his novel only after having started writing the work – when he could perhaps more easily put himself into the position of a potential reader.

One term which has, I think, a useful summarizing function here is *narrative situation*. We can indicate what this term covers by asking about the relationship *between the telling and what is told*. Is the narrator personified? If so, is he/she a character involved in the action of the work? Is the narrative dramatic and immediate or distanced? – and so on. Narrative situation thus includes both perspective and voice, and also a range of other matters such as tone, mood and frequency (see below for discussion of these terms, and also the separate Glossary entries).

Narrative technique and history

At the start of this chapter I reminded the reader that the craft of the novelist has its history, and that different narrative techniques emerge at different times in response to changes in the way people live and think. Thus the rise of the epistolary novel (see the Glossary) in the eighteenth century, for example, cannot be understood apart from the great importance of letter-writing at that time, while the emergence of the stream of consciousness novel in the twentieth century has to be related to the development of modern psychology and the increasing interest in mental operations that accompanies it. The following factors are all important in assessing the significance of a particular narrative technique.

- Changes in the dominant modes of human communication (think of the enormous effect that the telephone had on human communication during the first three-quarters of the twentieth century, and of the enormous reverberations of the computer revolution – including those of the Internet – since the late 1980s).

- The effect of different world-views, philosophies and ideologies (there is clearly a parallel between a belief in a God who sees everything, and novelists' use of omniscient narrators – witness Jean Rhys's phrase 'told in the third person with the writer as the Almighty' (p. 89). The widespread loss of belief in such a God seems to have been parallelled by a disenchantment with the possibilities of narrative omniscience).

■ Changes in readership patterns and habits (it is perhaps harder to feel intimate with a larger, more amorphous and anonymous set of readers).

■ Larger changes in human life and modes of consciousness (think of the growth of urban living, of mass communication, of modern science and politics).

Stream of consciousness and interior monologue

Let me at this point say a few words about *stream of consciousness* technique and the *internal* (or *interior*) *monologue* (terms also defined in the Glossary). The two need carefully to be distinguished. Strictly speaking, an internal monologue implies the use of *language*, and if an individual is 'talking to himself or herself', then that in turn presupposes a certain amount of consciousness of what is going on in that person's mind. Milan Kundera, talking about 'the fantastic espionage of interior monologue', claims that James Joyce set a microphone within his character Leopold Bloom's head (Kundera 1988, 28). The famous closing section of James Joyce's *Ulysses* gives us, essentially, the stream of Molly Bloom's consciousness, but in internal monologue; she is (I think) thinking to herself in words and is conscious of what she is thinking. I say 'I think' because novelists can transpose unverbalized thoughts and sensations into verbal statements which are attributed to the character in question, and it is possible that at least part of this chapter should be read in this way. The chapter opens:

> *Yes because he never did a thing like that before as ask to get his breakfast in bed with a couple of eggs since the City Arms hotel when he used to be pretending to be laid up with a sick voice . . .*

It is possible that the reader is meant to imagine Molly experiencing a primarily sensuous (visual/tactile) memory of the previous recumbent breakfast, and that the words we read are to be taken as a token of this set of sensuous, non-verbal memories. This seems unlikely though – first because the chapter in spite of its lack of punctuation has a logical structure and presents us with Molly's *arguments*, and it is difficult if not impossible to argue non-verbally, and second because Joyce typically presents thought processes as verbalized.

Consider the following passage – the first two paragraphs of D.H. Lawrence's short story 'Fanny and Annie' (1922):

> *Flame-lurid his face as he turned among the throng of flame-lit and dark faces upon the platform. In the light of the furnace she caught sight of his drifting countenance, like a piece of floating fire. And the nostalgia, the doom of homecoming went through her veins like a drug. His eternal face, flame-lit now! The pulse and darkness of red fire from the furnace towers in the sky, lighting the desultory, industrial crowd on the wayside station, lit him and went out.*
>
> *Of course he did not see her. Flame-lit and unseeing! Always the same, with his meeting eyebrows, his common cap, and his red-and-black scarf*

knotted round his throat. Not even a collar to meet her! The flames had sunk, there was shadow.

The passage is extremely complex, in part because it mixes what the narrator tells us and what Fanny is thinking, so that at several points it is hard if not impossible to tell whether what we are reading represents a narrative comment or Fanny's thoughts. I would like to draw attention to the fourth sentence ('His eternal face, flame-lit now!') and the whole of the second paragraph down to the end of the penultimate sentence quoted ('… to meet her!'). It seems to me highly likely that these sentences represent Fanny's stream of consciousness rather than the narrator's commentary, although some parts could be both or either. What seems almost certain is that Fanny is not thinking by means of the actual words we are given. She is not thinking 'His eternal face, flame-lit now! Of course he does not see me, flame-lit and unseeing! Always the same, with his meeting eyebrows, his common cap, and his red-and-black scarf knotted round his throat. Not even a collar to meet me!', although she may verbalize *some* of these thoughts by means of the words we read. What Lawrence's words do is to give us Fanny's stream of consciousness rather than her internal monologue. We can summarize and say that an internal monologue gives us a character's stream of consciousness (or at least part of it, if we imagine images accompanying words), but not every stream of consciousness is an internal monologue.

Free Indirect Discourse

The difficulty I mentioned above of distinguishing between what a narrator says and what a character thinks or verbalizes may become particularly acute with the use of a technique which is known by a number of different terms: 'Free Indirect Discourse (or Speech)', 'represented speech and thought', 'narrated monologue', or the German and French terms 'erlebte Rede' and 'style indirect libre'. The complications of terminology are worth wading through, for the technique itself is arguably one of the most important in the novel since Jane Austen. Look again at the opening of 'Fanny and Annie'. Who is it who says 'Of course he did not see her'? The grammatical structure of the sentence, with Fanny referred to as 'her', might suggest that it is the narrator (it cannot be Harry, the man, precisely because he has not seen her). Is it not rather odd for the narrator to utter this comment, as if Harry's behaviour were expected but nonetheless irritating, and as if the reader knew enough about Harry to legitimize that 'of course'? The same can be said of 'Always the same, with his meeting eyebrows, his common cap, and his red-and-black scarf knotted round his throat. Not even a collar to meet her!' Is it not odd for the narrator to say this, first because we do not expect an omniscient narrator to get so quickly irritated by a character, and second because the statement assumes that whoever hears this comment will be familiar with poor Harry's shortcomings? How do we know that Harry is always the same? This is the first time that we have encountered him!

In fact, as most readers have no difficulty in working out, it is not Lawrence's narrator but Fanny whose irritation at Harry's familiar inadequacies is thereby expressed. Typical of Free Indirect Discourse – to use what I now favour as the best term to describe this technique – is the use of the grammar of third-person utterance (with certain modifications) to present us with a character's speech or (verbal or non-verbal) thoughts. (As will be understood, terms such as Free Indirect Speech, represented speech, and represented thought have a more limited application than does the blanket term Free Indirect Discourse.)

The traditional way of defining what we can refer to as FID makes use of grammatical or linguistic evidence. This involves seeing FID as a midway point between Direct and Indirect (or Reported) Discourse (DD and ID), or as a combination of the two which blends their grammatical characteristics in a distinctive mix. Thus we can use the following simple illustration, in which one can note that the third example retains the third-person 'he' and past tense from ID, but in its truncation resembles the words in inverted commas in the DD example.

> DD: *He said, 'I love her'*
>
> ID: *He said that he loved her*
>
> FID: *He loved her*
>
> (example from Rimmon-Kenan 1983, 111)

What should strike us immediately about the third example ('He loved her') is that, like sentences in the passage from 'Fanny and Annie' at which we have already looked, in the context of a passage from a novel it could be ambiguous. It could either give us the consciousness of the 'he' referred to, his realization that he loves a woman, or it could give the reader a statement by a narrator about a character (who might not even realize, yet, that he loves the person concerned). This ambiguity is exploited by the most skilled writers of prose fiction, and very often allows them to move backwards and forwards between narrative comment and character consciousness, often with no apparent seams. Look again at the opening of Lawrence's story. It clearly gives us both (i) comment that comes from a narrator or source outside the depicted characters and events, and also (ii) what Fanny is thinking. It is nevertheless impossible to make a sharp distinction between the two such that one ends up with two neat piles, one labelled 'narrator's comment' and the other 'Fanny's thoughts'. This, I would argue, is a strength rather than a weakness of the passage; if you disagree, try rewriting it so as to exclude any ambiguity as to whom statements should be attributed.

Another example, this time another passage from Katherine Mansfield's 'The Voyage':

> *'How long am I going to stay?' she whispered anxiously. He wouldn't look at her. He shook her off gently, and gently said, 'We'll see about that.*

> *Here! Where's your hand?' He pressed something into her palm. 'Here's a shilling in case you should need it.'*
> *A shilling! She must be going away for ever! 'Father!' cried Fenella.*

The part of this passage to which I want to draw your attention is 'A shilling! She must be going away for ever!' Now you will note that (as with 'He loved her') these two utterances are ostensibly in the third person; Fenella is described as 'she' and inverted commas are not used. Even so, it is clear that it is Fenella's thoughts that are being given here as neither the narrator nor her father would be so surprised at her being given a shilling.

Let me return to the issue of the ambiguity associated with the technique, an ambiguity which sometimes makes it impossible definitively to attribute a statement either to narrator or character. Take this extract from Virginia Woolf's *Mrs Dalloway*:

> *Elizabeth rather wondered whether Miss Kilman could be hungry. It was her way of eating, eating with intensity, then looking, again and again, at a plate of sugared cakes on the table next them; then, when a lady and a child sat down and the child took the cake, could Miss Kilman really mind it? Yes, Miss Kilman did mind it. She had wanted that cake – the pink one. The pleasure of eating was almost the only pure pleasure left her, and then to be baffled even in that!*

Whose consciousness is represented in the last three sentences? Is it (1) narrator (2) narrator (3) narrator? Or (1) narrator (2) narrator (3) Miss Kilman? Or (1) narrator (2) Miss Kilman (3) Miss Kilman? It is even possible that these sentences give us Elizabeth's thoughts as she imagines what Miss Kilman is thinking. As with the opening of 'Fanny and Annie', these ambiguities do not constitute a flaw in the passage but quite the reverse: we know what Miss Kilman is thinking and we understand the narrator's attitude towards her and her desires without having to attribute a form of words either to the narrator or to the character. Note that a principle of inertia operates in our response to such passages: unless we are given good reason for changing the way we attribute statements to a particular source or consciousness, we tend to go on attributing them to the one already established as the operative one. The technical term for this 'principle of inertia' in narrative theory is *obstination* (see also the Glossary).

Another technique, one which has something in common with Free Indirect Discourse without having quite the grammatical specificity of this technique, is that of *coloured* discourse or narrative. This involves the 'colouring' of a piece of (normally but not necessarily) third-person narrative with words, phrases, expressions which the reader associates with the verbal habits of a particular character. The technique is closely related to techniques used to mock, mimic or satirize others in speech. The fiction of Dickens contains innumerable examples of it, from which the following (the opening of Chapter 25, 'Book the Second', of *Little Dorrit* (1857–8)) will serve as illustration:

> *The dinner-party was at the great Physician's. Bar was there, and in full force. Ferdinand Barnacle was there, and in his most engaging state. Few ways of life were hidden from Physician, and he was oftener in its darkest places than even Bishop. There were brilliant Ladies about London who perfectly doted on him, my dear, as the most charming creature and the most delightful person . . .*

The whole of this chapter is characterized by bitter and ironic mockery of the pretensions of those involved, but in this passage we see Dickens actually incorporating a verbal 'signature' from those he is mocking; 'my dear' is, we take it, the sort of frequent hypocrisy to be found in the conversation of the ladies being ridiculed, and its inclusion colours the narrative around it. (See also the entry for *colouring* in the Glossary.)

Tone and mode

Before we leave the general topic of narrative technique, two other important terms need to be mentioned: *tone* and *mode*. The term 'tone' refers to the attitude of the narrator (and sometimes, by implication, of the author) towards what is narrated. One fails to understand *Gulliver's Travels*, for example, if one does not perceive the satirical tone that pervades the whole work. In like manner, although it is true that a work like Kafka's *The Castle* suggests that life is meaningless and that communication between human beings is impossible, this aspect of the work has to be seen in consort with the tone of deep pity and sympathy for humanity which pervades the novel.

'Mode', however, refers to the type of discourse used by the narrator – the sort of issue we considered earlier in connection with discussion of the term 'point of view'. The term is taken from Continental narrative theorists and is sometimes rendered as 'mood', although as 'mood' has other meanings within literary criticism I prefer to use 'mode' in this context. We can sum up what is meant by mood/mode by saying that it refers to the *relationship* between the narrating and what is narrated in a broad sense – both in terms of *what* is perceived and reported and in terms of *how* this is treated. I will come back to this relationship and to other technical terms in the discussion of plot later on in this chapter.

If these (and other) terms confuse you, do not worry; remember that the important thing is not to learn a complicated set of terms but rather to become alive to the sort of distinctions the terms point to.

■ Character
Character and individuality

I suggested in Chapter 2 that it was a moot point whether much fiction from before the time of the modern novel could be said to contain characters as we understand the word. For us, 'character' is intimately bound up with individualism: a character is unique, not just the property of a person but somehow simultaneously both the person and the sign or token of the person. (See my comments in Chapter 2, p. 14, on the etymological connection with 'character' meaning 'handwriting'.) According to Clemens Lugowski, so long as human existence is dominated by myth (which is timeless and collective) rather than by history, 'there can be no individual characters', for instead of being autonomous individuals 'they are no more than components of a whole' (Lugowski 1990, 83). Myth takes, typically, an oral form, whereas the novel, as I have argued in my opening chapter, has an intimate relationship with writing and printing. No literary or artistic form has a closer relationship to what we now know and understand as character than does the novel.

If we can conceive of a time during which characters as we know them, both in life and in fiction, did not exist, then it will be easier for us to consider a number of other possibilities. First, that how human individuals are represented in books has some connection with how they are conceived by themselves and by others in real life. Second, that as our view of human individuality in the real world changes, so too may our view of fictional character. Third, that just as there are conventions which govern (or at least influence) how speech is represented in the novel (see the end of this chapter, p. 126), so too there are comparable and changing conventions which govern the depiction of character in the novel. Finally, that if there was a time in which human beings saw themselves in ways untouched by the individualism which forms an important component in the developing concept of fictional character, then there might just be such a time again one day, so that those elements which may strike us as strange and unnatural in the way in which individuals are represented in modernist and postmodernist fiction *may* be prophetic of some such change. (Needless to say, they may not!)

We should certainly not assume that because we can respond so fully to characters in the fiction of past ages there is, therefore, no change in fictional characterization from age to age. Not only are there technical changes in the way novelists learn to create and reveal characters, but also changes in human beings outside literature (or at least the belief that such changes have taken place) often inspire novelists to use new methods to produce a new sort of character.

In her famous essay 'Mr Bennett and Mrs Brown' (1924), Virginia Woolf states her belief that:

> *all novels ... deal with character, and that it is to express character – not to preach doctrines, sing songs, or celebrate the glories of the British Empire, that the form of the novel, so clumsy, verbose, and undramatic, so rich, elastic, and alive, has been evolved. (Woolf 1966a, 324)*

This does not mean that she sets up 'character' as a sort of human universal, or that she claims that the characters we find in books or in real life are always the same. Indeed, earlier on in the same essay she has already made the remark (doubtless part tongue-in-cheek) that 'in or about December, 1910, human character changed' (320). Woolf is of course exaggerating for humorous and other purposes, but it is clear that she is serious in the main point that she makes in the essay, that changes in human beings have taken place, and thus changes in the ways novelists represent human beings must also occur. Thus if we feel tempted to complain (as many *have* complained) that characters in the *nouveau roman* are less satisfying than those in Dickens's novels, we should pause to ask whether or not we would be happy with a situation in which the contemporary novel used only the methods of characterization used by Dickens. Would the novel help us to understand contemporary human beings if that were the case?

My earlier discussion of modernism and postmodernism should have suggested that recent fiction to which the labels 'modernist' or 'postmodernist' can be attached will be likely to portray the human individual in ways different from those to be found in the classic realist fiction of the previous century. This is indeed the case. What often seem to disappear in the characters we find in modernist fiction are individual coherence, self-knowledge and autonomy. Virginia Woolf's *The Waves* is a textbook example of this sort of change. Her character Bernard repeatedly utters statements such as 'I am not one and simple, but complex and many'; 'I am more selves than Neville thinks'; 'We exist not only separately but in undifferentiated blobs of matter'. Not surprisingly, Bernard repeatedly asks 'Who am I?', and even describes himself as a man without a self. It needs to be said that *The Waves* does not attempt to universalize Bernard's view of himself: other characters in the novel *do* have a sense of their coherent and autonomous selves. Nonetheless, the novel opens up the possibility that the classic realist view of character is either inadequate or historically limited – perhaps culture-specific. Other modernist novelists have also portrayed character as complex and problematic rather than simple and self-evident. Think of Klamm in Kafka's *The Castle*, who appears to be different to everyone who sees him and each time that he is seen. It seems clear that Kafka is concerned to open up certain conventional views of human individuality to renewed scrutiny by means of his character Klamm, both as these views operate in fiction and as they are circulated more widely in the world at large.

Postmodernist fiction generally takes this disintegration of character a stage further, playing with the conventions governing the representation of character in works of fiction so as to expose these to the reader's scrutiny. Thus a *cancelled character* (sometimes called an *erased character*) is a character in a postmodernist work who (or which) is introduced in order to make the reader accept him or her as a human individual, but who is later cancelled or erased and revealed to be only the creation of the novelist, a construct who (or, again, which!) has existence only in the pages of the work. Such a refusal to abide by established conventions has to be seen as comparable to the way in which modernist art frustrated realist expectations by perverting those conventions governing the representation of depth in pictures – perspective. The aim is also to make the reader or viewer think about the way in which these conventions govern our understanding both in literature and in the extraliterary world.

Cyberfiction takes some of these elements even further, imagining futures in which the grafting together of organic and non-organic materials is able to produce cyborgs, beings part-human and part-machine (see p. 185).

Types of literary character

These rather extended introductory comments seem to me to be necessary because 'character' may well appear to be one of the least problematic terms with which you have to deal in studying the novel. The proper names we encounter in a novel – Tom Jones, Anna Karenina, Daisy Miller, Huck Finn, Yossarian – seem very much like the proper names we meet in everyday life and by which we designate individual human beings.

Yet even if we stop at names we may realize that characters in novels are not quite like real people. In everyday life we sometimes meet a person with an unusually appropriate name: the very tall person called Long, for example. In novels it is different. The peculiar appropriateness of a name such as Heathcliff is surely hardly ever met with in real life. What about Dickens's Esther Summerson – who acts like a 'summer sun' in *Bleak House*, dispelling the shadows with which the work is, initially, filled? Even 'Tom Jones' with its resolute *lack* of connotations or associations seems extraordinarily appropriate a name for the non-aristocratic, normally healthy hero of Fielding's novel.

'Tom Jones' is a rather different name from 'M'Choakunchild' – the name given by Dickens to one of his characters – however, and this reminds us of an important point: there are different *sorts* of literary character. Of course there are different sorts of people in ordinary life, but it is not this sort of variation that I have in mind. Think of Meursault in Albert Camus' *The Outsider* and Mr Guppy in Charles Dickens's *Bleak House*. Both are young men who have problems communicating with others and have an odd relation to their mothers. There are also important differences between them, however, and if we were asked to explain these differences we would have to talk about them not just as if they were ordinary human beings but also in a way that recognizes that they are different *types* of literary character, existing within very unlike sorts of novel, very varied *narrative situations*.

A good test here is to ask to what extent a character from one literary work could be transplanted to another. We have little difficulty in imagining a meeting between, for example, the title character from Jane Austen's *Emma* (1816) and Mr Darcy from her *Pride and Prejudice* (1813, but written 1796/7). This is because the fictional worlds of these two novels are so similar that such a meeting, which is as much a meeting of fictional worlds as it is of characters, does not seem absurd. That is why we have films with titles like *Godzilla Meets King Kong*, but not, outside the realms of parody, with titles such as *Bambi Meets Godzilla*. (I have actually seen a very short film with this title, and of course knew from the title that it *had to be* a parody!)

If we go back to the young men from *Bleak House* and *The Outsider* we realize that Mr Guppy could not be transported to the fictional world of *The Outsider*; he could not survive in that novel as we know him in *Bleak House*. My concept of 'fictional world' is not just a matter of setting (about which I talk below). After all, the settings of *Clarissa* and *Robinson Crusoe* are very different, but there is a sense in which their fictional worlds are much less so. The concept refers, in other words, not just to the real-world elements (places, events, history) contained in the works, but also to the representational conventions governing the depiction of these and other things. *Bleak House* and *The Outsider* are, moreover, partly held together by philosophical and ideological elements: views of the nature of the world which enter into the very fabric and texture of the novels. Meursault lives in a world defined by the preoccupations of existentialist philosophy, and Mr Guppy does not. (Note that the important thing is not whether the *individual character* has certain philosophical or other concerns but whether their *presentation* and fictional existence accord with these concerns.)

Subsequent to my writing the previous paragraph I discovered Christine Brooke-Rose's novel *Textermination* (1991), in which a conference of characters out of the great works of literature is convened at the San Francisco Hilton, to pray for their continual survival in readers' minds. It is not exactly *Bambi Meets Godzilla*, but it does have Emma Bovary sharing a carriage with Jane Austen's Mr Elton. Of course, the characters' knowledge of themselves as literary characters gives them something in common and something which their originals lack; thus the fictional world of *Textermination* is one coloured and formed by the post-structuralist interests of its author. It is not in any way a simple mixing of the fictional worlds of the different characters – and nor could it be.

Let us try to explore some of the differences that exist between literary characters. We have some well-established terms to draw on initially: major and minor characters, flat and round characters, stock characters, 'types', and so on.

We can sum up one important distinction that has a bearing upon all of the above terms: is the writer interested in developing a character so as to *represent something*, or in order to present a *particular individuality*? The distinction is related to that between novels of 'life' and novels of 'pattern' to which I referred much earlier, for it is in novels of pattern that one is likely to find characters who stand for something (a giveaway feature is often the names) and in the novel of life that one finds characters possessed of a distinctive, idiosyncratic and unique individuality. However, even in the latter case we have to face the paradox that a highly individualized character may also stand for something: Dickens's Mr Toots in *Dombey and Son* and Dostoyevsky's Prince Myshkin in *The Idiot* (1869) are 'originals', yet they also stand for certain valuable qualities which contribute importantly to the themes of the two novels mentioned. Moreover, just because a character is a recognizable *type* (another of Dickens's grotesques, one of Dostoyevsky's eccentrics) does not necessarily mean that he or she cannot also be a realized individual personality in the work.

In his book *Aspects of the Novel* (1927), E.M. Forster uses Dickens's Mrs Micawber (from *David Copperfield*) as an example of what he calls a 'flat character': 'The really flat character can be expressed in one sentence such as "I never will desert Mr Micawber." There is Mrs Micawber – she says she won't desert Mr Micawber; she doesn't, and there she is.' Mrs Micawber does not change because she is not allowed genuine *interaction* with other people and situations; even though she has, as it were, dealings with them, she is independent of them.

We have now suggested three different ways in which a fictional character can be unlike a real person: first, by being defined by the philosophical or ideological underpinnings of their fictional presentation; second, by being limited to one essential characteristic; and, third, by being possessed of a constituting individuality that is unshakeable by events.

The term 'synonymous character' is often applied to recent, especially experimental, novels; synonymous characters are those which are possessed of essentially the same characteristics and functions in a piece of prose fiction, and are thus to all intents interchangeable. The term is very close to the more old-fashioned 'stock character'.

Functions and types

The word 'function' also deserves some attention at this stage. Its literary-critical usage is most associated with the analyses of folk tales carried out by the Russian theorist Vladimir Propp, who argued that all folk tales consist of a selection from a finite number of functions, a function being 'an act of a character, defined from the point of view of its significance for the course of the action' (Propp 1968, 21). Not all the available functions would be selected by the creator of the tale, but those which were selected had to appear in the tale in a strict order. Such a description seems foreign to those of us more familiar with the novel than with the sort of work with which Propp was concerned, but, just as I argued earlier that although the novel is to be distinguished from the romance, nonetheless romance-like elements can be found in the novel, so too it is worth remembering that although the modern novel is to be distinguished from the folk tale in terms of – among other things – its individual and individualized characters, nonetheless modern novelists are still capable of using characters as a means whereby an 'act significant for the course of the action' can be achieved. In other words, some characters are there to do things; they are primarily *vehicles*, and their significance is limited to what they do.

Thus although *in general terms* we can distinguish the novel from other fictional forms which represent human individuals but are less interested in their particularity and individuality than in what they do or stand for (the type-characters of the fable or parable, for example), we should recall that even those novelists most renowned and admired for their creation of living characters utilize recognizable types: think of Jane Austen and Charles Dickens. Indeed, because in real life we classify people ('a typical schoolmaster'), we should not automatically assume that depictions of realistic characters cannot also be representations of human types, or of characteristics typical of particular groups of human beings.

In recent years a number of critics have developed the concept of *projection characters*, that is characters into whom the novelist projects aspects of him- or herself – often aspects which cannot be acknowledged either to others or to the author him- or herself. (Psychoanalytic theories of projection lie behind the term, the idea being that what we cannot accept in ourselves we often project onto others.) In Charles Dickens's *Great Expectations*, for example, the character Orlick is like a dark shadow of the hero Pip, and seems almost a personification of Pip's repressed desires. He stands up to Mrs Joe (who treats Pip so unfeelingly) and eventually strikes her down, and he openly lusts after Biddy, for whom Pip eventually acknowledges his own desire. In a late, climactic scene he announces his intention of murdering Pip himself, thus dramatizing what otherwise would be a purely internal struggle in Pip. If we take into account the considerable extent to which Pip's portrayal (like that of David Copperfield) is modelled by Dickens on his own character and experiences, then we can understand that Orlick can be described as a projection character: whereas the similarities between Dickens and Pip are open and overt, those between Orlick and Dickens are concealed and even denied. (For a comparable application of the concept of the 'projection character' to another novel by Dickens – *David Copperfield* – see Roger Sell (1983).)

This means that a novelist may use a character for purposes quite other than 'characterization'; to say that there are different types of character is to say in effect that novelists portray human individuals for a range of different purposes. This is why it is a mistake only to talk about characters in a novel as if they were real people; clearly the novelist relies upon our knowledge of and reactions to real people in his or her creation of character, but characters are often created by novelists for purposes other than that of investigating human personality or psychology. They can be used to tell a story, to exemplify a belief, to contribute to a symbolic pattern in a novel, or merely to facilitate a particular plot development. (The same is true of, for example, descriptions of landscape in a novel. These are sometimes written for quite different reasons than to remind the reader what actual landscapes are like, and in such cases it would clearly be irrelevant to draw attention to the ways in which such a description failed to mesh with 'what real landscapes are like'.)

'Telling' and 'showing'

A classic but still useful distinction between two fundamental ways of creating (or 'revealing') character is that which we owe to Percy Lubbock's *The Craft of Fiction* (1921). Lubbock's distinction between 'telling' and 'showing' (a distinction he probably owed to Henry James) is very similar to that which Georg Lukács makes between 'narration' and 'description' in a famous essay entitled 'Narrate or Describe' (1936). (In neither case, it should be said, is the critic talking exclusively about characterization.) When Jane Austen opens her novel *Emma* in the following way, she is *telling* (or in Lukács's terminology describing) rather than showing us what Emma is like:

> *Emma Woodhouse, handsome, clever, and rich, with a comfortable home and happy disposition, seemed to unite some of the best blessings of existence; and had lived nearly twenty-one years in the world with very little to distress or vex her.*

Later on in the novel, however, when we witness the conversation between Emma and Mr Knightley in which he criticizes her rudeness to Miss Bates, we are *shown* the sort of person Emma is through her behaviour and her responses to him. It may be worth adding that Austen's use of the word 'seemed' in the above passage encourages the alert reader to wonder whether Emma's happy situation may turn out to contain some less positive elements.

Since Lubbock, critics have generally preferred 'showing' to 'telling' as a method of revealing character, believing that this method unlocks the life in characters rather than treating them (as Lukács puts it) as inanimate objects. Moreover we feel that we decide what a character is like when we observe him or her behaving in front of us; we can use our critical intelligence and our knowledge of human beings to reach an assessment of them, whereas when we are *told* something we can only take it or leave it. This is why, in real life, we prefer to make up our minds about people through personal acquaintance and observation rather than on the basis of others' assessments.

If we think of the most memorable literary characters we probably find that we remember them doing or saying things; we do not so much remember being told things about them. Where a narrative comment on a character does stick in our minds it is probably as a result of something other than characterization: irony, moral discrimination, or whatever.

So far as the creation of lifelike characters is concerned, it is very often the interplay between given and explained attributes that makes them fascinating. Think of Heathcliff in *Wuthering Heights*; we understand partly why he is as he is because we have witnessed key elements of his upbringing. Some attributes seem to be beyond such an explanation; they are presented as givens rather than as effects or results.

I repeat, however, that creating a lifelike character may not always be what a novelist is aiming at – even in pre-modernist or pre-postmodernist fiction. It is not lifelike for Gulliver to be so acute and humane at one part of *Gulliver's Travels* and so obtuse and unconcerned about talk of human suffering at others. It seems apparent that Swift's primary aim here is not the creation of a consistent and lifelike character so much as the creation of a character whose alternating qualities and abilities will represent different aspects of that 'human race' that is perhaps the real subject of *Gulliver's*

Travels, and the creation of a mechanism to display those aspects of humanity which he is anxious to expose to satire.

Methods of characterization

What are the most important methods of characterization available to the novelist? I would suggest four that are worth thinking about. First is *description* or *report*. In Conrad's *Heart of Darkness*, we know a very large amount about Mr Kurtz before ever he appears before us; other characters in the novella have talked about him so much, reporting his actions and beliefs, that we feel almost as if we had met him ourselves. The description of physical characteristics – and especially of physiognomy – is a very traditional means whereby the writer can suggest what sort of character we are encountering. Here is a description taken from the second paragraph of Philip Larkin's novel *Jill* (1946). The novel's main male character, John Kemp, is travelling by train to Oxford:

> *It looked cold and deserted. The windows of the carriages were bluish with the swirls of the cleaner's leather still showing on the glass, and he confined his eyes to the compartment. It was a third-class carriage, and the crimson seats smelt of dust and engines and tobacco, but the air was warm. Pictures of Dartmouth Castle and Portmadoc looked at him from the opposite wall. He was an undersized boy, eighteen years old, with a pale face and soft pale hair brushed childishly from left to right. Lying back against the seat, he stretched his legs out and pushed his hands to the bottom of the pockets of his cheap blue overcoat. The lapels of it curled outwards and creases dragged from the buttons. His face was thin, and perhaps strained; the expression round his mouth was ready to become taut, and a small frown lingered on his forehead. His whole appearance lacked luxuriance. Only his silky hair, as soft as seeding thistle, gave him an air of beauty.*

Just imagine that you have met someone on a train, and when discussing this meeting with someone you know, later on, you start to describe him. You would, I venture to suggest, hardly come out with something along the lines of the above paragraph. If you did, it would probably be because you were a student of literature indulging in a little parodic behaviour. To put the matter another way, we can say that Larkin's description of John Kemp depends upon certain fictional conventions which regulate the depiction of character, conventions which require that physical characteristics be seen to have a much more reliable function as indicators of non-physical characteristics (and even, perhaps, of past or future events and experiences) than they do in real life. (This is not to deny that the *sort* of observations we are presented with in this passage and the *sort* of deductions implied by these observations are closely related to those observations and deductions we make in real life. Railway journeys seem to encourage this sort of speculation about other people: Virginia Woolf makes this the basis of her essay 'Mr Bennett and Mrs Brown'.)

Thus from this passage we can detect that John Kemp is not rich, and is not a thrusting, self-confident youth ready and eager for heroic exploits. We assume that the journey he is making has not been made by him before, otherwise he would not notice so many details about his surroundings. (We are not told that it is he who sees and smells these details, but we are encouraged to assume this.) We deduce too that behind his lack of position and self-confidence there reside qualities which now are apparent only to the discriminating and which will allow him to deal well (finally, perhaps) with whatever trials he has to face. It is almost unthinkable that this is a description of a man who will turn into a pompous and conforming hypocrite, or whom the reader will end up hating. Behind his portrayal we may, even at this stage, recognize what can be called a mythic element: the unregarded person who has a potentiality that, when revealed, may surprise those who take him at face value. That silky hair of John Kemp's, along with the expression round the mouth and the frown on his forehead, betoken much more on the first page of a novel than they would in real life: they stand for that unregarded quality or virtue which exists only *in potentia*, whose emergence the novel will trace. As the description also insists on the shabby cheapness of Kemp's clothes and of the third-class compartment, we can feel reasonably confident, too, that the novel will pay particular attention to the problems raised by his background and social class – especially as the first paragraph of the novel has informed us that the train he is on is heading for Oxford. Notice how much we know of Kemp and how much we are already expecting – and he has said nothing and done nothing so far!

Second, character can be established by *action*; when Insarov in Turgenev's *On the Eve* (1859) throws the insolent German into the water – an action of which his effete Russian companions are palpably incapable – then we learn something about him which pages of description could not give us.

Third, through a character's *thought* or *conversation*. Dialogue in particular is a wonderful way of revealing character: think how much we learn about Miss Bates in *Emma* merely through her conversation – so much so that comment from Austen's narrator is really not needed. Modern novelists have shown how much we can learn about a character merely by following his or her thoughts; in Virginia Woolf's *Mrs Dalloway* (1925), Clarissa Dalloway and Peter Walsh actually *do* very little, but by the end of the novel we feel that we know them quite well just by having followed so many of their thoughts.

In the third paragraph of Chapter 2 of Jane Austen's *Sense and Sensibility* (1811), we learn as much as we feel we need to learn about Mrs John Dashwood through a report of her comments on her husband's intended generosity to his two sisters. Austen here uses that variant of Free Indirect Discourse known as represented speech (see p. 98), and as this is frequently used for ironic purposes, we are alert to the hints concerning the narrator's disapproval without their ever becoming overt and intruding directly. The paragraph reads:

> *Mrs John Dashwood did not at all approve of what her husband intended to do for his sisters. To take three thousand pounds from the fortune of their*

dear little boy, would be impoverishing him to the most dreadful degree. She begged him to think again on the subject. How could he answer it to himself to rob his child, and his only child too, of so large a sum? And what possible claim could the Miss Dashwoods, who were related to him only by half blood, which she considered as no relationship at all, have on his generosity to so large an amount. It was very well known that no affection was ever supposed to exist between the children of any man by different marriages; and why was he to ruin himself, and their poor little Harry, by giving away all his money to his half sisters?

In addition to represented speech, the passage contains a number of textbook examples of *colouring* (see p. 100); although the narrator is telling us about Mrs John Dashwood, the passage is full of what the reader recognizes as the character's own speech characteristics. We may observe how close the technique is to mimicry in spoken delivery.

The pleasure we get from such a passage is related to the fact that, while on the one hand we do not feel we are being told how to regard Mrs John Dashwood and coerced into a particular attitude towards her, we also feel that our amused disapproval of the character is shared by Jane Austen (through her narrative voice). The very omission of comment on Mrs John Dashwood's more outrageous statements indicates a narrative opinion that they *are* so outrageous as to require no comment.

Finally, the novelist can use *symbol* or *image* to reveal and develop a character. In Jean Rhys's novel *After Leaving Mr Mackenzie* (1930), the heroine, Julia, has just been to see a Mr James, shortly after visiting her dying mother and her spinsterish sister Norah:

She wanted to cry as he went down the stairs with her. She thought: 'That wasn't what I wanted.' She had hoped that he would say something or look something that would make her feel less lonely.

There was a vase of flame-coloured tulips in the hall — surely the most graceful of flowers. Some thrust their heads forward like snakes, and some were very erect, stiff, virginal, rather prim. Some were dying, with curved grace in their death.

The tulips present us symbolically with the varied fates of the different women in the novel: snake-like cunning and self-interested behaviour; prim and virginal lifelessness (like Norah); and death — like Julia's mother. Such a passage contributes to our knowledge of and attitudes to characters in the novel even though nothing is said directly about any character.

■ Plot

Let us start with a definition: a plot is an ordered, organized sequence of events and actions. Plots in this sense are found in novels rather than in ordinary life; life has stories, but novels have plots and stories (see the earlier comments on the double chronology of literary fiction on p. 6). As E.M. Forster puts it, a story is a narrative of events arranged in their time-sequence, whereas a plot is a narrative of events with the emphasis falling on *causality*. Not all commentators would agree that causality is the distinguishing feature, but all would agree that there is a necessary distinction to be made between the incidents about which we are told in a novel in their chronological order and the actual narrating of these events in perhaps quite a different order in the novel. I prefer the terms 'story' and 'plot' to describe these two, but some critics use terms created by a group of theorists known as the Russian Formalists (see p. 171), the terms 'sjužet' (plot) and 'fabula' (story).

Recent narrative theorists have performed a useful function in providing terms and concepts such that we can more accurately analyse how and why the plot of a novel deviates from strict and simple chronological progression.

Order

First of all are a number of terms connected to what is termed *order*. The plot of a novel may move backwards and forwards in time, instead of proceeding steadily forward in chronological order. Any deviation from such strict chronological progression is termed an *anachrony* by narrative theorists, and there are a large number of such deviations possible. The most frequent are *analepsis* (or flashback) and *prolepsis* (or flashforward). The italicized terms are perhaps to be preferred, as 'flash' suggests a rather short movement backwards or forwards in time whereas an analepsis or a prolepsis may be of very considerable duration. These terms are also utilized by some theorists when a past or future event is evoked rather than actually invoked or brought about. Thus the fate of the *gringos* who die searching for silver in the opening pages of Joseph Conrad's *Nostromo* (1904) is proleptic of much that follows in the novel, even though it does not technically involve events that take place after the time established at the novel's opening.

Ellipses

Second, a novel's plot may include gaps, omissions, absences. These can be referred to collectively as *ellipses* – the same term as is used to refer to the succession of dots in a text that indicates that something has been omitted. Thus in *Wuthering Heights* we never get to know what Heathcliff does after his sudden disappearance and up to the time of his reappearance. This is what can be termed a (relatively) *unmarked* ellipsis – in other words, the text does not display the fact that something is not there. But when in Charles Dickens's *Bleak House* Esther Summerson seeks to explain why she finds Mrs Woodcourt irksome, and breaks off with the words, 'I don't know what it was. Or at least if I do, now, I thought I did not then. Or at least – but it don't matter', then we have a clearly *marked* (or explicit) ellipsis: the reader's attention is drawn to the fact that something that is known to the narrator is withheld from him or her. A novelist typically uses a marked ellipsis to get the reader's imagination working: what has happened here? Why are we not told? An unmarked ellipsis usually involves the novelist's having skipped over a period of time during which nothing of artistic significance can be represented as having happened.

Duration

Third, the element of *duration* is also of great significance. Nearly all works of prose fiction vary the relationship between narrating and narrated time. (The term *tense* is sometimes used to refer to this relationship, although this usage – influenced by structuralist theorists – has not achieved general acceptance in Anglo-American circles.)

Whatever term we use, the essential characteristic involved is crucial to how novels work. A novelist can spend fifty pages to tell us about one day in the life of a heroine and then ten further pages to cover fifty years. Such extremes are sometimes referred by means of the linked terms *scene* (a passage in which there is a sort of equivalence between narrated and narrating time – for example a dialogue in which all the words exchanged are given) and *summary* (where it is clear that the narrative is reducing all the potentially available material to a descriptive outline). Within a single novel the ratio of narrated to narrating time can alter very substantially, and it is worth paying careful attention to such shifts.

In *Tristram Shandy*, for example, Laurence Sterne makes frequent jokes about the relationship between narrated and narrating time. At the start of Chapter 21 the text breaks off into a digression in the middle of a sentence uttered by uncle Toby, to utter which he has had to take his pipe out of his mouth. The digression finished, the text continues: 'But I forget my uncle Toby, whom all this while we have left knocking the ashes out of his tobacco pipe.' The suggestion that narrated and narrating time are coterminous is a joke, we know, because in many novels the narrator can leap over enormous gaps of time. Think how few pages are devoted to the period of Cathy's married life prior to the return of Heathcliff in *Wuthering Heights*.

Frequency

Fourth, narrative theorists also isolate the important topic of *frequency*, and note the following fundamental possibilities:

(i)   one event narrated once (*singulative frequency*)
(ii) a repeated event narrated the same number of times that it occurs (*multiple frequency*)
(iii) one event narrated many times (*repetitive frequency*)
(iv) many events narrated once (*iterative frequency*)

Probably the most usual of these is (i): many unique events that are depicted in a novel are recounted to the reader only once. The same event can however be recounted many times, as in (iii). Sometimes this has the effect of sharpening our understanding: the detective novel typically recounts the same events more than once, so that what was unclear the first time becomes clear in the detective's final version. In *Catch-22* (1961), as Snowden's death in the bombing raid is as it were 'replayed' repetitively through the anti-hero Yossarian's consciousness while the novel unfolds, the reader is reminded of a psychoanalytic patient recalling more and more of a repressed event. As the reader gradually comes to learn what happened, the repetition conveys the traumatic effect that the event has had on Yossarian. Sometimes clarity is not the intended result: the repeated but different depictions of the same events in Robbe-Grillet's *The Voyeur* (1955) lead the reader to lose confidence in the existence of a single, isolable series of events.

Many similar events may, as in (iv), be recounted as one. In Conrad's *Lord Jim*, Marlow's narrative is introduced as an *iterative* narrative – in other words, we are told that what we are about to read is an account that has been given many times. (The word 'would' often confirms that the account is an iterative one, as can be seen in the extract below from Guy de Maupassant's novel *Bel-Ami*.) By the time Marlow's account ends it has become a single, particular act of recounting. In the same novelist's *Nostromo*, the shifts between the singulative and iterative modes are technically contradictory, but they draw attention to important thematic concerns about the uniqueness of events and the repetitions of history. Conrad deliberately and repetitively frustrates his readers' expectations: passages change unexpectedly from singulative to iterative mode, and from iterative to singulative mode (I have written more on this elsewhere: see Hawthorn 1998).

The French narrative theorist Gérard Genette has isolated a variant on the above alternatives which he calls the 'pseudo-iterative'. According to his definition, the pseudo-iterative occurs when 'scenes presented, particularly by their wording in the imperfect, as iterative', are possessed of a 'richness and precision of detail [which] ensure that no reader can seriously believe they occur and reoccur in that manner, several times, without any variation' (Genette 1980, 121). Consider the following passage from Guy de Maupassant's novel *Bel-Ami* (in its original French this passage also contains examples of the pseudo-iterative, although perhaps because of the problems this mode presents to the translator, frequency in the English version does not match frequency in the French original exactly):

> *So they would go into low dives and sit down at the end of the squalid murky room on rickety chairs at decrepit wooden tables. An acrid cloud of smoke and the smell of fried fish filled the room; men in their working clothes were shouting at each other as they downed their glasses of raw spirits; and the waiter would stare at the strange couple as he put the two cherries-in-brandy down in front of them.*
>
> *Scared and trembling, but blissfully happy, she would begin sipping the red fruity liquid, looking around her, bright-eyed but uneasy: each time she swallowed a cherry she felt she was doing something wrong, every drop of the spicy, burning liquid that slipped down her throat gave her a sharp pleasure, the pleasure of forbidden fruit, of being naughty.*

> *Then she would whisper: 'Let's go.' And so they would leave. She*
> *slipped away hastily, tripping along and holding her head down, like an*
> *actress leaving the stage, between the drinkers sitting with their elbows on*
> *the table, who looked up with a suspicious, surly air as she went by. And*
> *when she was through the door, she gave a big gasp as if she had just*
> *escaped from some terrible danger.*
>   *Sometimes, with a shudder, she asked Duroy:*
>   *'What would you do if they insulted me in a place like that?'*
>   *He said airily:*
>   *'Defend you, of course!' (Maupassant 1975, 124–5)*

It seems clear that the detailed dialogue provided here is not fully reconcilable
with the suggestion that it represents what was said again and again on
different occasions. Maupassant wants to give the reader a sense of repeated –
even obsessively repeated – actions, while giving them enough individualized
flavour to dramatize them and to prevent the reader from getting bored. Note
that technically there is a change of frequency at the end of this passage from
'Sometimes … she asked Duroy' (iterative – she asked more than once) to
'He said' (singulative – he replied only once; we are not told 'he would say').
This oscillation between the iterative and singulative modes is often a sign of
the pseudo-iterative.

Why does Maupassant use the pseudo-iterative here? I think because the
technique allows him to combine the dramatic sense of a *particular* scene with
a thematic insistence upon repeated action.

Plots and purpose

When someone sees that we are reading a novel and asks 'What happens?',
we generally simplify its plot so as to bring it back more to resemble the story
behind the plot. It is often only when we do this that we recognize that
novels with very different plots may have rather similar stories. Thus if you
have read William Faulkner's novel *Absalom, Absalom!* (1936) and Jean Rhys's
novel *Wide Sargasso Sea*, it may have struck you that the stories in both novels
are remarkably similar (which you can confirm if you wish by writing them
both down in chronological order). The two plots, though, are very different,
so different that the similarity of the stories is not immediately apparent.

Again, if you have read Joseph Conrad's novel *Nostromo*, then you will
know that it has a very complex plot; the novel *could* have been told in a far
more straightforward chronological way. So why did Conrad tell it in such a
complicated, *unchronological* manner? Come to that, why did Emily Brontë not
have *Wuthering Heights* told to us in one consistent chronological sweep –
perhaps by having Nelly Dean recount it all at one meeting to Mr Lockwood?

The answer to such questions has to be complex. A novelist constructs a
plot in a particular manner so as to draw attention to certain things which
might otherwise escape notice, to produce a different effect upon the reader,
and so on. One result of the complex plot of *Nostromo*, for example, is that
Conrad deliberately kills what many novelists strive for: tension and reader

expectation. We know from early on in the novel what the eventual outcome of the political and military struggles in Costaguana will be. Why does he do this? One likely reason is that, as the reader has to devote less attention or expectation to *what* will happen, he or she is able to devote much more to *why* and *how* it happens. Tension may make us read quickly and carelessly, anxious only to find out what happens. (We rarely read the closing chapters of a detective novel with the attention that the opening chapters command.) Such a reading is actively discouraged by the way *Nostromo* is constructed. It is encouraged, in contrast, by the way in which most of Dickens's novels are constructed; Dickens wants to engage our sympathetic anxiety and so he sets puzzles, creates mysteries, which we read on in order to solve.

Chronology and coherence

If a novelist abandons strict chronology, how else can he or she retain coherence, make the novel hang together? Well, as Forster points out, *causality* is one important possible way. We are still interested as we read the final chapters of *Nostromo* because we want to see why things happen as they do; causal links are revealed to us.

Another technique is for a novelist to draw *parallels* and *resemblances* between characters, situations and events such that the novel has coherence even if it plots neither chronological sequences nor causal relationships. It is only to a limited degree that we believe that the experiences of the second-generation characters in *Wuthering Heights* are actually caused by the lives and actions of the first-generation characters. Even so, the parallels (with variations) and resemblances between the younger Cathy, Linton Heathcliff and Hareton Earnshaw and their parents suggest that this latter part of the novel continues themes and enquiries from the first part of the novel. It is important for the reader first to encounter the mature and embittered Heathcliff; this means that we see the young Heathcliff in the context of what we know he will later become, and thus our attention is focused in very particular ways as Nelly Dean starts to tell Lockwood of the childhood and young adulthood of Heathcliff and Catherine.

Alternatively, a novel can be held together by a common character or event. The picaresque novel and the *Bildungsroman* (see Glossary), for instance, are held together by the personality of the central figure. The extent to which this provides a complex or a crude unity depends to a certain degree upon the complexity of the central character.

It should be said that with modernism and postmodernism, the whole question as to whether a novel *should* compose a unity has been raised. Virginia Woolf argued against plot (in the sense of the traditional, well-structured, realist plot) as one of a number of distorting conventions in her essay 'Modern Fiction' (1919), and a novel such as Alain Robbe-Grillet's *The Voyeur* certainly lacks unifying elements as we have outlined them. The actual denial of causality as a reliable principle by many modernist and postmodernist novelists has, inevitably, affected the way they construct their novels.

Types of plot

We can categorize plots in two ways: either in terms of the dominant human activities which form the motivating principle in them or which are induced in the reader by them, or in more technical ways. In the first category we can include plots structured around _conflict_ as in many ways the plot of _Nostromo_ is; around _mystery_ as are many of Dickens's novels; around _pursuit_ or _search_ as is _The Castle_; around a _journey_ as is _Gulliver's Travels_; or, finally, around a _test_ as is Joseph Conrad's _The Shadow-Line_. Now of course these are very simplistic descriptions and we would want to say that all of these novels are structured around far more complex issues than the single topics mentioned. It is worthwhile remembering that a novel is often given force and coherence by a dominating element such as one of these plot types provides. _The Shadow-Line_ is structured around a journey as well as a test, but the theme of the test is a sort of archetypal bedrock within the organizing logic of the plot, and we should not be ashamed to see it as such.

A more technical classification of plots will provide us with terms such as 'picaresque/episodic'; 'well-made' (the traditional nineteenth-century realist plot); 'multiple' (many novels have two or more lines of plot, sometimes interconnecting and sometimes not). It is very often important to be able to single out a _main plot_ from its attendant _subplot(s)_ for the purpose of analysis.

You may recall that much earlier on in this book I quoted Johnson's remark that if one were to read Richardson 'for the story', one would be so fretted as to hang oneself. Plot and story fulfil different sorts of functions in different novels. According to Johnson, the story in a novel by Richardson is there only to give occasion to the sentiment; in other novels the tension and suspense relative to our desire to know 'what happens next' are an integral part of the appeal of the work. When the 'outer' or 'frame' narrator of _Heart of Darkness_ warns us (indirectly) that we are about to hear 'about one of Marlow's inconclusive experiences', we need to adjust our expectations with regard to the plot of the novella. Modernist works of fiction very often have inconclusive endings, endings which leave the reader perhaps puzzled and unsatisfied, but puzzled and unsatisfied in ways that are productive of further thought. You should, again, remember that such matters go beyond the merely technical. Novels without omniscient narrators and with inconclusive endings are perhaps less likely to betoken a conventionally Christian world-view in which everything is concluded in the manner in which God wishes; a novelist whose novels all have happy endings is unlikely to suffer from very much existential doubt. (See the entry for _closure_ in the Glossary.)

■ Structure

Structure and plot are closely related to each other, and it might have made sense to include this section as a sub-section of 'Plot'. However, critics often use 'structure' in a rather wider sense than such treatment might suggest. If we can think of the plot of a novel as the way in which its story is arranged, its structure involves more than its story, encompassing the work's total organization as a piece of literature, a work of art. Nor are the terms 'structure' and 'form' to be confused; the latter does not normally include thematic elements in the work (see my comments concerning theme later in this chapter) whereas these are involved in a novel's structure. Structure involves plot, thematics and form: it refers to our sense of a novel's overall organization and patterning, the way in which its component parts fit together to produce a totality, a satisfying whole – or, of course, the way in which they fail so to do.

Let us start by observing that different novels have very different sorts of structure. We feel, for example, that some parts of *Moll Flanders* or *Huckleberry Finn* (1884) could be shifted around in position without making too great a difference to the works in question: how many readers of the former work remember clearly whether Moll robbed the little girl of her necklace before or after she robbed the drunken man in the coach? But to shuffle around the parts of *Wuthering Heights*, or of Henry James's *What Maisie Knew* (1897), would, we feel, do something rather serious to the works in question. Clearly the fact that a novel has an *episodic* structure has an important bearing upon such issues; if a work is structured around a series of relatively self-contained episodes, then these can be assembled in different orders without making too much difference – just as on a modular degree scheme with self-contained modules one can often take different courses in any order one chooses.

The matter goes beyond plot, as I have suggested. In *Moll Flanders* there is very little alteration in Moll's character, or in the values the narrative underwrites, or in the symbolic meanings contained in the work (if there are any worth noting in this novel!). In short, *Moll Flanders* is consistently structured on the principle of 'repetition–with–slight–variation'. There is somewhat more development and change in *Huckleberry Finn* – in the characters and relationship of Huck and Jim, in the general *tone* of the novel before and after the return of Huck and Jim to 'civilization', and so on. Thus, although some of the scenes in this novel might be switched around without too much effect, such alteration would have to be more limited than with *Moll Flanders* if we wished to avoid damaging the work. The intricate patterning of a novel such as *What Maisie Knew* would, surely, be completely destroyed if we started to move sections of it from place to place.

Very often the *chapter* and *section* divisions made by the author impose a structure upon a work – or bring out one that is implicit but not overt in it already. It is interesting to read Conrad's *The Shadow-Line* in his manuscript version, in which there are no section divisions, and then to see how differently the published text of the novel reads with these divisions included. Very often such divisions perform the useful function of telling the reader when he or she can pause and put the book down for a bit, and, as it is at these points of time that we think backwards over what we have read and forwards to what we hope for or expect, such divisions can be very significant. It is doubtless for such reasons that Virginia Woolf (in her essay

'Modern Fiction') disapproved of the 'ill-fitting vestments' of the 'two and thirty chapters' of what she called the materialist novel. If clothes or vestments 'make the man' (or woman), then the wrong chapter divisions may make the novel something other than its author wants.

Order and *chronology* – issues upon which we touched when talking of plot – can be crucial to the matter of structure. The difference between a novel's 'story' and its 'plot' can tell us much about its structure. It is often an interesting exercise to map out a novel's story and plot in note form one above the other.

As I have argued, structure involves thematic elements too. Note how the repetition of thematic elements in Charles Dickens's *Bleak House* helps to structure that work. Just to take one example: Esther Summerson, like her mother Lady Dedlock, has to choose between two men: a rich, older, 'safe' one and a younger, less wealthy, more 'risky' match with more passionate potential. Whereas Lady Dedlock makes what we are led to see as the wrong choice in marrying the older man, Esther – after an initial false decision – makes what is clearly the right decision for her. Now this produces an element of *pattern* in the work which contributes to our sense of its structure, a pattern which blends in with other things in *Bleak House* to produce a satisfying work of art.

Take a different example. In Katherine Mansfield's short story 'The Voyage' we have a very simple story: a little girl leaves her father at a New Zealand port and travels by boat with her grandmother to the south island of New Zealand, to her grandparents' home. In the course of the voyage we discover that her mother has died, and the reader comes to understand what Fenella – the girl – has not yet realized: that henceforth she is to be brought up by her grandparents. What is striking about the story is that, whereas images of darkness and cold dominate the opening of the story, these gradually give way to images of light and warmth which (especially the images of light) dominate the close of the story. Now clearly this shift of images contributes to the structure of the story: without actually being told it directly we realize that Fenella is moving out of an unhappy period of her life into a potentially much happier one. The physical voyage is from one *place* to another, but this is complemented structurally by travel from one *state* to another.

Structure involves ideas and sensations of some sort of pattern: *completion, reiteration, contrast, repetition, complementarity* – all of these and others can be invoked by a work's structure. We should note too that the *frame* of a narrative – what constitutes its outer limits – can contribute importantly to our sense of structure. Consider the narrative framing of the 'tale within a tale' of *Heart of Darkness* and *The Turn of the Screw*. Think of the importance of the fact that the events recounted in James Joyce's *Ulysses* and Virginia Woolf's *Mrs Dalloway* take place within twenty-four hours. Note the thematic framing effect of our being told in E.M. Forster's novel *Howards End* that the work is not to be concerned with the very poor, who are 'unthinkable'. In each case our view of what is 'in' the novel is given structure by our sense of what is excluded from it.

■ Setting

'Setting' is one of those terms about which recent literary critics have felt increasingly uneasy. Does the term not suggest a perhaps too-simple relationship between characters and action on the one hand and the context within which these take place on the other? Does it not sound rather unsatisfactory to talk about the Nottinghamshire 'setting' of D.H. Lawrence's *Sons and Lovers* or the Yorkshire 'setting' of *Wuthering Heights*, as if the same actions might conceivably have taken place elsewhere – in Tunbridge Wells or Minnesota? The fact that so many characters in Emily Brontë's novel have names that are also the place-names of towns and villages around her native Haworth suggests a relationship between character and environment too organic, we feel, to be described with the term 'setting'.

There may well be other reasons why this has become a relatively unfashionable term of late. Much twentieth-century fiction, especially that which we can term modernist or postmodernist, presents a view of human beings as symbolically homeless, deracinated, alienated from their environment. That close bond between individual and place that is celebrated in the regional novel (see the Glossary) is harder to find in our own time than it was in the nineteenth century. As a result, many novelists present the reader with settings whose unfamiliarity and unwelcoming aspect is frequently generalized or universalized. If all large towns are unwelcoming and dehumanizing, then does it matter which large town one is in? It is surely an essential part of the force of Franz Kafka's *The Trial* (1925) that the setting is not specified in real-world or real-time terms. The point is that in our age the events depicted could take place in many different locations: our time is the time of universal human experiences.

Yet even today it is important to be aware of the context within which the action of a novel takes place – and this does not just mean its geographical setting; social and historical factors are also important. It is just as important to ask why the author has chosen the setting he has chosen when it is generalized (as in the case of *The Trial*) as when it is highly specific (as with, say, Walter Greenwood's *Love on the Dole* (1933)).

To start with we need to distinguish between realistic and conventional or stylized settings. The famous country house of the classic detective story is obviously a highly *conventional* setting; we are not interested in the particularity of such country houses and their environments – they serve, rather, the function of providing a stylized and familiar setting within which a conventional set of happenings can unfold. Many detective stories actually choose relatively artificial settings that have the function of isolating the characters (or suspects) from the outside world: the closed world of Agatha Christie's Orient Express stuck in the snow is a paradigm case.

At the other extreme we can cite highly realistic settings like that of the tuberculosis sanatorium that dominates Thomas Mann's *The Magic Mountain* (1924). Here, however, we need to tread carefully, for although this may be a realistic setting, it is a very *symbolic* one as well. It is not hard to see the sanatorium full of sick people as representative of pre-First-World-War Europe with its sicknesses and fatal illnesses. Authors are very often quite conscious of such symbolic meanings; in his essay 'Well Done' (1918), Joseph Conrad refers to 'the ship' as 'the moral symbol of our life', and clearly we need to take such a statement into account when looking at those of his works which are set on board ship.

Sometimes the choice of a suitable setting helps an author to avoid the need to write about things that he or she is not good at, or interested in, writing about. For instance, some commentators have argued that it was convenient for Conrad that merchant marine ships usually contained no women. A setting in the historical past can often help an author to avoid contemporary issues about which he or she feels confused; the setting that E.M. Forster chose for *Howards End* enabled him to avoid writing about the very poor. It is generally agreed that Jane Austen chose settings for her novels which allowed her to exercise her strengths and conceal her weaknesses so far as her knowledge of different sorts of people and of human experiences was concerned.

Dickens's frequent choice of London as the setting for his novels was convenient in other ways: the mass of concealed relationships, indirect forms of human communication and innumerable secrets to be found in London offered a perfect opportunity to a novelist whose plots contain all of these elements in abundance. (See also the comments on the passages quoted from *Moll Flanders*, *Oliver Twist* and *Austerlitz* on p. 29.)

Just as there are conventions relating to the description of individual human appearance (see the earlier section on character), so too descriptions of places and environments are conventionally seen to denote something about the people associated with them. Think of the symbolic force of the descriptions of Wuthering Heights and Thrushcross Grange in *Wuthering Heights*.

A setting can also be a crucial factor in the creation of *mood* or *moral environment*. If we think of *The Great Gatsby* we can see, I think, how a setting can make an essential contribution to a work's mood. This example reminds us that theme and subject and setting can be inextricably intertwined: you could no more set *The Great Gatsby* in the northern England of the 1930s than you could set *Love on the Dole* anywhere else.

Remember that there is a difference, in this context, between 'mood' and 'tone': the latter term involves narrative *attitudes towards* what is recounted and described. A setting may help to create a particular *mood* in a story, but only the narrative treatment can confirm a certain *tone*.

■ Theme

'Theme' is a much-used word in the literary criticism of the novel, and a favourite word for use by lecturers and teachers in essay and examination questions. 'Discuss the treatment of the theme of evil in *Crime and Punishment*'; 'Write about the theme of escape in *Huckleberry Finn*'; 'Examine the theme of alienation in *The Castle*', and so on.

Students often find such questions or topics baffling. What exactly is a theme? Well, the confusing answer to this question is that the term is used in a number of different ways.

Theme and thesis

Some critics find it useful to distinguish between theme and thesis. The simple distinction here is that, although both pose questions, a thesis also suggests or argues for answers. A theme, in contrast, can involve establishing a set of issues, problems or questions without any attempt to provide a rationale or answer to satisfy the demands these make of the reader. Traditionally, novels dominated by a thesis have been valued less highly than those in which certain themes are raised or treated: in contrast to earlier generations of readers perhaps, some recent critics have preferred our novels not to be overtly didactic, to be open-ended rather than pointed towards solutions at which the author has already arrived. We should ask whether such an attitude is always justified; novels that are fired with their creators' crusading zeal or commitment to a belief or a cause constitute a very substantial part of the body of fiction, and since its birth the modern novel has had a significant commitment to didacticism.

One problem with distinguishing between theme and thesis is that for some commentators 'theme' is something of an umbrella concept and includes what we have just termed 'thesis'. If we define theme in the former, weaker sense (distinguishing it from thesis) then we will not be surprised to discover that a large and complex novel can have a range of varied themes attributed to it. Charles Dickens's *Bleak House*, for instance, has been variously interpreted as containing the themes of 'parental responsibility', 'the heartlessness of the law', 'the evil of "causes"', 'the destructiveness of choosing money and position rather than love', 'the centrality of writing to Victorian society' – and many more. It needs to be remembered that a complex novel is likely to be susceptible to analysis in terms of numerous different – perhaps interlocking – themes.

Overt and covert themes

A theme may be overt or covert. That is to say it can be either consciously intended and indicated as such by the author or, alternatively, discovered by the reader/critic as an element in the novel of which perhaps even the author was unaware. (If we retain the distinction between theme and thesis then it will be understood that a thesis is much more likely to be consciously intended than a theme.) Thus although we can be pretty certain that Saul Bellow had the *carpe diem* theme ('Live today, while you can') consciously in mind in his novella *Seize the Day* (1956) – because the title makes this much clear – we cannot be so sure that Alan Sillitoe had the theme of working-class socialization equally in mind with regard to the writing of his _Saturday Night and Sunday Morning_ (1958). (We should also bear in mind the possibility that Bellow recognized his theme and chose his title after he had completed his story.)

■ Symbol and image
Symbol

Let us introduce this section with some concrete examples. In E.M. Forster's _Howards End_ the motor-car plays an important role. We could respond to this fact by pointing out that the car had not been around for very long at the time that the novel was written, and that Forster was merely incorporating a piece of contemporary reality into his novel for the purpose of increased verisimilitude.

Few readers of the work would find this satisfactory as an explanation. The motor-car in _Howards End_ clearly _stands for_ or _represents_ something; it is not merely a means of transport but a _symbol_ in the novel. By this we mean that it carries with it various ideas, associations, forms of significance that in ordinary life it might not have in people's minds: 'innovation and the destruction of tradition'; 'the mechanical as against the organic'; 'unfeeling social change'; 'violence and death'; 'the selfish pursuit of personal comfort by the rich' – and so on.

Notice that I have not suggested that the car in _Howards End_ stands for just one, fixed thing; it is characteristic of symbols that they do not have a simple one-to-one relationship with what they stand for or suggest. (In this respect a symbol can clearly be distinguished from an allegory, the secondary meaning of which is usually single and distinct. Thus the allegorical meaning of Bunyan's _Pilgrim's Progress_ (1676) is that life as a Christian brings problems comparable to those experienced by Bunyan's pilgrim.) The lighthouse in Virginia Woolf's _To the Lighthouse_ (1927) has obvious symbolic force in the novel, but it would be an unwise critic who stated definitively the one thing that it stood for. Perhaps the lighthouse does stand for the unfulfilled dreams of youth, or masculine aggressiveness – but part of its power comes from its multiple suggestiveness and indirect significance. Note that Forster's car and Woolf's lighthouse can be said to exist on two planes: on the realistic level they are what they are in the real world – a car and a lighthouse – while on the symbolic level they have meanings that cars and lighthouses do not necessarily have outside of fiction.

Symbols are not limited to literature and art: they are central to all known human cultures. When a woman gets married in white she makes use of the symbolic force of that colour of dress within our culture – a symbolic force that has existed for an extremely long time. Any writer who incorporated this convention in a novel would be taking what we can call a public symbol and adapting it for use within his or her work – just as a film-maker who produced a Western with a hero dressed in black would be challenging another (rather stale) convention.

Thus in James Joyce's story 'The Dead', we feel that the repeated references to snow have a symbolic force. This is partly because snow is referred to so repetitively and suggestively that the reader of the story cannot but feel that there is something significant in the function that snow performs in the story. It is also, of course, because we naturally associate snow with some things rather than others – especially in countries like Britain and Ireland where extensive falls of snow are relatively rare. Put briefly, we can suggest that in 'The Dead' snow stands for or suggests *death*: it is cold, it covers the graveyard, it affects the whole country just as death comes to us all, and so on. Now the justification for this interpretation is partly that snow is naturally associated with death, because it is cold like a dead body and because people lost in snow die. It is also that Joyce in 'The Dead' draws attention to certain of these qualities and associates them with other references in the story (not least with its title) so as to make these associations clear. If we think of the death of Gerald in the snow in D.H. Lawrence's *Women in Love* (1920) we will see, I think, that both Joyce and Lawrence are able to incorporate a public symbol into the private or internal world of meaning in their respective fictional works.

On occasions a writer will create a symbol that has the meaning and significance that it does have only in the context of one particular work. If we think of a green light, for instance, the natural symbolic associations that it has for most of us today are positive: advance, road clear, healthy environment – all of those extensions of meaning that have accrued from the greenness of nature and from our use of green lights in traffic regulation systems. It is arguable that none of these references or associations is active in our response to the repeated mention of the green light that marks out the quay by Daisy's house for Gatsby in Scott Fitzgerald's *The Great Gatsby*. What Fitzgerald succeeds in doing in this novel is to create a private symbol, something that has meaning only within the world of the novel. Similarly, it is arguable that few if any of the public symbolic associations of lighthouses are active within Virginia Woolf's *To the Lighthouse*; the significance of the lighthouse in that work (and by this I mean the significance for the reader – which is not necessarily the significance it has for the characters in the novel) is something that has to be decided upon on the basis of internal rather than public information.

A synonymous set of terms for public and private symbols is *motivated* and *unmotivated* symbols. In practice, of course, it is hard to find a completely public or a completely private symbol. I suggested, for example, that Forster's use of the motor-car in *Howards End* developed associations that 'motor-car' might not have in people's minds prior to their reading the novel. However, for *some* people the motor-car *might* have had these associations, and the symbolic force that the motor-car has in *Howards End* is, as it were, a potential force already implicit in the motor-car as it was experienced in Edwardian England. (Think of the role played by the motor-car in a work of fiction that is nearly contemporary to Forster's: Kenneth Grahame's *The Wind in the*

Willows (1908); Messrs Toad and Wilcox may belong to very different fictional worlds but they do have certain qualities in common.)

Before concluding, I should point out that, although I have chosen to discuss things or objects which have a symbolic force, actions and settings can be equally well possessed of this. When Hester in Nathaniel Hawthorne's *The Scarlet Letter* (1850) undoes her hair and lets it fall free, the action has an enormous symbolic charge: in a novel so concerned with repression and concealment it suggests a breaking of bonds, a triumph of natural and healthy impulse over artificial and corrupt restraint. Similarly, innumerable novels also make use of another symbolic potentiality involved in this scene in *The Scarlet Letter*: the contrast between indoors (representing society, the artificial, restraint) and outdoors – especially in a wild or undomesticated setting (representing pre-social impulses, the natural, the outpouring of feeling). Think of the role performed by windows as the dividing line between these two sets of associations in both Brontë's *Wuthering Heights* and Joyce's 'The Dead'.

Image

In passing from symbols to images I am in a sense going backwards, as an image is arguably a less complex form. I find, however, that 'image' is typically used in a looser sense and is easy to define in relation (and contrast) to 'symbol'.

I referred earlier to Katherine Mansfield's short story 'The Voyage', and commented upon the movement from dark and cold references at the start of the story to warm and – particularly – light images at the end. Let me quote a little from the close of the story:

> On the table a white cat, that had been folded up like a camel, rose, stretched itself, yawned, and then sprang on to the tips of its toes. Fenella buried one cold little hand in the white, warm fur, and smiled timidly while she stroked and listened to Grandma's gentle voice and the rolling tones of Grandpa.
>
> A door creaked. 'Come in, dear.' There, lying to one side of an immense bed, lay Grandpa. Just his head with a white tuft, and his rosy face and long silver beard showed over the quilt.

You will notice the recurrence of words that connote light and warmth here ('white', 'warm', 'silver', 'rosy'). These I would dub *images* rather than symbols. The distinction is not an easy one to explain, and there are differences of usage that complicate matters, but the following points are probably worth remembering.

■ Images are usually characterized by their evocation of *concrete qualities* rather than abstract meanings; images normally have a more sensuous quality than symbols – they call the taste, smell, feel, sound or visual image of the referred-to object sharply to mind.

■ Symbols, in contrast, because they *stand for* something other than themselves, bring to mind not their own concrete qualities so much as the idea or abstraction that is associated with them.

Thus in the extract from Katherine Mansfield the feel of the cat's fur, its whiteness and warmth, are brought sharply to our minds *in themselves* – we do not automatically wonder what they 'stand for' (note how this tactile sense is encouraged by the contrast with Fenella's cold hand). We do not experience sharp sensory responses to Gatsby's green light or Woolf's lighthouse: it is what these stand for or call to mind *apart from* themselves that is important. If we think of a continuum stretching from the sensuous to the intellectual, we can say that images are located towards the sensuous end while symbols are located towards the intellectual end.

With Joyce's snow and Forster's motor-car we may pause: in these cases we think both of what they stand for and of their individual sensory qualities. In these two cases, therefore, we may guess that the references have an imagistic function alongside their primary symbolic purpose.

This is not to say, incidentally, that images do not contribute to thematic elements in a work. Although it is true that an image is distinguished by its concrete qualities in an immediate sense, it sets up waves of association in the mind that have other than a purely concrete significance. Thus, as I have already suggested, the images in Mansfield's 'The Voyage' contribute importantly to our sense of the multilevelled nature of Fenella's voyage, away from unhappiness and suffering and to the promise of something more cheerful and enjoyable.

■ Speech and dialogue
The voices of the novel

According to Bakhtin:

> the decisive and distinctive importance of the novel as a genre [is that] the human being in the novel is first, foremost and always a speaking human being; the novel requires speaking persons bringing with them their own unique ideological discourse, their own language. (1981, 332)

This does not, however, mean that people in novels speak the same way as do people in the everyday, extrafictional world. It does mean that novels tend to have not one centre of authority – the narrator's or author's voice – but many such centres, centres which typically are in conflict with one another. For Bakhtin, it will be perceived, a voice is not just a mechanical means whereby thoughts are broadcast, it has an ideological dimension. Different voices in the novel represent and disseminate different points of view, different perspectives. Moreover, for Bakhtin different voices can be isolated even in a narrator's or a single character's words: when we speak, our utterances contain a range of different voices, each of which carries its own values, such that an utterance can represent a veritable war of different viewpoints and perspectives.

Speech in life and speech in fiction

Modern readers are fortunate in that we live in an age of tape-recorders and their digital successors. We can thus study normal, unselfconscious conversation in a way that our ancestors could not – and can thereby discover that nobody actually talks quite as people are portrayed as talking in novels. The conventions that govern the speech that is represented in novels cover technical matters such as the syntax of the sentences that make up separate utterances. They also cover matters such as the sort of things that can be talked about and the sort of language that can be used in such discussions – which have, of course, a significant ideological dimension. There is an amusing exemplification of this point in Josef Skvorecky's novel *The Engineer of Human Souls* (first published in Czech in 1977) in which a character, Mrs Santner, tries to defend the 'bad' language used in a novel by referring to how people in real life would actually speak if in the same circumstances as the novel–character in question:

> '*You have to read it in context,' she explains. 'After all, those words are spoken by an anti-Nazi revolutionary who's afraid the Gestapo will catch him. When people are afraid, they use strong language. It's a well-known phenomenon.'*
>
> *Her defence is too scholarly for Mr Senka. 'But this is a book, madame,' he cries. 'A book.'*
>
> *This time it is Mrs Santner's turn not to understand. For her the word 'book' has none of the sanctimonious overtones it has for Mr Senka, for whom a book is a household object to be taken up only on very special occasions. Mrs Santner's husband leans over her shoulder and whispers, 'Now, Betty, don't let's get into an argument,' but this only goads her on.*
>
> '*I can't help it. In context, language like that has a valid function. That's the way people actually talk in situations like that.'*
>
> '*But they don't talk like that in* books.'
>
> *Each is partly right, according to his experience.*

This is the sort of conflict towards which the realist imperative almost inevitably impels novelists and their readers. We want the novel to give us our recognizable, everyday world, warts and all: but that world includes taboos, prescriptions, repressions to which the novel is not immune.

One of the extraordinary achievements of realism (and not just in the novel) is that it gives us something that to us resembles the world even though it is formed and constrained by conventions of representation different from those that operate in the real world. In his book *Art and Illusion* (1960), Ernst Gombrich has explored at length the paradox that the world does not look like a picture, but a picture can look like the world. So far as the novel is concerned, we do not talk like people in books, but the dialogues in books seem to us to be like the conversations we have in real life. People in novels tend, unlike real people, to talk in complete sentences, with few indicated hesitations, mistakes of grammar, 'ums' and 'ers', and so on. As Skvorecky's narrator notes, perceptively, both Mr and Mrs Santner are partly right. Why is this?

The answer has to be that the novelist follows conventions in the representation of speech and dialogue with which we are so familiar that we are unaware of any conventionality. (Just as individuals from Britain or the United States are unaware that they follow conventions governing the nodding and the shaking of heads to mean 'yes' and 'no' – until they travel to a country like Turkey or Bulgaria where these conventions are reversed.)

The novelist has to convey exclusively in words what in ordinary conversation we convey by words, tone of voice, hesitations, facial expression, gesture, bodily posture – and by other means. Learning how to do so was not accomplished overnight, and we can note a great difference between the way novelists in most of the eighteenth century represented dialogue and the way later novelists have done so. If, for example, you open Henry Fielding's novel *Joseph Andrews* (1742) at Chapter 5, which is the chapter directly parodying Richardson's *Pamela* in which Lady Booby attempts to seduce her servant Joseph much as Mr B— in Richardson's novel had attempted to seduce Pamela, then you will notice something odd about the layout of the page. Although conversation takes place all through this short chapter, the prose is set out in one continuous unparagraphed stream. Thus Fielding has to keep including 'tag-phrases' such as 'he said' and 'she replied'. The result is not just that reading the chapter is rather hard work, but that the guiding presence of the narrator keeps intruding: we have narrative tag-phrases in addition to the actual words spoken by the characters.

By the time of Jane Austen's *Pride and Prejudice* a little over half a century later we see a very different picture. Dialogue is presented in a recognizably modern form, with each new utterance by a different character given a new paragraph. Here the narrator may intrude or remain hidden at will. If necessary the characters can be left to speak for themselves with no interruption from anyone. This certainly increases the *dramatic* effectiveness of scenes involving dialogue; we feel that we are actually witnessing conversations taking place rather than being instructed by an intrusive stage-manager who keeps pointing out what we have to notice.

The narrator can now use the different possibilities available to create an appropriate effect. Take the conversation between Mr Bennet and his wife that we are given on the first page of *Pride and Prejudice*:

> '*My dear Mr Bennet,*' *said his lady to him one day,* '*have you heard that Netherfield Park is let at last?*'
>
> *Mr Bennet replied that he had not.*
>
> '*But it is,*' *returned she;* '*for Mrs Long has just been here, and she told me all about it.*'
>
> *Mr Bennet made no answer.*
>
> '*Do not you want to know who has taken it?*' *cried his wife impatiently.*

'You want to tell me, and I have no objection to hearing it.'
This was invitation enough.

Note how Jane Austen wrings so much significance out of her use of Direct and Indirect Speech here. 'Mr Bennet replied that he had not' must be one of the most economically sarcastic lines in English literature: the shift to Indirect Speech somehow conjures up Mr Bennet's weary, long-suffering response to his wife's importuning. The narrative comments here are little more than touches on the tiller. To put it another way, we feel that we are witnessing a real conversation but with someone beside us whispering in our ear comments concerning the participants in the discussion.

Ivy Compton-Burnett's *A Family and a Fortune* (1939) shows what is perhaps near to the ultimate role that dialogue can play in a novel. At a rough estimate, 75 per cent of the novel consists of dialogue, and this dialogue performs a crucial narrative function in the work. The novel's heavy reliance upon dialogue is fascinating and revealing, but the final impression is of a writer rather straitjacketed by her narrative technique.

Representing speech or reproducing speech

Recent narrative theorists have pointed out that the writer of fiction has at his or her disposal a range of more or less distanced means whereby characters' speech can be rendered. In her *Narrative Fiction*, Shlomith Rimmon-Kenan reproduces a useful seven-element survey of the full continuum of possibilities open to the writer of narrative fiction. At one extreme we have what she calls *diegetic summary* (in her usage 'diegetic' means loosely 'of or within the story'). This is where the reader is given the 'bare report that a speech act has occurred, without any specification of what was said or how it was said'. Second there is *summary, less purely diegetic*, which 'to some degree represents, not merely mentions, a speech event in that it names the topics of conversation'. Third is *indirect content paraphrase (or: indirect discourse)*, 'a paraphrase of the content of the speech event, ignoring the style or form of the supposed "original" utterance'. Fourth is *indirect discourse, mimetic to some degree*, which is a 'form of indirect discourse which creates the illusion of "preserving" or "reproducing" aspects of the style of an utterance'. Fifth comes *Free Indirect Discourse*, which I have already discussed on p. 98 (and which, we should remember, can be used to represent more than just speech). Sixth is *direct discourse*, in which the actual words spoken are 'quoted', although, as Rimmon-Kenan points out, always with some degree of stylization. Finally there is *free direct discourse*, which is 'direct discourse shorn of its conventional orthographic cues', a good example of which would be first-person interior monologue.

If these descriptions are hard to follow, the examples provided by Rimmon-Kenan in her *Narrative Fiction* may make the distinctions easier to comprehend. All are taken from John Dos Passos's trilogy *U.S.A.* (1938):

1 When Charley got a little gin inside him he started telling war yarns for the first time in his life.

2 He stayed late in the evening telling them about miraculous conversions of unbelievers, extreme unction on the firing line, a vision of the young Christ he'd seen walking among the wounded in a dressingstation during a gas attack.

3 The waiter told him that Carranza's troops had lost Torréon and that Villa and Zapata were closing in on the Federal District.

4 When they came out Charley said by heck he thought he wanted to go up to Canada and enlist and go over and see the Great War.

5 Why the hell shouldn't they know, weren't they better off'n her and out to see the goddam town and he'd better come along.

6 Fred Summers said, 'Fellers, this war's the most gigantic cockeyed graft of the century and me for it and the cross red nurses.'

7 Fainy's head suddenly got very light. Bright boy, that's me, ambition and literary taste. … Gee, I must finish *Looking Backward* … and jez, I like reading fine, an' I could run a linotype or set up print if anybody'd let me. Fifteen bucks a week … pretty soft, ten dollars' raise.

(Rimmon-Kenan 1983, 109–10; her examples are taken from McHale 1978, 249–87)

Earlier I used the word 'continuum', and it is worth stressing the fact that, although many theorists quantify the possible variations according to grammatical distinctions, the novelist has a wide sweep of alternative possibilities from which to choose, ranging from a summary by the narrator which merely reproduces the gist of what a character has said (and not how it has been said), at one extreme, to a rendering which appears to have no narrator involvement and maximal mirroring of the character's speech in terms of both content and delivery at the other extreme.

As to *why* a novelist should choose to render speech at one point along this continuum rather than at another, a number of different explanations are possible. In one sense we are back to life and pattern; at the number 7 end of the continuum we have maximum life, we are close to the actuality of a character's living use of language. At the number 1 end we have at least maximum potentiality for pattern: the novelist can choose what lessons to draw, what moral to underline, as the character's speech is summarized. Here the novelist's or the narrator's view of the character predominates over the character's actual speech. You can probably think of many other reasons why a novelist may or may not wish to render a given character's use of slang, colloquialism or dialect. These evoke ways of life, values, cultural specifics which may or may not be what the novelist wants to bring to mind at a given stage of a narrative.

As Bakhtin has pointed out, a voice is not just a 'medium' or a channel of communication; it involves complex ideological elements as well. Take the following passage from Lewis Grassic Gibbon's *Grey Granite* (1934), the final part of the trilogy *A Scots Quair*. Ewan Tavendale is talking to a number of other apprentices, and one of them, Norman, reveals that, while he can never be bothered to go to a trades–union meeting, his father has a more positive attitude:

And he looked a bit shamed, He's Labour, you see.

Tavendale said There are lots of chaps that, my stepfather was, *and you all cheered up, sitting on buckets in the furnace room, a slack hour, and having a bit of a jaw, you were none of you Labour and knew nothing about politics, but all of you had thought that the Bulgars of toffs were aye Tory or Liberal or this National dirt. And somehow when a chap knew another had a father who'd been Labour you could speak to him plainer, like, say what you thought, not that you thought much, you wanted a job when apprenticeship was over and a decent bit time and maybe now and then a spare bob or so to take your quean to the Talkies – och, you spoke a lot of stite like the others did, about the queans that you'd like to lie with, and the booze you'd drink, what a devil you were, but if you got half a chance what you wanted was marriage and a house and a wife and a lum of your own. . . .*

Now it hardly needs saying that on a simple level the use of elements from Scots dialect gives this passage added verisimilitude. If we are not Scottish then we may be sent to a specialist dictionary to discover the meaning of some of the dialect terms in the passage, but most of us can probably guess at their meaning without too much difficulty, and British readers will probably work out that 'Bulgar' is a euphemism for 'Bugger' – a term that Gibbon's publisher would certainly have bridled at in 1934.

Beyond vocabulary, the language of the passage is crucial to certain other effects. We can say that it mimics the speech and thought patterns of a working man of the period, especially one talking among a group of his peers. The use of 'you' is especially interesting. On the one hand it represents an accurate piece of observation on Gibbon's part; in Britain men of this background will use 'you' as a generalizer where a person from a middle-class background would use 'one' (as Virginia Woolf does throughout her writing, and the British royal family do throughout their speech). On the other hand it involves the reader in a process of collective sharing of attitudes: we feel as we read that we are part of the group that is thinking out its beliefs; it is as if these beliefs come out of a group to which we belong. We thus experience the ideology of the group from the inside while having it displayed in a manner that allows us to look at it more objectively. The natural form of the work-group conversation conceals what is actually quite an unnatural process – whereby a group is made to speak those taken-for-granted items of ideological positioning that, just because they *are* taken for granted, are normally not spoken. (Virginia Woolf does something rather similar in *The Waves*, although revealingly the statements in this work are more individual and even individualistic; the class with which she is concerned lacks the collective voice and consciousness that Gibbon wishes to display.)

There is, in other words, a sort of sleight of hand in the above passage. Gibbon is actually in one sense telling us something about the working class from a vantage point outside of its typical self-knowledge. Because he dramatizes this telling in the form of a discourse that belongs to the class, however, the reader is given the impression that as we *experience* the ideology with the collectivity, so too we are simultaneously detached from it and allowed to look at it through its members' self-aware analysis of themselves. (One of the things that is being mimicked here is the style of a working–class anecdote. It is as if the reader is being addressed in an intimate way by the collective voice that is thus personified through the language that it speaks.) Gibbon could not have achieved such a complicated effect without having borrowed the language and habits of expression of the group, even if he uses these in a way that members of the group would not have done.

We should, in other words, be very suspicious of views which look upon the language that a novelist uses to represent speech and dialogue (or thought, or an unexpressed sense of identity even) as merely a medium. A medium is relatively untouched by what it transmits. Bakhtin has argued that 'the language of a novel is the system of its "languages"' (1981, 262) – in other words, that the action that takes place on the surface of a novel is only one level of the total action to be found within its pages. Below the level of literal event is the level of ideological action, an action in which the participants are not characters but positions encapsulated in language. For Bakhtin:

> *The word in language is half someone else's. It becomes 'one's own' only when the speaker populates it with his own intention, his own accent, when he appropriates the word, adapting it to his own semantic and expressive intention. Prior to this moment of appropriation, the word does not exist in a neutral and impersonal language (it is not, after all, out of a dictionary that the speaker gets his words!), but rather it exists in other people's mouths, in other people's contexts, serving other people's intentions: it is from there that one must take the word, and make it one's own. (293)*

This, surely, is what we see in the passage from Gibbon: men using other people's words, words which contain opinions that are not their own but which they are led to believe *are* their own, while they begin to discover their own views and interests, and begin to appropriate the word for their own uses.

Topics for discussion

- Do you prefer a novel to be told by an 'anonymous voice' or an identified character? Why?
- Take one or more novels you know, and imagine them as told in different ways by different narrators. Discuss the gains and losses of such changes.
- Why on earth should a novelist choose to use an unreliable narrator?
- Find examples of 'flat' and 'round' characters. Discuss their use.
- Find examples of 'showing' and 'telling'; is showing always preferable?
- 'The essence of telling a story is to keep some information from the reader.' Is it?
- List the themes of a favourite novel. Are you sure that they were all intended by the novelist? Does it matter?
- Find examples of symbols and images in a work of fiction. How do they differ?

7
Studying the novel

Preview

This chapter deals with:
- how to preserve your fleeting responses to a novel
- how to take notes and what to note
- how to choose critics; how to assess the significance of their affiliations
- using libraries and using computers
- writing essays: analysing topics, planning your response
- preparing for examinations and taking them

■ Reader and critic

Given that studying literature involves being conscious of many of those aspects of a literary work that operate on the 'common reader' without their being conscious of the fact, there is always an element of tension and even incompatibility between the activities of reading for pleasure and reading for study. Wordsworth's aphorism that 'we murder to dissect' has in some ways a greater force when applied to prose fiction than when applied to poetry. Moreover, because the novel is often read by those interested in 'losing themselves' in its pages – and some commentators have argued that the genre invites readers to read in this manner – maintaining an attitude of distanced observance of formal and technical issues can present greater problems to the novel reader than to the reader of poetry.

On the other hand, most students of literature find that, after a period of awkwardness, practice in analysing technical issues can lead to an enrichment of their reading pleasures. Being made aware of, for example, complex shifts in the manipulation of point of view in a novel can increase a reader's appreciation of a writer's skill without lessening those pleasures experienced by the common reader.

However, if the student of the novel must learn to combine a more detached appreciation of the skills of the novelist with an experience of those pleasures that do after all constitute the reason for finding the novel worth studying in the first place, he or she must also learn how to convince the teacher or lecturer responsible for grading essays or examinations that this state of grace has been achieved. Just as learning to pass the driving test involves not just looking in the mirror, but letting the examiner know that you are looking in the mirror, so too you need to be able to write essays and examinations in such a way that your skills of reading, analysis and discussion are displayed to the person with the red ballpoint pen. It is with the successful mastery of these three stages – attentive reading, controlled analysis and intelligent discussion – that this chapter is concerned.

■ Response: retaining the ephemeral

We may read a shortish novel in one sitting, while anything up to twenty or more sessions will be required for a long and complex novel such as Tolstoy's *War and Peace*. For those readers who read Victorian novels when they were first published in serial form there was no choice: they *had* to stop and wait at certain stages in their reading. When we pause in our reading of a novel we go over what we have read and we think forward to what we guess will happen or what we would like to happen. Frequently we will imagine ourselves in situations described in the novel; perhaps we will hold imaginary conversations with characters, or wonder what we might have done in their positions.

In other words, expectation, surprise, disappointment, foreboding, tension, suspense, imagination and fantasy all form part of our reading of a novel. To read a novel is to be involved in a *cumulative process*.

The problem which this raises for the study of the novel is that there are certain experiences in us, and certain events in the novel, which lodge far more permanently in the mind than do others. Indeed, it is part of the way that a novel works upon us – part of its power as a source of enjoyment – that some aspects of our reading experience should fade more quickly than others. Moreover, our memory plays tricks with us once we have finished a novel. If it is some time since you read *Wuthering Heights* then try this test on yourself: at what stage in the novel does the older Catherine die? I suspect that unless you are an unusually retentive and conscientious reader you are likely to place this event far later in the novel than it actually occurs.

The issue is complicated by the fact that we often read a novel more than once. On a subsequent reading we are normally less preoccupied with what will happen and so are able to read more carefully and notice many details that slipped our attention on first reading. To retain such details we need to take notes. Taking notes is actually a skilled operation and one that requires practice. It takes time to develop one's skill to the point at which it does not interfere with pleasurable reading.

■ How to take notes

Notes can be written either in the novel itself or in a separate notebook. The advantage of the former method is that it does not disturb one's reading too much; the disadvantages are that it spoils a book, it affects one's second reading, there is not always sufficient room for notes on the page, and *retrieval* of the notes afterwards for purposes of study is difficult. One way round these problems is to write very brief notes in pencil in a novel as you are reading, and then to copy these up and expand them in a separate notebook or folder later on. This also allows you to copy out brief extracts from the novel which strike you as important, and it means that you file for future reference only notes about which you have thought a second time after having finished reading the novel. Pencil marks can be erased once they have served their purpose.

If something in the text strikes you as important or significant but you do not want to puzzle over why, lest you break your train of thought, then mark or underline the passage in question, note the page reference on the inside back cover of the book, and come back to ponder the point once you have finished the novel.

■ What to note

Learning what is of significance in a novel, and in your response to it, is a matter of practice. Teachers and lecturers often ask for analyses of selected passages from novels, and undertaking such analyses is an excellent way of sharpening your eye for important detail in the reading of fiction. Such close reading is, however, only part of what constitutes a full critical reading of a novel, for in addition to responding to significant detail in the prose of a work of fiction, you need also to be able to perceive larger patterns and movements in the work as a whole, as well as connections to other works. The list that follows is intended to serve a double purpose. On the one hand I hope that it will be useful to work from when you are engaged in the analysis of a particular passage from a novel or a short story. In addition, however, I hope that its perusal will serve as a reminder of the sort of points that can be noted in the process of reading or rereading a work of fiction. The golden rule here is: if in doubt, then make a note.

Checklist

Narrative technique All information relating to the manipulation of narrative in the work: clues about the values or personality of the narrator; voice and perspective; what the narrator does *not* know; changes of narrator or narrative perspective; narrative intrusion or comment. 'Telling' and 'showing'.

Story and plot Sketch out what happens (i) in chronological order and (ii) as it is told. What differences are there? What is added, missed out, repeated?

Action Any information that advances the plot, gives significant new developments in human relationships or new events.

Tone Is it familiar or formal, intimate or impersonal? Who (if anyone) is apparently being addressed? Do the vocabulary or syntax suggest a particular style of delivery?

Characterization Information about *how* we learn about characters; any indication that characters are changing or developing; significant new information about a character; views as to what the writer is trying to achieve in the presentation of character.

Speech and dialogue Use of Direct, Indirect or Free Indirect Discourse. Do characters speak for themselves or does the narrator intrude, comment or direct? Is the dialogue realistic or conventional? What functions does it perform? (Development of character, of plot, introduction of dramatic element, discussion of theme[s].)

Thoughts/mental processes Do we 'get inside characters' heads'? If so, which heads, and how?

Dramatic involvement Is the reader drawn into events as they happen, or rather encouraged to observe them dispassionately? How is this achieved? (Manipulation of distance.)

Setting and description What is significant about where the action takes place, and about descriptions of people and places?

Symbol or image Anything apparently significant should be noted. Do symbols/images relate to others used elsewhere in the work?

Theme(s) Any development of themes dealt with elsewhere in the work; introduction of new thematic elements. Moral problems/issues raised for the characters or for the reader.

Your own response Strong personal preferences/responses the work evokes in you – or dislikes/disapproval. Mood. Strong identification with a character – or the opposite. Tension, desire to know what happens. Particular expectations (especially at the end of chapters/sections, or when a mystery or problem is presented). Any experience of bafflement or surprise; and points where you feel you disagree with or react against a narrative opinion (or the opinion of a character).

■ Using critics

A glance at the library shelves may convince you that you will never even scratch the surface of what might be read: even for a single major novelist it seems that a good library can provide weeks or even months of reading. How should you proceed?

The first thing to do is to heed the advice of your lecturers. Syllabuses and booklists generally contain advice on 'secondary reading', and this advice is based upon your lecturers' knowledge of the set texts and of your needs and capacities. Lecturers rarely expect you just to plough through everything on such a list: you have to be selective. Remember that it is possible to talk to even busy lecturers, and to ask them about the secondary reading that they have (and have not) recommended. Explain what your interests are, what essay you want to write, and ask for suggestions.

Any good academic library should subscribe to certain journals that are particularly concerned with the novel. Titles such as *Novel: A Forum on Fiction* or *Eighteenth-century Fiction* speak for themselves. Remember that even if you cannot see such journals on the shelves your library may subscribe to electronic editions, and even if it does not you may still be able legally to download electronic copies of articles (see below). Of course many important essays on the novel are published in periodicals with a less focused concern, and here electronic searches (again, see below) can be invaluable.

If you are not looking for help with a particular essay, but feel that you want to read some criticism on a novel or a novelist, then again it will probably be worth spending a bit of time planning. Remember that different 'secondary works' will be concerned with very different aspects of a writer or a text. Later on in this book (in Chapter 9) you will find a discussion of critical approaches to fiction, and this should help you to categorize the books and articles on your library shelves in a general way. A biography of Henry James may help you with material for your essay on *The Turn of the Screw*, but this material is likely to be very different from a recent psychoanalytic reading of James's novella, and both will differ from a New Critical essay on the tale written in the 1950s. My strong advice, then, is that you divide your search for secondary works up into two stages, following your reading of the 'primary text' – the literary work itself. If you look at a scholarly edition of a novel, such as the highly respected ones published by Norton, you will note that normally the text of the novel comes right at the beginning of the book, preceded only in certain series by a brief note on the text. Material on 'backgrounds', contemporary responses, critical essays and debates – all these come *after* the text of the novel. This is because almost every authority believes that a relatively open-minded reading of the actual text should come before the reading of biographical, contextual or critical material.

So, you have read the novel. What next? *Stage 1* of your search for secondary material should involve two things: first, a listing of all the questions that your reading of the novel has raised, and, second, a general survey of the matters discussed and debated by critics. If as I have recommended, you have taken notes while reading the novel, you should have a basis for constructing a list of issues arising from your own reading, especially those concerned with *problems* or *puzzles* – questions that you want answers to. Here for example are the issues about which I felt I wanted to read more when I had finished a first reading of Ford Madox Ford's novel *The Good Soldier* (1915). The points are adapted from notes I found scribbled in my copy of the work, and are listed in the order in which I found them.

- The narrator Dowell: how much are his shortcomings recognized or shared by Ford? How much does Ford expect the reader to be critical of him and his values (his leading the life of the idle rich, his violence (two physical assaults on others), his report that 'This is the saddest story I have ever heard')?
- Ditto the characters: I am not positively inclined towards any of them. Is that a comment on me, or is Ford writing a sort of social satire that requires the reader to be distanced from the characters being satirized?
- Religion: clearly crucial for certain characters (Catholicism and Protestantism). Is the reader free to situate him- or herself with regard to religious/spiritual issues, or does the novel adopt a standpoint and impose this on the reader?
- Novel published at the start of the First World War. Easy to see it in terms of Ford's portrayal of a way of life that is now threatened or destroyed – but is this the effect of hindsight?
- Lots of references to 'hearts' – thematic importance?
- American/English contrasts: Ford writing in the shadow of Henry James?

Now you may well not have read Ford's novel, but even so I think that you should be able to recognize that the issues raised for me by a first reading of this novel are of very different *sorts*. Some are what we can term *textual* or *interpretative* – for example the issue of 'hearts'. In this case I would be likely to receive help from more interpretative or analytical studies of the novel that pay detailed attention to elements in it that may well have thematic or symbolic significance. Such studies are often referred to as *textual* studies.

My puzzlement concerning Ford's narrator is also in part a textual matter, but we can term it as much *technical* as thematic, and a study of Ford's *narrative technique* is likely to be of use to me here.

So far as the issue of religion is concerned, a good biography of Ford is likely to let me know what Ford's own religious position was when he wrote the novel, although this may not help to isolate the function that religion plays in the novel. A good biography may also help to fix Ford's attitude to the lives of the idle rich, and it may tell me something of the effect of the war on the novel's composition, although again this may not answer all the questions raised for the reader by these matters. (In Chapter 9 you can read about some of the problems of using biographical information to illuminate a literary work; see p. 177.)

If biographical information has its limitations, it can be supplemented and often corrected by more interpretative or analytical studies of a work that attempt to isolate themes (see p. 121) and patterns of meaning. Thematic studies of *The Good Soldier* are thus likely to have much to say about the importance of religion in the novel – and about the significance of the fact that the novel defines characters not just in terms of their religion but also in terms of their nationality, their wealth and their cultural traditions.

If you look at a modern scholarly edition of *The Good Soldier*, such as the Norton Critical Edition edited by Martin Stannard (1995), you will find, in addition to the text of the novel and commentary on textual issues, sections containing contemporary reviews of the work, a long section on literary impressionism, and a section containing biographical and critical commentary. My questions concerning the narrator and Ford's narrative are the easiest to find answers to: other readers of the novel have needed to investigate Ford's use of – and attitude towards – Dowell, and their discussion helps me to explore this matter. I also find discussion of the issue of 'hearts', and some concern with issues of religion – although not as much as I feel the need for.

Let us leave my reading at this stage, and ask how you can start to get a sense of the tradition of critical discussion associated with a particular novel. After you have looked at the titles of essays reprinted in scholarly editions such as the Norton or the Bedford ones, pull a few books off the shelf of the library. Look at the titles, chapter titles and index entries in a range of critical works. Consult works such as *The Year's Work in English Studies*, which give useful summaries of critical responses to particular works. Electronic bibliographies and databases now offer continually updated material that can be accessed speedily online. See the sub-section on using computers below.

Now you can move to *stage 2*. You have your two lists; compare them. To what extent will some of the sequences and traditions of critical discussion that you have uncovered help you with the questions that your own reading has thrown up? You are now better able to start looking for particular essays or books that you can use to deepen your involvement in the novel you have just finished reading. You should find that a brief survey of the critical debate around a particular writer or work will actually open your eyes to issues of which you have been unaware, issues which do not feature on the list you compiled on the basis of your reading notes, but which you recognize to be important once your attention is drawn to them.

Thus when I started to look at critical responses to Ford's *The Good Soldier*, I found discussion of some issues that my own reading of the novel had not raised for me: Ford as impressionist writer, for example, and articles which see *The Good Soldier* as comedy (in one case) and tragedy (in another). These articles sent me back to the novel to reconsider my reading, to look at certain scenes and passages again – and generated a checklist of issues to consider on a rereading of the work. Critics do not just provide answers to questions; they also provide questions for you to answer.

If you have been given an essay topic and a deadline for submitting the finished essay then you may be under more pressure. But you should not just rush to the library with a list of words from the essay topic that you then attempt to find in the table of contents or the index of a succession of critical works. Spend some time *analysing* your essay topic: this will help you in your literature search. You will find more advice on this below (p. 148).

At the end of stage 2, you should have a shortlist of books and articles that you can now proceed to read. Remember that you may not be able to obtain all of them in time (inter-library loan can take many weeks if an article is not in your library, and you may have to pay a fee). Remember too that as you read criticism you will refine your shortlist: some new references that you may want to consult are likely to be thrown up, and you may also be sent back to reread parts of the literary text with which you started.

■ Using computers

The Internet now offers a range of facilities that both supplement and extend those available in conventional libraries, but not all of these services are free. Some of the most useful tools – such as databases like the Chadwyck-Healey Literature Online database – are expensive to subscribe to and generally beyond the pockets of individual student subscribers. Not even all university libraries have subscriptions to all such commercial databases, so you should find out exactly what your college or university library (and also your public library, if you live in a large town or city) does subscribe to. But if you can access a database like Literature Online, it is worth learning how to exploit what it has to offer; there is no doubt that such tools, sensibly used, are enormously useful.

Many of the electronic services that are aimed at individual student subscribers need to be either avoided completely or treated with great circumspection. In the 'not to be touched at any cost' category are the straightforwardly dishonest – companies that sell either pre-written or written-to-order essays for cash. Your institution will almost certainly have a regulation concerning plagiarism and using such companies will risk contravening this regulation. Remember that academics and university administrators are getting clever at detecting web plagiarism and cheating, and there are now programs that will help your teachers to find out if you have cheated.

Then there are those companies that, for a few pounds (or, more usually, dollars) will sell you a text that gives you a plot summary of a novel, with commentary on characters, narrative technique, historical background, and so on. If you do not actually quote directly from these you may escape being accused of cheating, but it is clear that such material is designed to enable you to avoid reading and thinking about the text in question, so that if it is discovered that you have used such material, you may end up failing an assignment and sullying your reputation with your teacher.

Having said that, there is much that can be accessed via a PC and an Internet connection that can be very useful to you in your study and that can quite legitimately be used in writing an assignment if properly acknowledged. Remember that it is always better to err on the side of caution and to be as open and comprehensive as possible in your acknowledgements. And if you are in any doubt, talk to your lecturer in person.

I list below some of the different ways in which you can use your PC as a study tool. All of these require an Internet connection, although you can download material and then use it on a PC without such a connection.

1   Many of the novels and short stories you study can be downloaded as complete texts and saved on the hard disk of your own computer. A simple web-search along the lines of <nostromo + electronic> will soon establish whether there is an available and downloadable electronic text of Conrad's novel (there is). Remember that if the work was first published, or its author died, fewer than seventy years ago (fifty in the United States), then the work will be in copyright and you will be unlikely to be able legally to download a free electronic text of it.

If you call up the text of all or part of a novel into even a standard word-processing program, it will allow you to do such things as find all examples of a particular word or phrase, or to compare – say – the average sentence length in two short stories by the same or two different authors. Because novels are generally longer than poems or plays, this facility is particularly useful for the student of the novel.

If for example you think that you remember (as I once did) that Chablis wine is described as 'straw-coloured' in Henry James's *The Ambassadors*, then the computer will locate the reference in seconds (I had searched for hours in the printed text, but had been looking in the wrong place). Remember that not all electronic texts are reliable, and even a reliable text may be based on a different edition from the one on your syllabus (see the discussion of different versions of the same work on p. 154).

Imagine that you are struck by the phrase 'paradise of snakes' in Joseph Conrad's *Nostromo*. Does this betoken a concern to link the development of the silver mine in that novel with the expulsion of Adam and Eve from the Garden of Eden? In a matter of a very few minutes you can electronically search through the text looking for words such as 'Eden', 'fall', 'snake', 'serpent', 'Adam', 'Eve', 'Satan', 'Devil', 'tree', 'forbidden', 'fruit', and so on. Whatever you do, don't think that you can just list the results of such searches in an essay! You need to *think* about what such searches uncover, and relate the results to your reading of the work as a whole and to what critics have written about it.

2 I mentioned above the Chadwyck-Healey Literature Online database. This is mostly what is known as a full-text database, meaning that it will allow you to search – for instance – for examples of the word 'photograph' in a very large number of – again, for instance – nineteenth-century poems. Its coverage of fiction is at present less comprehensive, but it is a very good place to start looking for criticism. If you search for <author: Fielding> and <keyword: picaresque>, it throws up a list of four articles, three of which can be downloaded in full-text format. With a more open search you can get a good sense of the critical issues associated with a particular text. Thus a search for <author: Ford, Ford Madox> and <keyword: good soldier> throws up the titles of 112 items ranging from reviews through articles to books. Just looking at the titles of these items will give you a sense of the different emphases in criticism of this novel over the past four decades, and many of the articles listed can again be immediately downloaded free in full-text form.

More specialist databases are available. To take a representative example, ECCO – Eighteenth Century Collection Online – offers at present 'full-text searchable facsimile page displays of approximately 24,000 books published in Britain and its colonies during the 18th century', with the long-term aim of raising the number of books covered to 150,000.

Both the British Modern Humanities Research Association (MHRA) and the American Modern Library Association (MLA) produce annual bibliographies. ABELL (Annual Bibliography of Language and Literature) is compiled by scholars under the direction of the MHRA, and provides information concerning the sorts of issues critics have been concerned with from year to year and from country to country. Most academic libraries should be able to provide access to these databases – either online or on CD-Rom.

I should stress that any material you obtain from any of these databases is just as respectable as it would be had you obtained it in hard–copy form, and you need in no way feel that you have to conceal the fact that you obtained it online. Literature Online gives you two ways of downloading texts: either as 'full text' or as 'page image'. The latter option gives you an article paginated exactly as it is in the printed version, so references can be given precisely as they would for an article consulted in a printed journal. 'Full text' downloads enable you to quote accurately, but you need to reference the fact that the pagination quoted is for an electronic download.

3 Electronic discussion groups on e-mail or the Internet allow you to follow debates between other students all over the world (although, at the time of writing, often mainly in the United States) about a particular novel. You can also submit questions to such discussion groups, although, if participants think that you are trying to get them to do your work for you, you will get the cold shoulder. Specialist questions can often get useful replies: if you want tips on essays dealing with a relatively specialist topic, sometimes a discussion group can help where a scholarly bibliography cannot.

4 Even the general 'search' function in an Internet search engine (such as Yahoo or Google) can throw up useful leads. One Sunday, when the library was closed, I found very useful scholarly material on Thomas Hardy's short story 'An Imaginative Woman' merely by searching for <Hardy + Imaginative> on my PC. Often lecturers put out material on their departmental or university web page which is well worth consulting. You may well be able to access useful material put out for students in other universities. It is absolutely acceptable to use such material in an essay *provided you acknowledge where you got it from and furnish a web-page reference*.

If you want more detailed information about using the Internet which covers such topics as the different ways to refine web searches, how to assess the academic reliability of web pages, and how to reference web material, you can consult the second section of Paul Goring, Jeremy Hawthorn and Domhnall Mitchell, *Studying Literature: The Essential Companion* (2001) entitled 'Guide to the Use of Electronic Media'.

■ Revision

If you have taken full notes from your reading of novels and your study of critics then the process of revision should be easier for you. Always study your notes in conjunction with the novel concerned; it makes no sense to memorize a set of notes if you have forgotten the salient details from the work itself.

You may take an examination requiring knowledge of a number of novels up to a year after you have read some of them. Full rereading is impossible, and some elements will certainly have slipped your memory. Do *not* try to skip-read the whole work again, but concentrate upon reading selected passages with care. These should always include the opening and closing pages of the work – beginnings and endings of novels are invariably revealing. Is the opening dramatic or descriptive? Does it plunge the reader into the middle of things, or carefully establish a scene? Does it set a dominant tone, and establish the narrative perspective or personality of the narrator? Is the reader addressed directly, and are we given an indication of what sort of reader (or reading) the narrative invites or appears to assume? Is the ending happy or sad? Why does the author choose to make it so? Does it tie up all the loose ends or leave many questions unanswered? With what effect?

Apart from opening and closing pages, you should pick some key passages – either those that have seemed important to you, or those which critics have found of great interest. Pick a couple of passages at random, preferably ones that seem unfamiliar on leafing through the work. Analyse these in detail.

If it makes you feel easier, construct a list of character names (just the main characters) for each work prior to an examination. If you forget a name in an examination do not panic, just leave a blank and go on writing. If the name does not come to you by the end of the examination then asterisk the gap and write in a footnote explaining that you have forgotten the character name and indicating who the character is by other means such as relationships to other characters.

So far as critics are concerned, it is useful to be able to situate their arguments and positions – both in the context of critical debate about the work in question, and also in the context of the critic's own principles and theoretical allegiances (see my comments on p. 171).

■ Essays and examinations

Some rules concerning the writing of essays are not specific to study of the novel. There are a number of textbooks that will advise you on such matters, and you should find out which if any of these your lecturers recommend. But the best way to learn how to write an essay is to read articles in respected academic journals and note the conventions that they follow. The tips below are not specific to essays or examination answers on the novel, and you may find them irritatingly basic. But if you have not previously been aware of their importance you should pay careful attention to them.

- If you are using a computer you should *never* submit an essay without spell-checking it. It takes very little time, and reduces the risk that an irritated teacher will mark you down for careless spelling.
- I am much less enthusiastic about the grammar-checkers contained in basic word-processing programs. But if you know that you regularly make basic grammatical mistakes, then the grammar-check facility can help you to guard against them.
- I am a strong believer in the use of sub-headings. This is partly because they help whoever reads your work to find his or her way through your

argument, and partly because they may reveal to you that a particular section or paragraph in an essay would be better placed in another position. Similarly, remember to use paragraphs sensibly. If you are not sure about the conventions governing paragraphing, consult a more specialist book on the writing of essays.

- Try to use an appealing layout. Heed your teachers' advice on such things as line-spacing, reference systems, bibliographies.
- Always start your essay or examination answer by making it clear which question or topic you are addressing (but you do not need to copy the whole question out on the first page).

When it comes to writing essays and examination answers there is no substitute for practice: the more that you write, and have your writing commented upon, the more clearly and easily you will come to write. The following advice picks up what in my own experience are the most common sorts of weakness in essays and examination answers dealing with the novel, but it is important to listen to the advice of your teachers.

Be relevant

You will be responding to a specific question or topic. Do not just pick out a couple of words from it and proceed to write all you know about the text(s) mentioned. (This is known as the sack–of–potatoes method: you spend months gathering in the potatoes, and then the first time you eat you slit the sack open and spill them all out all over the table. Remember that an essay or answer is like a meal: selection, preparation and order are necessary if the result is to be pleasing.) Use coloured pens and underline key words in the question. If the question has several points then *number* these. After every second page you write, look back to make sure that what you are writing is of relevance to the topic or question.

Argue a case

A question requires an answer, not just a response. You will be expected to take up a position in relation to what has been asked, and to argue your position as logically as possible. Do not be afraid to express a personal opinion, but, if you do, say that it is a personal opinion and justify it (see below). If you refer to the opinion of others (critics, for example), say whether or not you agree with them, and why. If the question or topic includes a quotation, remember that you may disagree with the opinion of the person quoted. (Very often the person who has written the question expects you to do this.) Remember, however, that if you are to argue successfully, you need to ...

Plan your answer

If you only have a very short amount of time, you may have to restrict this to a five-minute sketch of what you intend to say, but if you are writing an essay in your own time then you should plan more carefully. With an essay, you can afford to restructure what you have written for its final presentation, such that the introduction and conclusion can be added on at the end in case your argument has become modified or more complex in the course of writing. Because essays are now usually written on a PC you may get used to moving material around on screen. Remember that you cannot do this in an examination, which means that examination answers need to be more carefully planned. In an examination you may find as you write that your answer is moving in a rather different way from that laid out in your introductory paragraph. If so, the best thing is to admit to this change of direction, and even to explain why.

A good essay or examination answer should have an introduction which explains what attitude you are taking to the question asked, and how you are going to answer it. This need only be half a page long. You should then provide, in as ordered a way as possible, evidence to substantiate the position you have taken up. At any stage in an essay or examination answer, the person reading it should know (i) what you are trying to argue, and (ii) how this argument fits into your general thesis or response to the question. Anyone who has marked examinations knows that a sure sign that there is something wrong is when you have to flip back to page 1 to check exactly which question the script is supposed to be answering. See below for some further suggestions on how to make a positive impression with the opening sentences of your essay or answer.

Back up your arguments with evidence

There are different sorts of evidence that can be adduced in an essay or an examination answer. Unless the question specifically focuses upon extratextual matters, the most important evidence that you can bring forward is likely to be *textual*. The general rule about textual evidence is that it should be *detailed* and it should be *analytical*. In an essay you should quote enough to make your point, and you should *never* assume that a quotation speaks for itself. Every time you quote from a novel or a short story in an essay you should explain what it is in the quotation that is important – pointing to *particular* words, *particular* phrases, *particular* techniques (such as those outlined in my suggested checklist).

This is especially important in writing on the novel, because there is a tendency to assume that the language of a novel speaks for itself. The language of many novels seems almost transparent – we look through it at 'what happens' and are not arrested by it *as language* as we typically are when reading a poem. You have to learn to resist this process and to 'look at' that which in the past you have 'looked through'.

Examinations may present a different problem. If your college or university is an enlightened one you may be allowed to take unmarked copies of texts into examinations. Generally speaking, examinations have to be written without access to the novel or short-story texts on which they are based. I do not recommend that you spend hours learning selected passages by heart. Not only is this extremely time-consuming, but there is also a tendency for those who have shed blood learning long quotations to insist on demonstrating the fact in the examination room, and the quotations that have been learned may well not be relevant to the question asked. But, even if you cannot quote at length from a novel, you can still be detailed in your reference to it. Refer to particular *scenes*, isolate the operative *events*, *actions* and *utterances* (you do not have to quote to do this), draw attention to relevant aspects of *narrative technique*, and comment upon such things as *symbolism* and *imagery* if they play a significant role. If you can refer to particular words and phrases used, all the better.

In addition to textual evidence, there are various forms of extratextual evidence that can be incorporated in an answer: comments and opinions from critics, statements from or about the work's author, parallels with other works either by the same author or by others, information of the sort mentioned in my brief discussion of 'the sociology of literature' (p. 174), information about relevant social, historical and cultural events or states of affairs. In all of these, two issues should be borne in mind: *influence* and *relevance*. You may reproduce a lot of accurate facts, but did they have any influence on the writing (or do they have any influence on the reading) of the work? Are they relevant to the question asked?

Do not tell the story

I suppose I ought to concede here that it is possible that one day you might encounter an essay topic or examination question which starts, 'Tell the story of *Wuthering Heights* and then proceed to comment on …', but 99.9 per cent of essay topics and essay questions do not require you to open with an obligatory three-page précis of what happens in the novel in question. You have to assume that the person marking the essay or answer has read the work and knows what happens: he or she will be irritated, and not impressed, by such a plot summary.

Remember that the characters are not 'real people'

Although it is quite legitimate at times to discuss the characters and actions in a novel as we discuss the people we know in real life (all critics do this at some time or another), you should also indicate clearly that you are aware that what we read are words that have been created and crafted by an author. Peter Lamarque has suggested that the reader of fiction needs to be able to combine the imaginative involvement of an internal perspective with the awareness of artifice of an external perspective (1996, 14), and you should make sure that the person reading your essay knows you are aware of this difference.

Arouse your reader's curiosity

Compare the following selection of opening passages for an essay on Virginia Woolf's novel *Mrs Dalloway*.

1. Virginia Woolf was born Virginia Stephen in 1882. Her father was Sir Leslie Stephen, famous for his work on the *Dictionary of National Biography*. She had periods of mental disturbance all her life; the first in 1913 and the final one associated with her suicide in 1941. She was a member of the so-called Bloomsbury Group, and is credited with being one of the most important forces behind the modernist novel in England.■

2. Towards the end of Virginia Woolf's novel *Mrs Dalloway* we follow Clarissa Dalloway's thoughts as she considers Sir William Bradshaw, 'a great doctor, but to her obscurely evil, without sex or lust, extremely polite to women, but capable of some indescribable outrage – forcing your soul, that was it ...'. The words take the reader aback: it is as if being without lust is presented as a negative quality. What lies behind this attitude?■

3. The very brief opening scene of Marleen Gorris's 1998 film of *Mrs Dalloway* shows Septimus on the battlefield in Italy in 1918. He shouts 'Evans! Don't jump!', but a massive explosion and his look of horror reveal that he has shouted in vain. The scene is not to be found in Virginia Woolf's novel, which opens with the words, 'Mrs Dalloway said that she would buy the flowers herself' in the novel's 'present' of June 1923. The film-maker's instinct that in Woolf's novel the past is always there, influencing the present, is however perceptive.■

4. *Mrs Dalloway* is the first novel by Virginia Woolf that I have read. I had been looking forward to reading this novel because I had heard that Woolf was a fighter for women's rights and a major influence on feminist thinkers during the twentieth century. My first reading of the novel came as something of a shock: how could feminists respect a writer capable of producing such a negative, stereotyped portrayal of a lesbian character as Woolf does with Miss Kilman?■

I venture to suggest that any teacher who has pulled the first of thirty (or 130) essays off a pile to be marked and has read opening number 1 will feel his or her heart dropping. This is not because there is anything wrong, or even irrelevant, about the information it contains, but because it suggests very strongly that it has been copied straight out of a reference book by someone who does not have a burning desire to propose an original response to whatever question has been asked. Anyone marking a large number of essays on *Mrs Dalloway* is likely to encounter more than a few that begin much like this.

In contrast to opening number 1, openings 2, 3 and 4 all suggest that the writer does have something interesting and original to say. Moreover they all raise issues, problems, questions that stimulate the reader's curiosity. We want to read on to find out how the writer deals with the problem that he or she has outlined. We are hooked. Consider the different techniques involved in examples 2, 3 and 4: raising a textual or interpretive problem (2); using a film adaptation of a work to illuminate aspects of the original (3); starting with a report of a strong personal reaction that you then use to lead into an issue relating to the text or its critical history (4).

Now care is needed here, because if there is one standard failing for which essays and examination answers are marked down in literary studies, it is that of failing to answer the question. So that immediately after an opening along the lines of alternatives 2 to 4 the writer needs to establish that he or she is indeed going to tie in a resolution of the problem raised with a relevant response to the chosen question.

Perhaps I can conclude by attempting to exemplify some of the things that I have been recommending. Imagine that you are writing a response to the following question: 'Discuss Kingsley Amis's humorous techniques in *Lucky Jim*, drawing attention to the stated or implied values that underpin them'. First of all, you need to spend some time analysing this question – and this is where your collection of coloured pens can be useful. Using the colour you have set aside for primary issues, you should first mark the word that sums up the *type* of essay or exam answer that you are being asked to provide. My suggestion is as follows:

> **Discuss** Kingsley Amis's humorous techniques in *Lucky Jim*, drawing attention to the stated or implied values that underpin them. ■

I have started off by marking the word 'discuss' in bold, because this word asks for something slightly different from those other words that lecturers are fond of: 'consider', 'define', 'contrast', and so on. 'Discuss' allows you more freedom to manoeuvre than many of the alternatives, but it is *not* the same as 'describe'. In other words, the question wants more than (i) a list of humorous techniques, and (ii) a list of the values that you believe to underpin them. Discussion involves considering alternative possibilities, and suggesting perhaps why you prefer some to others.

Now you need your second coloured marking pen, to mark the main theme(s) of your response, the central topic(s) that you are expected to discuss. Here is my suggestion:

> **Discuss** Kingsley Amis's HUMOROUS TECHNIQUES in *Lucky Jim*, drawing attention to the stated or implied VALUES that underpin them. ∎

I have marked 'humorous techniques' and 'values' in small capitals because the person who set the topic seems most to be interested in your (i) showing that you can isolate and describe Amis's humorous techniques, and (ii) demonstrating that you can relate these techniques to particular values. To write about Amis's humorous techniques it is necessary to stand back a bit from the text, and to generalize; you will need to see what different funny scenes or amusing episodes have in common in terms of the writer's deliberate method. The other word or phrase I have marked here is 'values': this is the second essential element that whoever marks your essay or examination will be looking for in your response. To say nothing about values would be deemed a serious omission. Note that the whole thrust of the question is in the direction of your *relating* humorous techniques to values; the question does not actually use a word such as 'relate': this is where marking two elements in the question in the same colour helps to remind you that you need to provide more than a list of humorous techniques and an unrelated list of values.

Now you need your third coloured marking pen. Subsidiary elements in the question need to be marked as well. Here is my suggestion.

> **Discuss** Kingsley Amis's HUMOROUS TECHNIQUES in *Lucky Jim*, drawing attention to the <u>stated or implied</u> VALUES that <u>underpin</u> them. ∎

The words that I have underlined here have the function of *refining* the essential concern of the question: the values that you discuss in relation to humorous techniques do not have to be overtly stated in Amis's text; they may only be implied. This indirect relation between value and technique is also hinted at in the word 'underpin'; the values are not necessarily part of the humour, but the reader's sense that they are there in the background helps to anchor the humour to a more serious sense of moral discriminations.

Let us imagine that your examination question asks that you use the following quotation from the second page of the novel as a basis for your comments. The anti-hero of the novel, the university assistant lecturer Jim Dixon, is talking to his professor, Welch. Welch starts off describing a musical evening that had taken place at his house, 'with a tremolo imparted by unshared laughter':

'There was the most marvellous mix-up in the piece they did just before the interval. The young fellow playing the viola had the misfortune to turn over two pages at once, and the resulting confusion ... my word ...'

Quickly deciding on his own word, Dixon said it to himself and then tried to flail his features into some sort of response to humour. Mentally, however, he was making a different face and promising himself he'd make it actually when alone. He'd draw his lower lip in under his top teeth and by degrees retract his chin as far as possible, all this while dilating his eyes and nostrils. By these means he would, he was confident, cause a deep dangerous flush to suffuse his face.

Welch was talking yet again about his concert. How had he become Professor of History, even at a place like this? By published work? No. By extra good teaching? No in italics. Then how? As usual, Dixon shelved this question, telling himself that what mattered was that this man had decisive power over his future, at any rate until the next four or five weeks were up. (ellipses in original)

Here is my stab at a brief answer that does everything wrong in terms of the advice given above:

> *Lucky Jim* by Kingsley Amis is the story of a young history lecturer who is scared of losing his job. He tries to make his professor like him and want to keep him in his department, but he does everything wrong. He gets drunk and burns the sheets at his professor's house, falls in love with the professor's son's girlfriend, and gets drunk again giving a public lecture. But everything comes out all right in the end.
>
> Amis makes him think lots of funny things which make us laugh. Also the tight spots he gets into are funny.
>
> This passage shows us how laughable the professor is. Jim also imagines funny things here, like pulling a silly face. I think that anyone reading this passage will see how funny it is. This shows that Amis likes Jim and doesn't like Professor Welch. Perhaps Professor Welch did something nasty to Mr Amis once.
>
> I like this book, and the passage shows why.

This can hardly be said to qualify for a pass grade. It does not *discuss* anything except on the most trivial level, it fails to describe any humorous *techniques* (a précis of a funny scene is not an account of a technique), and it says nothing about any implied or stated *values* that could be said to lie behind the comic elements that it singles out. Furthermore it treats the characters as real people with whom author Kingsley Amis might have interacted, and it assumes that the passage in question speaks for itself and does not need to be analysed.

Compare the following short answer, which attempts to provide what the question asks for.

Anyone who has not read *Lucky Jim* might suspect that a novel in which the hero writes 'Ned Welch is a soppy Fool with a Fase like A Pigs gum' in the steam on the mirror in his professor's bathroom is not a sober discussion of issues of human conduct. Indeed, according to F.R. Leavis, 'the spectacle of an academic critic going out of his way to pronounce a Kingsley Amis novel a "serious study in amorality", would have been possible only in a period marked by a collapse of standards' (Leavis 1969, 56). But Leavis's marked lack of enthusiasm for Laurence Sterne's *Tristram Shandy* suggests that Leavis had difficulty in appreciating that the childish may be profound and that the comic may engage with serious issues concerning moral conduct. In what follows I shall argue that the humour of *Lucky Jim* does indeed rest on the reader's perception of certain underlying values, and that our ability to respond to the humour of the novel is related to our approval or disapproval of these values.

What strikes us straight away if we look at the passage in question is that, whereas Professor Welch's speech is quoted but his private thoughts are not revealed (if he can be imagined to have any), Jim Dixon says nothing out loud but the reader is given access to a succession of his unexpressed thoughts. One obvious source of humour is the use of sharp *contrast*, between what Jim is thinking and his public appearance. The contrast is backed up by verbal wit – 'Quickly deciding on his own word' allows the reader to feel enticed into an alliance with Jim; the suggestion is that because we think along the same lines as he does we do not need to be given Jim's 'own word', and the author thereby drags us into complicity with Jim.

This is a pattern that continues throughout the novel up to the dramatic point, in Jim's final confrontation with Bertram, when Jim thinks something to himself and then, for the first time in the novel, utters the same words publicly. We note that Welch's tremolo is 'imparted by unshared laughter'; he is wrapped up in himself, unaware of Dixon's lack of interest in his tedious stories. He is not just absurd, he is also objectionable: behind the humour lies a revulsion against his self-importance and lack of interest in Jim and his views. Amis's use of ellipses at the conclusion of Welch's speech is indicative of the character's mindless self-obsession: the recalled scene is amusing to him and he does not feel impelled to explain why it is amusing to his companion; because he is really only reliving the experience for himself he judders to a halt without making a point – his egocentricity does not require that verbal precision that would communicate something specific to Jim.

The three quoted paragraphs show an interesting progression from direct speech (paragraph 1), through reported speech (paragraph 2; the 'speech' is, of course, Jim's inner speech), moving eventually to Free Indirect Discourse (specifically, represented (verbal) thought) by the second sentence of the third paragraph. This is not accidental: in the first paragraph we are put into the position of listener to Welch's banalities, we are outside, being ignored by him as Jim is ignored. In the second paragraph we go inside Jim's mind, but still as an observer, able to contrast the absurdity of his wild and physical imaginings with Welch's tedious and petty ramblings, but by the end of the third paragraph we *are* Jim: the narrated thought recreates Jim's thought processes in our own reading minds. Thus the reader is encouraged to look at Welch from the outside but to experience with Jim from the inside. We understand that Jim has to talk to himself, to engage in a question-and-answer dialogue with himself, because proper communication is impossible with a man so self-important and so uninterested in others as is Welch.

I have used the word 'wild'. We can note that there is a wild, physical, anarchic element to Jim's fantasies: Jim is recurrently associated with a free physicality that contrasts with the polite sub-academic drawing-room conventionality of Welch. Note the use of a word such as 'flail' to describe his face-pulling, and the detailed physical description of the actions associated with the planned face-pulling. Physicality in novels often stands for 'natural' as against 'artificial' or 'conventional' behaviour. In Jim's case, though, physicality is inner, secret, repressed: thus we may suspect that behind the reader's laughter lies a sympathy with the natural man forced to repress a native honesty and lack of pretension in a context demanding adherence to artificial forms of polite deception. This, we may note, is a standard component in the literary works associated with the so-called 'angry young men' of the 1950s. In the work of all of these, including *Lucky Jim*, there is an anger at certain failings such as hypocrisy, privilege, convention, which may be portrayed as individual failings but which are also seen by their accusers as faults endemic in British society of the immediate post-Second World War period. We should remember, then, that behind our pleasure at the attack on Welch may be a belief that he represented (and perhaps still represents) a set of social ills from which our age has yet fully to free itself.

In conclusion, we may note that, although comedy has often been considered to represent a lower, simpler and more basic form than tragedy, we should not make the mistake of assuming that humour is a matter only of the surface, that what makes us laugh has no depth. We would not laugh as we read this passage if we rejected the values that underpin Amis's descriptions. If we felt Jim to be an outrageous, rude, ungrateful and hypocritical lout who should show more respect to such a decent and lovable man as Professor Welch, then this passage would not make us laugh. (It and others apparently did not make F.R. Leavis laugh.) It is only by succeeding in making common cause with the reader through a shared set of human values that Amis succeeds in making him or her laugh.

While I am not putting this forward as a perfect answer, I hope you will agree that it is more analytical than the previous version.

Topics for discussion

- 'Lecturers say they want our personal responses, but really they want us to repeat what they have told us.' Do you agree?
- What is the best way to revise a long novel that was read six months ago?
- How does writing an essay with access to text and notes help prepare us to write exams with access to neither?
- Is it useful to 'learn quotes'?
- What is the best way to prevent 'exam panic'?

8
Versions and adaptations

Preview

This chapter deals with:
- ■ the difference between a version and an adaptation of a novel
- ■ different types of adaptation
- ■ gains and losses in film adaptations

■ Versions

We generally refer to novels and short stories by means of their titles – *Bleak House*, or *Ulysses*, or *Lucky Jim*, or *Do Androids Dream of Electric Sheep?* For convenience we often abbreviate the titles under which novels were first published, so that we talk not of *The Personal History, Adventures, Experience, & Observation of David Copperfield the Younger of Blunderstone Rookery (Which He never meant to be Published on any Account)* but more manageably of just *David Copperfield*. Abbreviated or not, however, our use of such titles betrays a confidence that novels have a fixed identity that is not eroded or confused by many printings and editions. It is true that sometimes our attention is drawn to the fact that there are textual issues associated with novels: recent editions of Charles Dickens's *Great Expectations* generally print both of the endings that Dickens wrote for this novel, and the influential *Norton Anthology of American Literature* has included quite significantly different versions of Mark Twain's 'The Celebrated Jumping Frog of Calaveras County' in successive editions. Generally speaking, though, we discuss novels and short stories as if their titles denoted unambiguously single texts. But the reality is rather more complex than this, and I would like to illustrate this by means of a representative example.

In September 1907 the first English book edition of Joseph Conrad's novel *The Secret Agent* was published. If you study this novel you will probably read it in a modern paperback that is based upon this edition. Critical essays concerned with this novel will also almost certainly be based on an edition that descends in one way or another from the first English book edition. But behind this seeming unanimity a much more complex reality can be revealed. It is as if this single text is the visible part of a verbal iceberg, one that has a massive hidden presence extending backwards and forwards in time rather than in space.

If you consult the scholarly 'critical' edition of *The Secret Agent* published by Cambridge University Press in 1990, you will find in it a dense ninety-two-page discussion of the novel's textual history. From this you can determine not only that the novel was first published in a considerably shorter periodical version, in instalments, but also that it was published in separate book editions in Britain and America. Behind these published editions a web of manuscripts, typescripts and corrected proofs has been uncovered by the editors of this edition, a web so complex that it is represented in their discussion by a sequence of graphic representations resembling a map of the London underground system. Establishing who made changes to these various texts and when is often difficult, as later printings of the first edition seem on occasions to reintroduce earlier formulations that Conrad had altered.

In November 1922, just over fifteen years after *The Secret Agent* was first published in book form, an adaptation of the novel for the stage opened in London at the Ambassador's Theatre. The adaptation had been written by Conrad himself. Not only did this dramatization remove many scenes present in the novel, in transforming the work from a *narrative* to a *play*, it also completely removed the 'extradiegetic' narrator along with his ironic perspective on the events recounted – perhaps the most radical change that transformation from printed novel to performed play entailed. It also changed some aspects of the story, so that the character Winnie Verloc does not commit suicide but instead goes mad at the end of the work. The play was not a great success, and ran for only a week. But in the audience for one of the few performances sat a young man named Alfred Hitchcock, who was shortly to begin a career in the film industry (see Spoto 1983, 62). Fourteen years later, after having directed a film entitled *The Secret Agent* that had nothing to do with Conrad, Hitchcock directed a film entitled *Sabotage* that included the acknowledgement 'From the novel "The Secret Agent" by Joseph Conrad' in the opening credits, but that transposed the action to the present day and made very significant alterations to the setting and story of both Conrad's novel and his stage adaptation. Sixty years after Hitchcock's film was first shown, a new film entitled *The Secret Agent*, written and directed by Christopher Hampton and starring Bob Hoskins and Patricia Arquette, was released in the United States. Both Conrad's own dramatization of his novel and Hampton's screenplay have been published and can be consulted.

Instead of a single text, then, we now have a bewildering succession of texts, not all of which have survived. How should the poor student of the novel cope with this diversity?

By convention these varied texts are divided into separate categories. All of the variants and versions associated with Conrad's writing of the novel are usually deemed to be the preserve of the textual editor. Unless you are writing an advanced thesis on *The Secret Agent*, you will not be expected to pore over periodical and book versions of the novel in their British and American editions, nor to sit in front of a microfilm reader or PC deciphering the handwriting of Conrad's manuscript. Nor is it likely that you will be expected to read the novel in a full critical edition such as the Cambridge edition mentioned above. But you may – and in my opinion should – be expected to read the novel in a modern edition with a text based upon the results of recent scholarship. Such an edition will draw your attention to substantial variations in the text of the novel, and it should also allow you to ponder the significance of some of Conrad's own textual revisions. Recent editions of classic novels published by reputable firms such as Norton, Penguin and Oxford World's Classics will almost certainly be reliable – that is to say they will not give you texts that repeat mistakes or changes unauthorized by the writer after these have been pointed out by scholars, and they will contain information about the textual history of the work and about important textual variants.

■ Adaptations

But what about those later versions that we generally refer to as adaptations? And what is the difference between a version and an adaptation? Although the two terms overlap, generally speaking we call a rewriting of a novel or short story an adaptation when it does not seek to *replace* a known work ('known', typically, because it has been published or performed), but to be treated as a new work, one that it is hoped will have a life of its own *alongside* that of the work of which it is an adaptation. It is usual for an adaptation to involve some generic change – from prose fiction to play or film, for example – so that we may find that a play that is based on another play is termed 'a modern-dress version' rather than 'a modern-dress adaptation'. Conrad, like most novelists, was very keen to establish just one authoritative text of his novels, but he did not want people to stop reading *The Secret Agent* once he had dramatized it, and neither we assume did Alfred Hitchcock after he had made his film *Sabotage*.

Some introductory questions

There are many different ways in which a short story or a novel can be adapted. Let me try to list some key general issues here.

1 *How great an involvement in the adaptation does the author or the source text have?*
  If for example the author writes a one-person monologue based on a short story and then directs him- or herself in a performance of this monologue, the involvement is very considerable. If the adaptation is written and performed after the author's death by someone with only the original story or novel as basis, this involvement is non-existent.

2 *How different are the medium and genre for which the adaptation is produced from those of the source text?*
  Although a play is written to be performed, its reliance upon language is generally greater than is the case for a film. And the collective nature of film production inevitably reduces the importance of the writer's role when set against the writer's dominating importance for a novel. Remember that a basic issue such as the length of time available for a dramatization will vary between a film and a television series. Adapting John Galsworthy's *The Forsyte Saga* for a two-hour film would be a very different task from adapting it for a television series of many instalments. See below for more detailed comments on such issues.

3 *How long a time is there between the writing and publication of the source text and the writing and publication or performing of the adaptation?*

A director who wishes to film *Hamlet* today must contend with issues of cultural change that do not arise in the case of the filming of a Harry Potter novel. A similar point applies to the production of an adaptation in a different culture from the one to which the source text belongs, even if there is a small gap in time between the writing of source and of adaptation. *The Seven Samurai* and *The Magnificent Seven* are not so far removed in time or in medium and genre, but the cultures within which these two films were produced, and the cultures that they depict, are radically different. The term 'reculturation' has been applied to such adaptations. Remember that this issue arises even if an author adapts his own work: *The Secret Agent* was performed as a play sixteen years after Conrad's novel was published, in a very different England and world from those in which the novel was written and first read.

4 *How well known is the source text?*

Anyone adapting *Hamlet* for a new film cannot ignore the fact that almost everyone who sees the film will have *some* idea of what Shakespeare's play is about. But many films based on relatively unknown literary works can be made on the assumption that most of those who see the film will not have read the source text beforehand and will probably not read it afterwards either. A director may choose to satisfy or challenge an audience's expectations but he or she cannot ignore them completely. No director could make a film of Tolstoy's *Anna Karenina* which ended with Anna marrying Vronsky and settling down to a blissful married life without taking into account that a very significant number of those who saw the film would be aware that this ending is quite different from the ending of Tolstoy's novel. But when Conrad changed the ending of *The Secret Agent* in adapting it for the stage, he may well have assumed that the plot of his novel would not be familiar to his London theatre audience. And when Beeban Kidron filmed Conrad's much less well-known short story 'Amy Foster' as *Swept from the Sea* in 1997, she almost certainly assumed that only a few members of her film's audience would know anything of the source text.

5 *Does the adaptation display or conceal its relationship with the source text?*

Clearly the starting point here is the title, followed shortly afterwards by character names. A change of title (from *The Turn of the Screw* to *The Innocents*, for example) may signal a desire on the part of writer, director or producer to establish greater distance between the film and Henry James's novella than might have been implied by retaining his title for the film adaptation.

6 *What sort of adaptation are we dealing with?*

There are many ways of categorizing adaptations; one of the most influential has been Dudley Andrew's distinction between adaptations that 'borrow', 'intersect' with and 'transform' their sources (see Andrew 1992, 422–3). Andrew glosses these terms as follows.

Borrowing: Andrew describes this as 'the most frequent mode of adaptation. 'Here the artist employs … the material, idea, or form of an earlier, generally successful text.' Citing Richard Strauss's *Don Quixote*, Andrew comments that there is 'no question of replication of the original', but instead 'the audience is expected to enjoy basking in a certain pre-established presence and to call up new or especially powerful aspects of a cherished work'.

Intersecting: Andrew notes that 'here the uniqueness of the original text is preserved to such an extent that it is intentionally left unassimilated in adaptation'. An adaptation in the intersecting mode tends to 'present the otherness and distinctiveness of the original text', thus initiating a dialectical interplay of literary and cinematic forms. An example of this ambitious form of adaptation is Francis Ford Coppola's *Apocalypse Now*, although as Jakob Lothe points out, this film – which did not on first release acknowledge its debt to Joseph Conrad's *Heart of Darkness* – 'could be seen as an example of borrowing as well as intersecting' (Lothe 2000, 88).

Transformation: 'Here it is assumed that the task of adaptation is the reproduction in cinema of something essential about an original text.' Andrew finds that as transformations tend to be faithful to the literary text, they may 'become a scenario written in typical scenario form'. Yet it does not follow that this kind of adaptation is artistically inferior to the two other variants. An example of a successful adapation in the fidelity and transformation mode is John Huston's 1987 film *The Dead*, which closely follows the plot of James Joyce's short story.

The economy of Andrew's tripartite distinction stands in sharp contrast to Robert Stam's mention of 'a whole constellation of tropes – translation, reading, dialogization, cannibalization, transmutation, transfiguration, and signifying'. Indeed, later on in the same article, Stam adds yet more terms when he proposes that adaptation be seen as 'a matter of a source novel hypotext's being transformed by a complex series of operations: selection, amplification, concretization, actualization, critique, extrapolation, analogization, popularization, and reculturization' ('hypotext' in this context means the underlying, or foundational text that is the basis for later adaptations or transformations). If the issue of fidelity, of how much of the source text the adaptor wishes to preserve – ranging from 'little' through 'to some extent' to 'something essential' – is central to Andrew's tripartite distinction, a much greater range of other issues is introduced by Stam's extended lists.

How relevant are adaptations to the study of prose fiction? The answer to that question depends very much on the context of your study – put simply, on the sort of course you are taking – and on the nature of the adaptations with which you are concerned. If you are studying a novel as part of a literature course then the sort of adaptation that you are most likely to face on a syllabus will be a film or television adaptation of a novel or a short story. Adaptation can go in the opposite direction, but prose fictional adaptations of films and television series have generally been accorded little academic respectability: the 'spinoff' and 'tie-in' have not so far been deemed worthy of serious academic study. If you are taking a conventional course on the novel, but have been advised to watch a film version of one of the set texts, then the film may be treated almost as if it were a piece of literary criticism. By this I mean that it may be used to make you more aware of aspects of the novel: what is omitted, what is added, what is altered and what is concretized – and what the effects of these changes are.

'Omitted', 'added', 'altered', 'concretized': let us look at these different forms of transformation. The most obvious omissions will probably relate to excisions from the plot and from the cast of characters – especially if we are dealing with a narrative film that is based on a longish novel. By convention films are not normally more than about three hours long, and even adaptations for television have less space for long complex plots and large character casts than do novels. While noting this fact it might be worth pausing a moment to ask why this is so. Why are we prepared to extend our reading of a long novel over several weeks if necessary, while anything over three hours in a cinema feels excessive? A simple answer to this involves the fundamental point that we have control over our private reading of a book in a way that we do not have over a film: we can pause, flick back to refresh our memory of earlier scenes, increase or decrease the speed of our reading – or even stop and think about what we have read or talk about it with a friend – so that we can pace ourselves as we read and adjust our reading to our mental state. But this is only part of the story, since electronic versions of films and television adaptations have enabled us to do much the same with a film, although with somewhat less ease than we do with a printed source. It is of course possible that as more and more people have access to films on mini personal computers then films may start to extend in length and to take as long to watch as it takes to read a novel; but I rather doubt this – not least because films are expensive things to create, and making them very much longer will increase their cost dramatically. Even long television adaptations are typically shown in instalments rather than in, say, a continuous six-hour session, and this suggests to me that there is something fundamentally different in the way that we experience a silently read novel and a dramatization or a performance, and that this is one of the factors that lies behind the issue of length.

Whatever the reason, a filmed or televised version of a novel is likely to involve very significant abridgement, and a first point of interest in the study of adaptation has to be: 'What has been cut?' In the case of the adaptation of a long novel, it is almost certain that a number of scenes, and a number of characters, will disappear. Why have the screenwriter or director chosen to cut this rather than that scene, this rather than that character? What effect do such cuts have?

Abridgement need not involve elements of the plot or characters – it can also involve aspects of a novel that are integral to its narrative. In discussing Free Indirect Discourse, for example, I noted how the examples I chose (from Katherine Mansfield's 'The Voyage', Virginia Woolf's *Mrs Dalloway* and D.H. Lawrence's 'Fanny and Annie') managed to present a particular scene in such a way as to combine what a narrator tells us and what a character is thinking. Let us look once again at the first two paragraphs of Lawrence's short story 'Fanny and Annie' (1922):

> *Flame-lurid his face as he turned among the throng of flame-lit and dark faces upon the platform. In the light of the furnace she caught sight of his drifting countenance, like a piece of floating fire. And the nostalgia, the doom of homecoming went through her veins like a drug. His eternal face, flame-lit now! The pulse and darkness of red fire from the furnace towers in the sky, lighting the desultory, industrial crowd on the wayside station, lit him and went out.*
>
> *Of course he did not see her. Flame-lit and unseeing! Always the same, with his meeting eyebrows, his common cap, and his red-and-black scarf knotted round his throat. Not even a collar to meet her! The flames had sunk, there was shadow.*

How could one film this scene? Clearly a skilled film-maker could depict Fanny's irritation as Harry fails to see her, and could reproduce some of the effects of flame and shadow that the passage presents. But how could a filmed adaptation of this scene convey the fact that 'the nostalgia, the doom of homecoming went through her veins like a drug', when we are not even sure that Fanny herself is aware of what is happening to her? How could the film-maker convey her sense of his unchangingness ('His eternal face'; 'Always the same') without the crudity of a voice-over? In his introduction to *Aren't You Rather Young to be Writing Your Memoirs?* (1973), the novelist B.S. Johnson has commented with regard to film that it 'is an excellent medium for showing things, but it is very poor at taking an audience inside characters' minds, at telling it what people are thinking' (Bradbury 1990, 166). In his *Narrative in Fiction and Film*, Jakob Lothe draws attention to the difference between Gabriel *thinking* that his next visit to the Morkans will be occasioned by death in 'The Dead', and John Huston's film of Joyce's work *showing* a brief proleptic glimpse of Gabriel in a situation of mourning (Lothe 2000, 155).

What about additions? Some of these may well be straightforward: added scenes or new characters. But some additional elements can be the inevitable result of the 'concretization' that film involves. Here is critic Robert Stam again, considering exactly this issue in a discussion of John Ford's realist adaptation of Steinbeck's novel *The Grapes of Wrath* (1939). Stam comments in detail on a passage in which the character Ma Joad contemplates her memorabilia just before leaving her Oklahoma home for California. The passage in Steinbeck's novel reads as follows:

> *She sat down and opened the box. Inside were letters, clippings, photographs, a pair of earrings, a little gold signet ring, and a watch chain braided of hair and tipped with gold swivels. She touched the letters with her fingers, touched them lightly, and she smoothed a newspaper clipping on which there was an account of Tom's trial.*

Stam comments as follows.

> *In the film we see Ma Joad sit down, open the box, and look at letters, clippings, photographs, and so forth. But even here the 'cinematization' generates an inevitable supplement. Where Steinbeck wrote 'photographs,' Ford had to choose specific photographs. The mention of 'earrings' in the novel does not dictate Ford's choice of having Ma Joad try them on. The newspaper account of Tom's trial requires the choice of a specific newspaper, specific headlines, specific illustrations, and specific fonts, none of which is spelled out in the original. (2000, 55–6)*

Let us pause at this point just to absorb the force of some of Stam's discussion. We may be tempted to suggest that it is almost as if with Steinbeck's text we have a 'script' on the basis of which the reader can mentally perform the scene in question, whereas with Ford's film we have a single performance of the scene. I would not want to reject such a view entirely, but what is questionable about it is the assumption that every detail that is concretized in the film is also given a sort of mental concretization in the mind of the reader as he or she reads the scene in Steinbeck's novel – and this seems to me unlikely. When we read the words 'Inside were letters, clippings, photographs, a pair of earrings, a little gold signet ring, and a watch chain braided of hair and tipped with gold swivels', surely we do not imagine these listed items in the same sort of concrete specificity with which they are presented in Ford's film. We may have certain imagined visual or tactile sensations (compare the discussion of images on p. 125), but they will, surely, be much more generalized and imprecise than the graphic representations presented to us in a film. Imagine reading this passage, then having someone snatch the book away and demand: 'Describe the earrings!' Surely we would not be able to do so, and neither would we have imagined the wording of the newspaper clippings. The filmed version of this scene *has* to add detail that is not present in the written text and is not even 'performed in' by a reader. Concretization requires addition. One of the important things to note here is that the writer of prose fiction can ensure that only that which is relevant to his or her artistic intention is conveyed to the reader. The writer can state: 'He sat down.' But the film-maker has to decide on what sort of chair, with what sort of movement he sat down. The economy of prose fiction contributes fundamentally to its artistic focus.

Stam also reminds us that there are other necessary additions in any filmed version of this scene.

> *Nothing in the novel prepares us for the idea that Ma Joad will look at the memorabilia by the light of a fire or that the fire's reflection will flicker over her face. Nothing dictates the point-of-view cutting that alternates close shots of Ma Joad's face with what she is looking at, the contemplative rhythm of shot and reverse shot, or the interplay of on-screen and off-screen space, all of which is arguably in the spirit of the novel but not literally in the written text. Nor does the Steinbeck passage mention music, yet the Ford version features a melancholy accordion version of a song ('Red River Valley'). And even if the text had mentioned 'Red River Valley,' that would still be quite different from our actually hearing it performed. And even if the passage had mentioned both the music and the firelight and the light's flickering over Ma Joad's face, that would still not be anything like our seeing her face (or [actress] Joan Darwell's) and hearing the music at the same time. (56)*

Stam contrasts the 'single-track, uniquely verbal medium' of the novel to a 'multitrack medium such as film', and the distinction is worth bearing in mind. We are used to metaphorical accounts of novels, or of our experience of them, as 'rich', of their 'complex texture', and so on. These metaphors are not inaccurate, as we build up a sense of varied patterns and impressions in the course of our reading, and these different elements do combine in rich and complex ways. But if we exclude for the time being the issue of illustrations, the traditional novel is 'single-track' in the sense that everything that we experience in our reading of a novel comes from words and the arrangement of words. A film, in contrast, has many 'tracks' (Stam again provides a useful list: 'moving photographic image', 'phonetic sound' – by which he presumably means speech – 'music', 'noises' and 'written material' (59)).

A brief case study: Henry James's *The Turn of the Screw*

Henry James's *The Turn of the Screw* is a much-adapted work. In addition to Benjamin Britten's opera and a number of less well known adaptations for the stage, there are at least ten film or television-film adaptations of the work. Not all of these are readily available; among the lost adaptations is a 1959 live television play with Ingrid Bergman playing James's unnamed governess. Even so, anyone prepared to scour video libraries and retailers should be able to find five or six adaptations of the tale on video or DVD, along with a 1972 'prequel' starring Marlon Brando as the living Quint entitled *The Nightcomers*. Two adaptations of the story have been released with different titles: *The Innocents* (1961) and *The Haunting of Helen Walker* (1995).

   The existence of so many film adaptations of the same story illustrates an essential point. A single adaptation, like a dramatic performance, never exhausts the dramatic potential of the original. Put another way: any adaptation is partial, both in the sense that it has its own interpretive preferences, and also in the sense that it displays only a part of the complex richness of the original. This reminds us of an important difference between narrative and performance to which attention has already been drawn. Because a dramatic or film performance *concretizes* characters, events and settings, it necessarily reduces the play of possible variety that a written narrative possesses. A few lines above I noted that concretization required addition; without wishing to confuse you, I must now add that it also involves the exclusion of certain responses open to the reader of the printed text. We may read one line of dialogue in our heads in a large number ways, with different emphasis, intonation, and so on. But a line delivered in a film can be said in only one way. When we read 'the coachman' in a story we can imagine the individual in all sorts of ways; when we see him in a film he can look like only what he does look like.

Culture, convention and adaptation

One of the terms that I quoted above from Robert Stam was 'reculturization'. In a straightforward sense a film adaptation can accommodate a story to a new culture by changing its setting. Thus Rusty Lemorande's 1992 version of *The Turn of the Screw*, which sets it in the 1960s and has a female narrator (played by Marianne Faithfull) tell her story to a woman's therapy group, clearly 'reculturizes' the story. But an adaptation does not have to change the setting of a story to reculturize it. Adaptations are like forgeries and translations: they always seem to bear traces of the cultures from which they have emerged. Unless it has been produced by a real master-forger, a sham Modigliani painting produced in the 1950s now strikes us as inescapably '1950s'. We see marks of the time of its production in it that were invisible to all but experts in the 1950s. Similarly, a translation of a Tolstoy novel dating from the 1920s will bear the marks of its translator's age and culture, which is why even the best of translations will never last as long as the original. So far as James's novella is concerned, what seems in particular to have interested so many film-makers during the past four or five decades is its underlying suggestion of sexual corruption. It is hard to imagine that so many adaptations would have been made had the Freudian interpretations of the novella – which, broadly described, see the ghosts as hallucinations produced by a sexually frustrated governess – not drawn attention to hints not just of sexual frustration but also of paedophilia, homosexuality and extramarital sex in James's text. James's text is also full of religious elements and suggestions, and some adaptations do try to do justice to these, but the relative weight accorded to these two aspects of the novella in many recent adaptations reflects the cultures of the adapters rather than the cultures in which James lived and about which he wrote.

By common consent one of the best film adaptations of the novella is the 1961 *The Innocents*, directed by Jack Clayton from a screenplay written by William Archibold and Truman Capote. In its own way the film is a splendid example of successful adaptation, and a number of the terms suggested by

Robert Stam could be appropriated to describe it, including perhaps 'amplification, concretization, actualization, critique, extrapolation, analogization, popularization, and reculturization'. *The Innocents* stars Deborah Kerr as the governess, and (again by common consent) one of the most shocking moments in the film is when the young Miles kisses the governess goodnight on the lips, but extends the kiss in what is unambiguously a sexual manner. It seems clear that this is an element in the film that comes from the culture of the 1960s and not of 1898 when the novella was first published. It is not that the novella contains no hints that the young pre-adolescent children have had some sort of sexual relationship with adults, but that the way in which this element is presented in the film bears the mark of a culture later than James's.

This is perhaps an obvious example. But to stick with *The Innocents* we might mention a couple of things about the film that are less obvious. At the time Deborah Kerr made the film she was about forty years old, whereas the governess in James's story is, we are told, twenty years old at the time of the events she reports in her narrative. It is hard to be sure, but my suspicion is that when *The Innocents* was made it would have been more generally accepted that a 'frustrated, hysterical, unmarried governess' was in her late thirties or forties than just twenty years old. The one-sentence summary of the film given in the 1999 edition of *Halliwell's Film and Video Guide* reads: 'In Victorian times, a spinster governess in a lonely house finds her young charges possessed by evil demons of servants now dead.' The word 'spinster' is used neither in the film nor in James's tale. It is certainly the case that the age-span for the role of 'lead actress' in 1961 was greater than it is now. Although this may have had something to do with the greater ease with which advancing years could be concealed in black and white than in colour films, it probably has more to do with the way in which age and female sexuality were related in 1961 and how they are related today.

This takes me to my second point. Filming *The Innocents* in black and white would have been more obviously a *decision* in 1961 than it may appear today. Films were still being made in black and white at this time, and *The Naked Edge* in which Kerr also starred in 1961 was also made in monochrome. But the five films in which Kerr starred before these two films were in colour, and by 1961 to make a film in black and white bespoke either a desire to save money or a decision that monochrome was somehow fitting. I suspect that the conventional associations of monochrome were deemed appropriate to the filming of a ghost story designed to scare the viewer: Alfred Hitchcock's *Psycho*, released a year earlier in 1960, was also filmed in monochrome.

Narrative and performance

The case of *The Turn of the Screw* is particularly useful in illustrating some of the crucial differences between a narrative such as James's novella and a performance such as one of the film adaptations of the work. This is because the fact of narrative in *The Turn of the Screw* is so central to its artistic effect. In the opening pages of the novella an unnamed 'outer' narrator reports on a scene (set, we presume, in the present day of the time at which it was published – 1898) in which a group of adults exchange ghost stories on Christmas Eve. One of these adults, a man named Douglas, mentions a story concerning two children who witness some ghostly apparition. He agrees to tell the story, which he explains was told to him forty years earlier, by a woman who experienced these events and who was not just his own governess but the twenty-year-old governess of the story itself. Some days later her written account is delivered, and he reads this story over several evenings to those assembled. The frame narrator explains that what the reader will then be given is a transcription of the governess's written account which Douglas passed on to him, but this is preceded by the frame narrator's summary of Douglas's introductory comments, which describe a meeting in London between the governess and her employer-to-be, the uncle of the two children in the story.

The previous paragraph may strike you as long-winded, but even it compresses and simplifies the chain of connections necessary for the narrative to be delivered to Douglas's listeners and to the reader of James's tale. What is interesting is that film adaptations of the story typically simplify this chain of transmission. In *The Innocents*, for example, the Christmas Eve ghost-story session is missing completely – which means of course that the 'outer' narrator and Douglas, and their exchanges and comments, are also absent. The film's opening credits actually run alongside an image of a woman's hands clasped in prayer. After a while the hands are seen in a new shot to belong to the character who we later learn is the governess, played by Deborah Kerr. She changes the position of her hands from 'clasped in prayer' to 'clasped anxiously'. On the soundtrack a sort of sobbing, accompanied by birds twittering, can be heard. The shot changes from profile to full-face, and the woman says: 'All I want to do is save the children, not destroy them. More than anything I love the children. More than anything.' The scene then fades into the governess's interview with the uncle. At the end of this interview the governess agrees to accept the position on the difficult conditions specified, and the film then moves to the governess's arrival at Bly, where the main action takes place.

What difference do these changes make? Perhaps their most important effect is, I think, to remove that combination of distance and claustrophobic imprisonment that James's original gives the reader. The distance comes from the fact that when we *read* the account of the governess's experiences we seem to be at the end of a long chain of narrative transmission. The governess told her story – which took place forty years before the opening of the tale – to Douglas, who repeats it to the gathered guests after the governess's death. The frame narrator receives the governess's written account from Douglas shortly before the latter's death. We are cut off from the source of the narrative by time and death. We have only the words, written ostensibly by the governess. Neither she nor Douglas is alive to explicate them. In the first few pages of the novella the reader learns that the governess is dead; at the start of *The Innocents* she is very much alive, there, in front of us. In the film there is one 'present time'; in the novella there are many.

The reader's sense of claustrophobia comes from the fact that everything we read after the frame narrator's introductory pages comes from the governess, and is given in her words. We are imprisoned in her account, in her way of seeing things. We can no more see her from the outside than we can see ourselves.

In the film our sense that what we are seeing is *the governess's version* is more or less impossible to retain. Right from the start we look *at* and not *with* her. The short opening scene of her praying and agonizing about the children raises an issue of which the first-time reader of James's novella becomes aware only towards the end of the tale: that in trying to protect the children she may actually destroy them. In the subsequent scene with the uncle there is no suggestion that what we see may not actually have occurred – there it is, taking place before our eyes. But in James's novella, we learn of this scene through Douglas's report and not as part of the governess's account, even though, logically, Douglas can have had his information only from the governess. What the reader gets is Douglas's report of what the governess must have remembered about her interview with the uncle and told him. What the film viewer gets is the interview itself. The tale gives us a report, a version, while the film gives us the scene itself, however much the use of camera angle, cutting, and so on may encourage us to perceive the scene in a particular manner.

Because film *enacts* rather than *tells*, in other words, the governess is shown as a character along with other characters, and not as the source of all our knowledge about characters and events. It is true that by means of a variety of technical and artistic methods, a good film-maker can cause us to sympathize with the governess and to adopt her point of view, but we never actually see things through her eyes and understanding in the way that we do when reading James's story. (There is even a scene in the film in which we observe the governess while she is asleep.)

The director of *The Innocents* does manage to keep the viewer in a certain doubt as to whether the ghosts are really there or are a product of the governess's imagination. But it is much more difficult for a film-maker than for a writer to sow doubt as to whether something 'really happened'. Alfred Hitchcock has a nice comment in an interview in which he admits that in his film *Stage Fright* he made a mistake in putting in a flashback that was a lie. His comment draws attention to a key difference between films and written stories:

> *Strangely enough, in movies, people never object if a man is shown telling a lie. And it's also acceptable, when a character tells a story about the past, for the flashback to show it as if it were taking place in the present. So why is it that we can't tell a lie through a flashback? (Truffaut 1986, 275)*

This brief comment isolates a crucial difference: a lie can be *told* but it is very difficult for it to be *shown*. When the real crime documentaries shown on Discovery Channel dramatize accounts told by suspects, they very often have the word 're-enactment' superimposed on the screen so as to prevent the viewer from making the automatic assumption that if we see it then it really happened. When we do see things happening on screen it is very hard, and often impossible, for us to perceive them as someone's report, or memory, or hallucination. Films concretize. Even in the age of digital image manipulation, our senses tell us that the camera cannot lie.

In James's novella the reader learns that the previous governess, Miss Jessel, has died. The cause of her death is never given, even though – tantalizingly – when asked in the opening pages what she died of, Douglas replies: 'That will come out.' But it does not. In the course of her narrative, the governess (who has just learned that the housekeeper, Mrs Grose, does not share Douglas's view of the previous governess's respectability) asks the housekeeper about her death:

> 'Poor woman – she paid for it!'
> 'Then you do know what she died of?' I asked.
> 'No – I know nothing. I wanted not to know; I was glad enough I did n't; and I thanked heaven she was well out of this!'
> 'Yet you had then your idea – '
> 'Of her real reason for leaving? Oh yes – as to that. She could n't have stayed. Fancy it here – for a governess! And afterward I imagined – and I still imagine. And what I imagine is dreadful.'
> 'Not so dreadful as what I do,' I replied; on which I must have shown her – as I was indeed but too conscious – a front of miserable defeat.

What seems obvious here – and this is amply confirmed by Henry James's own comments about his strategy in this tale (from which I quote briefly on p. 50) – is that the aim is to get the reader to *imagine* why the previous governess had to leave and how she died. An unwanted pregnancy, suicide – these are possibilities that inevitably spring to the reader's mind. But in James's text these imaginings are never confirmed, and they have to be set against Douglas's statement in the opening pages of the tale that Miss Jessel 'had done for them [the children] quite beautifully – she was a most respectable person – till her death ...'. Note too that the reader has to guess not just what happened to Miss Jessel, but also what both Mrs Grose and the governess *imagine* happened to her.

In *The Innocents* all of this indeterminacy is lost. Mrs Grose tells the governess: 'Miss Jessel put an end to herself; she was found in the lake.' In the film Mrs Grose also tells the governess that after Peter Quint died, Miss Jessel went into the blackest mourning, and that she 'died of a broken heart', although in James's tale it is never made clear whether Quint or Jessel dies first. A later film version of James's novella – Ben Bolt's 1999 television film *The Turn of the Screw* – actually opens with a shot of Miss Jessel committing suicide by jumping into water. Accordingly when we see the ghost of Miss Jessel in this later adaptation we have already seen her in life. As the 'ghost' is clearly the same as the person we saw committing suicide, a person who in life has *not* been seen by the governess, the viewer must assume that there really is a ghost and it really is Miss Jessel.

My emphasis up to this point has been on what can be achieved in prose fiction that is beyond the ordinary scope of film. Clearly there is another tale to be told. Film can do much – enormously much – that is beyond the scope of the printed page. Just the ability to combine moving pictures, sound and language opens up for complex effects of potentially great artistic significance. The way in which the soundtrack at the start of *The Innocents* combines speech, the sound of sobbing and the twittering of birds establishes complex associations that are subtly developed as the film proceeds. We can see and hear Miles playing the piano, and piano music can later be used to suggest his presence even when he is off-screen. Film is not a less subtle medium than prose fiction, but its subtleties are of a different order. In comparing an adaptation such as *The Innocents* with its source in a work of prose fiction we can learn to appreciate the unique potentialities of two different media, two related but independent artistic traditions.

Topics for discussion

- 'Short stories make better films than do novels.' Do they? If so, why?
- Should a film-maker try to be faithful to the novel he or she is adapting?
- Do you agree that the biggest problem a film-maker faces is that in a film private experience cannot be shown and the public life cannot be hidden?
- 'In comparison to novels, films leave too little to the imagination.' Do they?

9
Critical approaches to fiction

Preview

This chapter deals with:
- classifying criticism into schools and approaches
- textual approaches (Russian formalism, New Criticism, structuralism, narratology, post-structuralism and deconstruction)
- contextual approaches (sociological criticism, cultural materialism and New Historicism, postcolonial theory, generic criticism, biography, psychology and psychoanalysis)
- ideological approaches (Marxist, feminist, Queer Theory)

This chapter is not meant to substitute for a more detailed and comprehensive introduction to different literary theories and approaches. It is rather designed to help you to recognize these theories and approaches in the books and articles you consult, while at the same time providing some information concerning their particular relevance to the study of the novel and shorter fiction.

■ Categorizing criticism

Critical books and essays, unlike chocolate bars, are not required by law to contain a list of ingredients. In some cases the titles chosen by critics are helpful: 'A Postcolonial Reading of *Jane Eyre*' or *Queer Henry James* leave little doubt as to the critical approach and theoretical allegiance of the writer (do not look for these in the library as I have invented them, but you will find many similar titles in bibliographies). If you are looking for criticism of *Jane Eyre* or of James's *The Turn of the Screw* that has a lot to say about narrative method then these titles are not too promising – although of course you cannot rule out stumbling across some striking insights about narrative technique in a book or an article with a similar title. A title such as 'The Personified Narrator in Charlotte Brontë and Henry James' is likely to indicate a work of much more use to you.

This much is relatively simple. If you can pull a book off the library or the bookshop shelf then a skim through the contents list, the index and a few pages will help you to decide if it is worth more serious reading. What students often find more difficult is the process of using a *categorization* of a particular critic's approach as a basis to *assess the force* of that critic's comments on a particular work.

Let me give a particular example. The third edition of the Norton Critical Edition of Joseph Conrad's novella *Heart of Darkness* reprints a chapter of a book on Conrad by Robert F. Haugh to which the Norton editor has given the title '*Heart of Darkness*: Problem for Critics'. The essay pours some scorn on the argument that Conrad's novella is a critique of Belgian imperialism, suggesting that this reveals a superficial understanding of the work, and concludes by arguing that the Conradian hero (such as Kurtz in *Heart of Darkness*) 'in his remarkable actions ... defines the mortal condition, and in his last moment of vision ... sees all the scheme of the universe; and we share it in a moment of tragic exaltation' (quoted in Conrad 1971, 163).

Let us imagine that you are writing an essay on *Heart of Darkness*, and in the course of your argument you state that Conrad's novella is not primarily a critique of Belgian imperialism but rather represents a tragic view of the mortal condition, and you quote from Haugh's chapter to back up your argument. What is problematic about this is that it does not assess Haugh's contentions in context: his book was published in the United States at a time (1957) when, because of the dominance of New Critical ideas, it was extremely fashionable to play down the extent to which works of literature engaged with specific socio-political situations or events, but it was more common to argue that 'great' literature draws our attention rather to the human condition in general. This does not mean that we can just dismiss Haugh's arguments out of hand. It does however mean that they have to be assessed in the light of Haugh's apparent critical beliefs and of the time at which he wrote. If you want to strengthen the force of your argument you need other substantiating material: the views of critics who have taken a different view of *Heart of Darkness*, quotations from Conrad himself and from contemporary responses to the work, and renewed analytical attention to the literary text itself.

Being able to categorize critical approaches should not mean that one prejudges the worth or the relevance of a book or an article, but it does help in assessing the force of a given critic's argument.

I started this book by drawing attention to the importance of the distinction between historical and structuralist (or synchronic) approaches to the novel. In my introduction I pointed out that structuralist narratology was often, in the Anglo-American critical tradition, associated with those techniques of close reading and detailed textual analysis inherited from the Russian formalists and (especially) the Anglo-American New Critics. Because most undergraduate study of the novel involves writing essays or examination questions on individual novels or short stories, I start with this particular *textual* tradition, because it is likely to be of most immediate use to you in the course of such undergraduate study.

■ Textual approaches

Textual critics concentrate on the actual words of the novel(s) they are studying rather than bringing what is called *extrinsic* information into their criticism. Textual critics thus pay little or no attention to biographical information about the author (including other writings by him or her), information about the author's society and historical period, the history of readers' responses to the novel, and so on. Critics known as *formalists* take a particularly exclusivist attitude to the text. A formalist critic is one who pays great attention to the *form* of a literary work, but the term has been applied mostly to two groups of critics: the Russian and Czech formalists whose most influential work was written in the second two decades of the twentieth century, and the Anglo-American New Critics who flourished in the 1940s and 1950s.

Russian formalism

The importance of Russian formalism for critics of the novel is that members of this critical and theoretical grouping paid serious attention to the novel, and developed an analytical terminology which has remained important. It is the Russian formalists whom we have to thank for the distinction between *fabula* and *sjužet* (story and plot in my terminology), and for a range of other important concepts and terms such as *defamiliarization* (see the Glossary for definitions of these terms). In addition to its debt to structuralism, modern narratology owes a substantial debt to Russian formalism, for the Russian formalists conducted much ground-breaking work on various aspects of narrative technique, often involving important works of English prose fiction such as *Gulliver's Travels* and *Tristram Shandy*.

New Criticism

The New Critics – to oversimplify somewhat – at least in theory rejected what they termed 'external' or 'extrinsic' information more or less *in toto*, preferring to concentrate upon 'the work itself' in relative isolation. In terms of *method* they often use what has been called *close reading* – taking a small section of a novel or a recurrent verbal feature and analysing this in exhaustive detail, drawing attention to the sort of issues that I outlined in the checklist in Chapter 7. Because the New Critics (unlike the Russian formalists) developed their critical ideas and practices mainly in connection with the interpretation and analysis of poetry, they tended to bring to the criticism of the novel a new concern with such matters as linguistic detail, paradox, tension, irony, symbolism, and so on. The title of an essay written by the New Critic Robert Heilman and first published in 1948, ' "The Turn of the Screw" as Poem', can be seen to announce a representative critical trajectory.

Such critics have, by common consent, contributed enormously to our understanding of the complexity and subtlety of great works of fiction, moving us away from merely discursive discussion of plots and characters and demonstrating that the novel is as receptive to detailed analysis as is poetry. Chapter 6 here, 'Analysing Fiction', could not have been written without the work of such critics. Many more recent critics who are by no means formalists have been significantly influenced by the practice of the New Critics. To take one highly recommended example: David Lodge's *Language of Fiction* (1966) is one of the major critical studies of the novel of the past four decades. Lodge's analysis of Charlotte Brontë's *Jane Eyre*, for example, is a masterly isolation of patterns of reference and connotation in Brontë's novel, treating it almost as a poem that can be analysed in terms of its imagery as much as in terms of its plot and characters.

Structuralism

Structuralist critics are, to start with a generalization, interested more in what makes meaning possible than in the different meanings that can be found – whether in the novel, in complete cultures (structuralist anthropology), or in a range of more specific cultural activities. We can use the analogy of the distinction within linguistics between grammar and pragmatics. Whereas pragmatics focuses on particular utterances, the grammarian is concerned more with those rules and conventions that allow verbal meanings to be generated.

Structuralism is characterized by a general belief that the structural study of language offers a paradigm (or model) for the study of other systems of meaning, including literature and the novel. This relationship is most clear in the work of a theorist mentioned earlier in this book – the Russian folklorist Vladimir Propp (see p. 106). Propp was interested not in any particular folk tale, but in the system that allowed a given folk tale to generate meaning. What appeared to be a surface difference between different folk tales – one about a princess, one about a miraculous goose – could be argued to involve an identity at a more fundamental level (both tales are to do with a pattern involving challenge, defeat and final victory, for example). Propp's 'functions' were like grammatical functions: they could be actualized through a range of different examples just as the grammatical function of 'noun' can be actualized with 'dog' 'pig', or 'magistrate' in sentences with the same grammatical structure.

Structuralism in its purer form focuses far less on the detail of individual works than on the manner whereby they exemplify a set of possibilities open to the genre as a whole. Like the variant of linguistics upon which they are based, literary-critical structuralisms tend to be ahistorical, concentrating upon systems as they operate at a given moment of time rather than on their modification over time. In certain ways structuralist approaches resemble formalist approaches: they pay little or no attention to extrinsic factors, and consider either 'literature' or a genre such as the novel as a self-enclosed system that can be studied in terms of itself. Thus, just as the New Critics argued against 'The Intentional Fallacy' of granting extratextual statements of intent any prioritized weight in interpreting that text, so too structuralist critics have followed Roland Barthes in agreeing to announce 'The Death of the Author' (see Glossary) so far as the interpretation of his or her text is concerned. For students of the novel, structuralism is most important because of its crucial contribution to the formation and development of modern narrative theory, or narratology.

Narratology

A founding principle of narratology (the term was apparently coined by the theorist Tzvetan Todorov in 1969) is that it is not committed to distinguishing _literary_ narratives from other narratives, but seeks to investigate common elements in all forms of 'telling'. Much narratology is based on the structuralist linguistics of Ferdinand de Saussure, and just as Saussure attempted to study language as a working system, so too narratologists attempt to study either narratives in general or particular individual narratives as working systems. The result of this work has been a much more detailed vocabulary and conceptual apparatus for the _analysis_ of narratives. Many of the terms included in the Glossary in this book come from narratology – among them such terms as _frequency_, _analepsis_ and _prolepsis_, _focalization_ and _distance_ – and we have to thank narratologists for developing and refining our understanding of narrative techniques such as Free Indirect Discourse, and of the ramifications of the distinction between story and plot.

Post-structuralism and deconstruction

For the purpose of a brief survey such as this, 'post-structuralism' and 'deconstruction' will be treated as synonymous. However, certain usages distinguish between the two terms in important ways and make post-structuralism a more general position of which deconstruction represents one possible variant.

Again, to simplify, we can say that post-structuralism extends and even universalizes the structuralist assumption that no element in a system of meaning has significance in and for itself but only as part of the system. If this is so, then there are (or should be) no elements in any text whose fixity of meaning can be used as a foundation stone or interpretative bedrock. Jacques Derrida, the French high-priest of deconstruction, calls such a desired point of stability in the swirl of meanings generated by the play between the different components of the system a _transcendental signified_, in other words an element that has meaning in and for itself rather than meaning defined by relations to other elements. For Derrida, meaning is always relational, and thus when he, famously (or infamously) declared that there was nothing outside of the text, he was arguing that there was no such fixed, extratextual point by reference to which the meaning of a text could be plotted and fixed.

Deconstructionists are accordingly committed to the unweaving of apparently firm and solid interpretations through a display of the way in which such interpretations rely upon such a transcendental signified. Examples of such transcendental signifieds in the criticism of the novel would be such things as 'the intended meaning of the author', 'how contemporary readers read the work', 'what the work means to a competent reader', and so on. In practice, deconstructionist readings very often involve dispensing with such traditional critical points of reference as these, and responding to the work in a way that is unconstrained by them.

At an early stage in undergraduate study such post-structuralist readings are either terrifying or exhilarating or both. The terror can be reduced by noting that post-structuralist readings often rely upon relatively simple processes of de- or recontextualization of a work or an element in a work, playing with the interpretations that can be generated once the work or the passage is unhooked from a textual or other context that restricts its possible meanings. The exhilaration can be eye-opening, revealing how our readings and responses are often channelled into familiar paths by reliance upon familiar but unregarded anchor-points. Too much indulgence in the activity of what a work or passage *could* mean may irritate your teachers and is in the end worthwhile only if it can be shown to generate readings and responses that are as rich and as sophisticated as those obtained by more traditional means.

■ Contextual approaches

If the most valuable aspect of the work of textual critics has been their development of methods of critical analysis, the aspect of their work which has gone least unchallenged by others has been their rejection or playing down of 'extrinsic' information as an adjunct to the reading and criticism of literature.

Socio-historical approaches

Sociological and historical critics have placed great stress upon the need to understand the context of the author's own society and his or her position within it, both as an individual (a member of a particular social group or class) and as an author (a member of a literary group, relying on certain publishers, libraries, readers, and so on).

Take Joseph Conrad's *Heart of Darkness*. Recent critics have suggested that the novella can only be fully appreciated in the context of what European powers were doing in Africa in the last part of the nineteenth century, and in particular in the context of statements made by prominent Belgians – including King Leopold – concerning the Belgian exploitation of the Congo (in which Conrad himself had worked). Thus some of Leopold's statements concerning the (extremely brutal) Belgian exploitation of the Congo include comments about opening to civilization the only part of our globe where Christianity has not penetrated, and piercing 'the darkness which envelops the entire population'. Conrad's ironic use of words such as 'civilization' and 'darkness' in the novella, it has been argued, can only fully be appreciated in the light of his aim to mock and expose statements such as Leopold's.

Some contextual critics argue that more than this is needed. The narrative indirection in the novel – Marlow's inability to tell the truth to Kurtz's 'Intended' and his feeling that he cannot make himself understood to his auditors – mirrors a situation in which comfortable Europeans who had never witnessed colonial brutality at first hand in Africa were unable to hear the truth spoken by such as Marlow. This argument raises some problems in its turn. Conrad deliberately left out localizing information such as the name of the European country or the part of Africa in which the novella was set, and with regard to his short story 'Youth', he made it clear that he very much objected to having such information reinserted (Curle 1928, 297). Novelists themselves tend, like Conrad, to be suspicious of critics who fill in background information claimed to be relevant to their works. Asked whether it is important to know the history of Czechoslovakia to understand his novels, Milan Kundera replied: 'No. Whatever needs to be known of it the novel itself tells' (Kundera 1988, 39). Key issues to be confronted are: what information points to material that had a *determining* effect on the writing of the work? What information is *relevant*?

Sociological critics have also drawn attention to the important influence that factors referred to collectively as the 'sociology of literature' can have on the creation of works of literature: publishers, patronage (see Glossary), literacy rates, readership profiles, libraries, booksellers, and so on. It is clear that if only a part of society is literate and can read novels, then this will affect the sort of novels that are written – as was the case in eighteenth-century England. If the habit of listening to novels read aloud by a friend or family member becomes customary in a society, this will alter the importance of the fact that many members of that society are illiterate. If success as a novelist depends upon having your work accepted by the circulating libraries, and these do not accept anything that does not conform to a set of rigidly moralistic views, then the reader should know this before expressing dissatisfaction with the portrayal of sexual relationships in a novel – and should also be on the lookout for concealed hints and suggestions!

Cultural materialism and New Historicism

Cultural materialist and New Historicist critics allow some of the insights (or claims) of post-structuralism concerning the difficulty or impossibility of confronting or interrogating reality other than through texts of some sort, while retaining a degree of what we can call a realist commitment – a belief that reality is not just texts or closed systems of meaning. New Historicists typically juxtapose literary and non-literary texts in ways that produce unexpected and frequently highly illuminating flashes of insight. Cultural materialists are especially interested in following the life of literary works through successive ages and varied cultures, and often responses to and interpretations of a literary work are as much of interest to them as is 'the work itself'. It has to be said, however, that up to now these critics have paid proportionately less attention to the novel than to other literary genres.

Postcolonial theory

The field of postcolonial theory is fashionable, fast-growing and riven with debates. At its best it has confronted readers and critics with the hidden or unstated implications of colonial and imperialist relations between lands and people for the reading and interpretation of literary works. Thus my earlier discussion of the way in which Jean Rhys's *Wide Sargasso Sea* interrogates Charlotte Brontë's *Jane Eyre* owes much to the new perspectives brought to literary and cultural criticism by postcolonialism. A key text is Edward Said's *Orientalism* (1978), which attempted to describe how Western domination of subject lands required not just physical force but also a discourse, a system of ideas by which European culture was able to manage and even to produce 'the Orient'.

Following Said's example, many writers attempted to use the vantage point of a period after colonialism ('post' colonialism) to interrogate literature written both during and after the classic forms of colonialism, and also to draw attention to the silenced voices of those who wrote from the standpoint of the oppressed.

This much is unproblematic – but much else is not. Earlier in this book (p. 41) I made reference to Ngũgĩ Wa Thiong'o's dedication of his novel *Devil on the Cross* 'To all Kenyans struggling against the neo-colonial stage of imperialism'. If there are such things as neo-colonialism and imperialism, is not the 'post' in postcolonialism a little optimistic? Does it refer to a historical or merely a mental and ideological supersession of colonialism? If Australia and the United States are just as much postcolonial countries as are Kenya and India, then is not the term in danger of becoming so all-embracing that it loses any effective specificity? Many have pointed out that the term has become very popular precisely because few objections to it are raised in the academy: it avoids sensitive words such as 'imperialism' and it raises the topic of colonialism only to suggest that all that is safely in the past.

For all this, postcolonialism has generated a number of extremely valuable studies and readings, and it represents a corrective to too-unthinking an imposition of privileged viewpoints on the interpretation of literary works which touch on and were directly or indirectly supported by the under- or unprivileged. Postcolonialist critics of more canonical works have also been active in drawing attention to the existence in them of gaps and omissions (or ellipses – see the Glossary) concerned with relationships between European powers and their colonial possessions.

Generic approaches

A genre is a type or kind of literature, and we often refer to prose fiction itself as one of the three main literary genres, along with poetry and drama. There are many different ways to classify literature generically, and the novel has been divided into a number of sub-genres by various critics – the gothic novel, the epistolary novel, the postmodern novel, and so on. Note that these generic divisions involve different sorts of category: there is no single set of principles that are available for dividing novels into sub-genres, and as a result a single novel can usually be classified in more than one way.

A generic approach to prose fiction insists that we cannot begin to read or understand a novel until we are clear as to what *sort* of novel it is. This typically means getting clear about the author's intentions with regard to his or her work, although it can also involve seeing how successive generations of readers have classified a work. Thus – the argument goes – unless we understand the picaresque tradition (see Glossary) within which Defoe's _Moll Flanders_ is written, we will run the danger of misreading and misunderstanding this novel.

I list this under 'Contextual approaches' because a genre is a sort of context: it helps us to understand the aims of a writer and the expectations of readers, to recognize conventional elements as well as divergences from what is conventional. Obtaining a better understanding of a work's generic associations can often be one of the most useful benefits of reading critics.

Biographical approaches

A writer's life is also a sort of context. The more books by the same novelist that we read, the more we become conscious of common or similar elements in them (as well as of contrasts, new directions, surprise variations), and the more we begin to build up a picture of the man or woman behind the printed text, constructing an idea of his or her values, interests and attitudes. We can, in short, start to use the life as a sort of explanatory context for the work.

Such an interest in an author can lead us to want to know more about the person in question in his or her own right, and then we may start to read the novels in the light of what we have learned about the author – even in terms of what he or she has said about them explicitly. Such a biographical approach to the study of the novel – reading fictional works with explicit reference to the life, personality and opinions of the author – seems straightforward enough, yet it is fraught with problems and has involved many sharp debates. In a piece entitled 'The Spirit of Place', D.H. Lawrence advised: 'Never trust the artist. Trust the tale' (Beale 1961, 297), and generations of critics have pointed out that novelists _can_ be very bad guides to their own work.

Why should this be so? We can isolate a number of possible explanations. First is that of _inspiration_. The writer seems often not to use the conscious and rational part of his or her mind for literary composition – something that has been appreciated since the days of antiquity when a term equivalent to 'inspiration' was first used. As a result, secrets of the created work may not be accessible to the rational, enquiring mind in the same way that details of other actions and utterances are. Second is that the author may want actually to _conceal_ something: a real-life model, a confessional element in the work, or whatever. Third, the author may comment on his or her work a very long time after writing it.

When it is a matter of relating a novelist's work to his or her life, similar problems may emerge. How do we know which experiences in a writer's life were reflected (or transformed) in his or her work? Experiences which seem minor to us may have been crucial to the person who had them – but, even so, they may not have influenced the writing of a given work.

If all this sounds like a counsel of despair I should add that it is not meant to be: I _do_ think that biographical information can be of very great help in enabling us to respond more fully to a novel or a short story. We should be fully aware of the problems involved in such critical procedures, and we need always to be sensitive to what the work itself can tell us.

Take D.H. Lawrence's novel *Women in Love*. It seems very likely that Lawrence's experiences in the period of the First World War had a crucial effect on the writing of this novel even though the war is not mentioned at all in it (in spite of the fact that it was written in the middle of these experiences). Lawrence was medically unfit for service in the war, and came under suspicion from the authorities for his anti-war views and because his wife Frieda (*née* von Richthofen) was the cousin of 'the Red Baron' – a man notorious for shooting down scores of British aeroplanes. Lawrence and Frieda were even forced to leave their cottage on the Cornish coast, allegedly because they were suspected of signalling to German U-boats. Now although none of this is directly referred to in *Women in Love*, it is arguable that much of the tone of that novel – in particular its dismissive remarks about England – can only be fully understood in the light of these experiences of Lawrence's. Moreover, the comments in the novel by Birkin about the destructiveness of the 'mechanical principle' have, too, to be seen in the context of Lawrence's complex responses to the slaughter of the war – a slaughter that is not mentioned directly in the novel at all.

Psychological and psychoanalytic approaches

In broad terms the distinction between psychology and psychoanalysis is that between theories of how the mind functions and theories of how the secrets of the mind can be unlocked through analysis. The question is then: which mind – the author's, the reader's or a character's? Let us again consider Henry James's novella *The Turn of the Screw*. A succession of critics has attempted to psychoanalyse the governess in this tale, finding evidence of mental instability of a sort that leads her to hallucinate and to imagine the ghosts that she reports on to the reader. But given James's clearly reported intention to make the reader 'think the evil' in this tale, it is possible to concentrate on the way in which readers and critics have responded to and interpreted the work, and to thus use the *work* as a way of analysing *readers*. (Compare the way in which the Rorschach 'ink-blot test' is used; the interpretive responses of different individuals to the same 'blot' are used to tell us something about these individuals rather than anything about the blot itself, which is normally possessed of an appropriately Jamesian ambiguity.) Finally, it is possible to use James's novella as a way of psychoanalysing James himself, and there is no shortage of critics who have attempted to do just this.

Certain short stories and novellas have been much used by psychological and psychoanalytic critics: Sigmund Freud wrote an influential essay on E.T.A. Hoffmann's 'uncanny' tale 'The Sandman', while Marie Bonaparte's study of the tales of Edgar Allan Poe remains much-quoted. More recently Jacques Lacan's analysis of Poe's 'The Purloined Letter' has confirmed the American writer's work as a richly seamed mine waiting for psychoanalytical excavation.

Children's literature (fairy tales) and folk tales have also provided material for analysis by writers such as Bruno Bettelheim and others. Generally speaking, though, psychological and psychoanalytical criticism has had most impact on criticism of the longer novel through incorporation in other approaches, such as those of feminism and deconstruction.

■ Ideological approaches

I choose the word 'ideological' for want of a better one, but I recognize that the problem with it is that it has a pejorative ring, suggesting narrow-mindedness and a lack of impartiality. These suggestions are not intended: all that I want to imply by my choice of this word is that certain critical schools and approaches carry with them an overt and conscious commitment to ideas, values, systems of belief that generally have a wider scope than the purely literary. Putting the matter crudely, knowing that a critic is a narratologist or a psychoanalytic critic does not help us to work out how they would vote or whether they are in favour of equal rights for men and women, whereas knowing that a critic calls him- or herself a feminist does give us information that may be relevant to an enquiry into such questions.

'Ideological' schools and approaches are often accused of imposing beliefs and positions onto innocent and resisting literary works, and there is no doubt that such accusations are sometimes justified. On the other hand, an ideologically committed critical approach may just as well illuminate something in a novel or a short story that has gone unnoticed by more seemingly impartial critics. In my personal opinion, for example, much criticism that can loosely be associated with Queer Theory (see p. 181) has indubitably revealed aspects of the work of canonical writers that has lain undiscovered for many years, and much the same can certainly be argued about feminist criticism.

Marxist approaches

Like sociological critics, Marxist critics are interested in relating literary works to the societies in which they were written. Marxism is a materialist philosophy, one which insists upon the primacy of material living conditions rather than ideas or beliefs in the life of human beings. It sees history as, in Marx's words, 'the history of class struggle' – the history of struggle for control of the material conditions upon which life rests. It is on the basis of these material conditions, and in response to the struggle for them, that ideas, philosophies, mental pictures of the world develop – as secondary phenomena. These secondary phenomena may provide human beings with an accurate picture of reality, including themselves and their situation, but they may not. Ideologies are all related to class positions and thus, in turn, to material conditions and the struggle for their control, but this is not to say that they provide a reliable picture of these. Traditional Marxists have laid great stress upon the distinction between base (or basis) and superstructure, seeing the social base as essentially economic in nature, and the superstructure as constituting the world of mental activities – ideas, beliefs, philosophies, and (in the opinion of some but not all Marxists) art and literature.

Marxists have been particularly interested in the novel because the novel can be argued to have emerged in response to a changed social situation and to the needs of an emergent class – the bourgeoisie in the capitalism that replaces feudalism. The Hungarian Marxist Georg Lukács, who remains an important critic of the novel, clearly also values the novel because of its association with realism, an association that holds out the promise of finding accurate rather than distorted analyses of social structures within realist (or 'classical') novels. More generally it seems clear that the novel typically (although not inevitably) raises issues concerning the relationship between the individual and society in a more historically detailed and specific way than do poetry or drama.

The interest of Marxists in ideology and in the distinction between base and superstructure means that although they typically attempt to relate novels and aspects of novels to the social conditions surrounding their creation, the relationship argued for is normally an indirect or a mediated one.

Feminist approaches

Over seventy years ago Virginia Woolf's *A Room of One's Own* (1929) startled readers by claiming that they lived in a patriarchy and that this fact conditioned the ways in which novels were written (or not written) and read. In more recent years a growing number of feminist critics have offered challenging accounts of the novel in general and of particular novels. Feminist critics have argued that not only have women had to overcome severe difficulties to become writers but also that once they have produced novels, these have consistently been read in negative ways by male readers. Thus once a woman had managed to become literate (no easy matter in the past), she had to overcome all sorts of male prejudices in the reception accorded to her work. As Virginia Woolf expresses it in her extended essay *A Room of One's Own*, 'This is an important book, the critic assumes, because it deals with war. This is an insignificant book because it deals with the feelings of women in a drawing-room.' Moreover, as Woolf points out, it may be difficult for a woman to write about such things as war because of the domestic role to which she has been confined, and she declares that a woman could not have written *War and Peace*.

Feminist critics have also done much to show the ways in which male views of reality have dominated much fiction – especially, of course, that by men, and especially their views of women. Women are typically portrayed *in relation to men*, and are often seen in certain stereotyped ways – as passive, hysterical, emotional, 'bitch' or 'goddess'. Thus it seems fair to say that it is only as a result of the efforts of feminist critics in recent years that the portrayal of women in D.H. Lawrence's major novels has been questioned and criticized, and that many other authors have been looked at with new eyes.

One of the works which introduced the new wave of feminist literary criticism was Kate Millett's *Sexual Politics*, first published in 1970. Millett's book is divided into three connected sections: 'Sexual Politics', giving a theoretical basis for what follows; a section on the historical background detailing the movements towards female emancipation and those seeking to reverse their effects; and finally a section entitled 'The Literary Reflection'. In this final section Millett looks at the work of D.H. Lawrence, Henry Miller, Norman Mailer and Jean Genet. In the writing of all of these she detects what we now familiarly refer to as patriarchal ideas – frequently linked to portrayals that debase, ridicule and humiliate women. The following comments on Lawrence's *Lady Chatterley's Lover* are representative:

> In Lady Chatterley, *as throughout his final period, Lawrence uses the word 'sexual' and 'phallic' interchangeably, so that the celebration of sexual passion for which the book is so renowned is largely a celebration of the penis of Oliver Mellors, gamekeeper and social prophet. While insisting his mission is the noble and necessary task of freeing sexual behavior of perverse inhibition, purging the fiction which describes it of prurient or prudish euphemism, Lawrence is really the evangelist of quite another cause – 'phallic consciousness'. This is far less a matter of 'the resurrection of the body', 'natural love', or other slogans under which it has been advertised, than the transformation of masculine ascendancy into a mystical religion, international, possibly institutionalized. (1971, 238)*

Millett's book is a fine piece of polemic, and one which jolted both men and women into reconsidering various canonical authors from previously unconsidered perspectives.

A variety of feminist criticism which believes 'gendering' to take place at a fundamental level concerns itself with what, using a French term, is termed *écriture féminine* – 'feminine writing'. Theorists of *écriture féminine* believe that men and women use language in fundamentally different ways, and that the task of the feminist critic is to give women writers the self-confidence to write as their femaleness requires, and not to ape the writing habits and style of men. As the term suggests, the concept in its modern form has originated in France, especially in the writing of Hélène Cixous. It has, however, antecedents and parallels outside France, and it is interesting in this context to see how many of the recent formulations about 'writing and the body' have parallels in Virginia Woolf's essay 'Professions for Women' (1942).

A further task undertaken by feminist critics has been that of the 'rediscovery' or reinstatement of a number of (mainly women) writers whose works have been undervalued or forgotten.

Queer theory

If Marxist criticism has sought to expose hidden links with class or economic interests in novels and short stories, Queer Theory attempts to expose different sorts of concealed or disguised elements in literary works. Although 'queer' was originally used as a term of abuse to stereotype homosexuals, it has now been reclaimed by gay men and women and used to express pride in their sexual identity.

Since the legalization of homosexuality in Britain, the United States and many other societies, it has been possible to write far more openly about issues of sexual orientation. This, combined with the fact that many writers in the past have *not* enjoyed this freedom, has meant that criticism aimed at exposing gay sub-texts in the works of canonical writers has flourished in the course of recent decades. When I was an undergraduate studying English in the 1960s, no one mentioned the fact that E.M. Forster was homosexual, and no one considered the extent to which this might have a bearing on the novels that he wrote. Today this is a factor that it is hard not to take into account in reading and responding to Forster's novels, and this shift of reading perspective has illuminated aspects of these novels that had previously gone unregarded.

On a rather more sophisticated level, Queer Theorists have done much to destabilize our sense of the fixity of gender divisions – partly by drawing attention to the sort of gender destabilization that can be traced in important novels and short stories. Much very important recent work on the fiction of Henry James is of this sort, and goes far beyond the treatment of James's tales and novels as a sort of homoerotic *roman à clef* (see the Glossary). Instead, the binary gender divisions fixed by social convention are seen to match up very imperfectly with the personal gender preferences and identities of James's characters, while the interplay of gender, class and culture can be traced in the convolutions of Jamesian narrative. Here for example is a passage that I have discussed elsewhere, from James's short story 'The Death of the Lion' (1894). In this story, the narrator discovers that a newspaper journalist named Guy Walsingham is actually a woman, while one named Dora Forbes is referred to as 'he'.

> *I was bewildered: it sounded somehow as if there were three sexes. My interlocutor's pencil was poised, my private responsibility great. I simply sat staring, none the less, and only found presence of mind to say: 'Is this Miss Forbes a gentleman?'*
>
> *Mr Morrow had a subtle smile. 'It wouldn't be "Miss" – there's a wife!'*
> *'I mean is she a man?'*
> *'The wife?' – Mr Morrow was for a moment as confused as myself. But when I explained that I alluded to Dora Forbes in person he informed me, with visible amusement at my being so out of it, that this was the 'pen-name' of an indubitable male – he had a big red moustache.*

While not rejecting a more traditional reading that sees this and comparable passages as examples of James's whimsical humour, Queer Theorists have shown how effectively (and, I think, deliberately) they chip away at a conventional sense that the sexual diversity of the human race can be neatly divided into two standard genders.

Topics for discussion

- Are the most useful critics the ones who share your own beliefs and opinions?
- 'If I want to quote a critic, should I say something about his or her theoretical position? How do I find out what it is?'
- When two critics disagree about a novel, how are we expected to decide who is right?
- 'I dislike feminism: why should I read a feminist critic?'
- 'I always want to find out more about the author, but my lecturer disapproves of this approach.'

Glossary of terms

Where terms have been defined and discussed in earlier chapters, I limit entries to a brief comment and a cross-reference to the relevant page(s). Cross-references within the Glossary are indicated by the use of small capitals. To avoid repetition, terms such as 'novel', 'short story', and 'fiction' are not cross-referenced.

ACHRONICITY/ACHRONY Achronicity is a state in which temporal relationships cannot be established; applied to a NARRATIVE it implies the impossibility of establishing an accurate chronology of EVENTS. An achrony is an event in a narrative which cannot be located on a precise time scale, and cannot be temporally related to other events in the narrative.

ANACHRONY Also, following Bal (1985), *chronological deviation*. Any lack of fit between the order in which EVENTS are presented in the plot or *sjužet*, and that in which they are reported in the story or fabula, is termed an anachrony. Both ANALEPSIS AND PROLEPSIS are examples of anachrony. See also STORY AND PLOT.

Bal isolates two sorts of anachrony: *punctual anachrony*, when only one instant from the past or future is evoked, and *durative anachrony*, when a longer span of time or a more general situation is evoked.

ANALEPSIS AND PROLEPSIS Both terms denote a divergence from strict chronological sequence in a NARRATIVE. An analepsis (otherwise flashback) moves out of the present of STORY-time to describe or evoke something from the 'past' of the story being told. A prolepsis (or anticipation) moves out of the present of story-time to describe or evoke something from the 'future' of the story being told.

ANISOCHRONY See ISOCHRONY.

ANTI-NOVEL A now somewhat outdated term used in the mid-twentieth century to describe experimental fiction that frustrated reader expectations by refusing to conform to accepted conventions – often by containing self-contradictions which could not be resolved by the reader. Compare NOUVEAU ROMAN.

BILDUNGSROMAN The German term *Bildungsroman* is now generally used in English to denote that sort of novel which concentrates upon one CHARACTER's development from early youth to some sort of maturity. Goethe's *Wilhelm Meister's Apprenticeship* (1795–6), Dickens's *David Copperfield* (1849–50) and James Joyce's *Portrait of the Artist as a Young Man* (1916) can all be described as examples of the *Bildungsroman*.

This type of novel clearly attracts the writer interested in depicting the close relationship between early influences and later character development, and its emergence can be related to the growing interest in the THEME that 'the child is father to the man' which accompanies the late eighteenth- and nineteenth-century interest in the young.

CAMPUS NOVEL A novel which takes place within a university or college, or which involves CHARACTERs drawn from such an academic milieu.

CHARACTER An actor in a literary NARRATIVE. If this seems like stating the obvious, it should be pointed out that genres such as science fiction provide borderline cases of entities which from a narrative point of view function as characters (they initiate actions, engage in communication or even speech, and form relationships) but are non-human in other ways.

E.M. Forster's *Aspects of the Novel* provides the now-clichéd distinction between the round and the flat character; the former having depth, complexity and unpredictability, and the latter being reduced almost to a single quality. Flat characters are often compared to *types*. See the extended discussion on p. 106.

A *chorus character* is a character used by a writer to comment authoritatively on EVENTS; for *cancelled* or *erased character* see p. 103. For *synonymous character* see p. 106. For *projection character* see p. 107.

CHARACTER ZONE A term coined by Mikhail Bakhtin to describe the way in which a fictional CHARACTER is surrounded by various verbal and stylistic elements which create a 'zone' that is 'the range of action of the character's voice, intermingling in one way or another with the author's voice' (quoted in Todorov 1984, 73).

CHRONOTOPE Coined by Mikhail Bakhtin to designate 'the distinctive features of time and space within each literary genre' (Todorov 1984, 83).

CLOSURE That sense of satisfying or reassuring finality that accompanies the end of a traditional REALIST novel, when no problems remain to be solved. It is typical of MODERNIST and POSTMODERNIST novels that they postpone or frustrate closure by having *open endings*.

COLOURING The alteration of the language of (say) a NARRATOR by the linguistic characteristics of (say) a CHARACTER. Also referred to as the 'Uncle Charles Principle', after a sentence in James Joyce's *A Portrait of the Artist as a Young Man*: 'Uncle Charles repaired to the outhouse', in which the word 'repaired', which is typical of Uncle Charles's usage, 'colours' the narrator's description. See also the discussion on p. 100.

CONTE The *conte* was originally distinguished from the novel by its (often quirky) wit and its more fantastic, less REALISTIC nature, and by a strongly didactic element normally focused in a moral point or use of allegory. Typical examples are two works both first published in 1759: Samuel Johnson's *Rasselas* (first published as *The Prince of Abissinia. A Tale*) and Voltaire's *Candide*. For the past century or so, however, the term in English has become roughly synonymous with 'short story', although Frank O'Connor (whose views on the short story I discuss in Chapter 3) categorizes Robert Browning's poem 'My Last Duchess' (1842) and Ernest Hemingway's 'Hills Like White Elephants' (1927) as *conte*s (O'Connor 1963, 26).

COVERT PLOT See SUB-PLOT.

CYBERPUNK/CYBERFICTION In both terms the 'cyber' is taken from the word 'cybernetics', itself a coinage by Norbert Wiener, whose book *Cybernetics: or Control and Communication in the Animal and the Machine* was first published in 1949. 'Cyber' comes from the Greek word for 'steersman', and Wiener's book was particularly concerned with what are known as feedback systems. The yoking together of animals and machines in Wiener's title may be one reason why 'cyber' has been hooked onto 'punk' and 'fiction' to refer to recent developments of SCIENCE FICTION that involve various graftings of the inorganic onto the human or organic. According to Austin Booth and Mary Flanagan, cyberfiction is 'writing that explores the relationship between people and virtual technologies' (Booth and Flanagan 2002, 1), but some works defined as cyberfiction, especially earlier ones, are concerned with technology rather than virtual technology.

So far as cyberpunk is concerned, the second part of the term focuses attention on the 'young male outlaws who hack and crack computer networks to steal, manipulate, or erase the information they find' (Booth and Flanagan 2002, 7). Such works are generally set in the desolate urban spaces of technologically advanced but culturally and morally decayed societies of the future, and they implicitly draw critical attention to what are seen as negative trends in today's world, in which large impersonal corporations control more and more of human life. The American Marxist critic Fredric Jameson has suggested that cyberpunk 'is fully as much an expression of transnational corporate realities as it is of global paranoia' (Jameson 1991, 38).

The term 'cyberpunk' seems first to have been used by the writer Bruce Bethke, who published a story of this name in the magazine *Amazing* in 1983 (Butler 2000, 9). The most influential early cyberpunk author, however, is generally agreed to be William Gibson. Cyberpunk has moved from being the preserve of a small band of enthusiasts to a more widely known genre as a result of the very successful filming of certain key cyberpunk texts. Philip K. Dick's 1968 novel *Do Androids Dream of Electric Sheep?* was made into the blockbuster film *Blade Runner* (1982, directed by Ridley Scott).

Apart from its debt to science fiction, the style and ambience of cyberpunk owes much to the so-called 'hard-boiled' detective fiction and its cinematic offshoot *film noir*. But going further back, the PICARESQUE NOVEL also shares common elements with cyberpunk: in particular, the central figure of a mobile, outcast young male. There are also intriguing parallels to be argued concerning the way in which both of these sub-genres seem to have been inspired by major social changes.

Cyberpunk has attracted the attention of women writers, who see in its concern with bodily modification and gender adaptation possibilities for feminist development. Again in the words of Booth and Flanagan, '[w]omen writers are

appropriating the cyberpunk aesthetic – metaphors of jacking in, figures of outlaws and outsiders, and film noir rhetoric – for their own ends' (2002, 2). The work of writer Donna Haraway is often seen as forging a bridge between cyberfiction ('cyberfeminism') and postmodernism. Haraway has fixed on the concept of the cyborg – part human, part machine – as a figure that uses technology to break down divisive binaries, especially those connected with gender. It is interesting to note that the work that can claim to have had a founding function so far as the concept of the cyborg is concerned – Mary Shelley's *Frankenstein* (1818) – was also written by a woman.

Haraway's optimism has not been shared by all: others have suggested that bodily modification is today more testimony to the control of women's bodies by patriarchal forces than evidence of a potential liberation.

DEATH OF THE AUTHOR A phrase taken from an essay by Roland Barthes, 'The Death of the Author' (1977, in French 1968). A recent commentary (Carlier, 2000) has suggested that Barthes' essay had a satirical intention, but for many years it has been taken as a serious argument advocating that the author be granted no power over his or her work once it has been published, and that it is language, rather than the author, that speaks in a work. Barthes' arguments are often associated with those of his fellow countryman Michel Foucault, whose essay 'What is an Author?' was also published in English in 1977.

DEFAMILIARIZATION From the Russian meaning 'to make strange', the term originates with the Russian formalists and, in particular, the theories of Viktor Shklovsky. In his essay 'Art as Technique', Shklovsky argues that perception becomes automatic once it has become habitual, and that the function of art is to challenge automatization and habitualization, and return a direct grasp on things to the individual perception. Of interest to students of the novel is that the Russian formalists exemplified defamiliarization by reference to the work of novelists such as Tolstoy, and Boris Tomashevsky, one of Shklovsky's fellow Russian formalists, refers to Swift's defamiliarizing techniques in *Gulliver's Travels* in his essay 'Thematics' (the scene in which the Lilliputians discover Gulliver's watch and describe it without understanding what it is – thus encouraging the reader to see something familiar as if it were strange).

DEIXIS Those features of language which fasten utterances temporally or spatially: 'here' and 'now', for example. Deictics, or deictic elements (deictic can perform as either noun or adjective) play an important role in NARRATIVE; they constitute an important token of Free Indirect Discourse, for example.

DELAYED DECODING A term coined by Ian Watt in his *Conrad in the Nineteenth Century* (1980) to describe a particular impressionist technique used by Joseph Conrad by means of which the experiences of a CHARACTER who understands what is happening to him or her only while these experiences are taking place (or afterwards), is recreated in the reader. Thus in Conrad's *Heart of Darkness*, we share Marlow's belief that lots of little sticks are dropping on the ship, up to the point when Marlow realizes that the 'sticks' are in fact arrows, and that the ship is being attacked.

DIALOGUE The standard meaning of this term with regard to prose fiction concerns the representation of the speech of CHARACTERs, either interactively between two or more characters, or monologically addressed by one character to him- or herself. See the extended discussion on p. 126, and compare also INTERNAL/INTERIOR DIALOGUE.

The writings of Mikhail Bakhtin have helped to make the term fashionable by suggesting that language itself is naturally dialogic, and that all use of language involves interaction with those others who have stamped themselves on words and phrases by their use of them.

DIEGESIS AND MIMESIS These are terms that present a number of problems of usage, as the meanings attached to them have changed since first they were used in the third book of Plato's *Republic*, in which Socrates uses them to distinguish between two ways of presenting speech. For Socrates, diegesis stands for those cases where the poet himself is the speaker and does not wish to suggest otherwise, and mimesis stands for those cases in which the poet attempts to create the illusion that it is not he who is speaking. Recent usage among critics and theorists of prose fiction is rather different: diegesis is commonly used to denote 'the world of the story'. Thus in *Wuthering Heights* we can describe Lockwood and Nelly Dean as intradiegetic NARRATORs, because they are also CHARACTERs occupying the same reality as Heathcliff and Cathy. The narrator of Fielding's *Tom Jones*, in contrast, clearly belongs to a reality that represents the STORY he tells as fictional, and thus he is described as an extradiegetic narrator.

In like manner, mimesis has come to be used to describe the more general capacity of literature to imitate reality, and has on occasions accumulated a somewhat polemical edge as a result of its use by those wishing to establish imitation as central or essential to art – by Marxist critics intent on stressing that literature and art 'reflect' extraliterary reality, for example.

For *autodiegetic* and *homodiegetic*, see p. 86.

DISTANCE A term used in a number of different ways to suggest varying levels of involvement (emotional, intellectual, ideological) with what goes on in a STORY on the part *either* of a NARRATOR *or* a reader. See also p. 94.

DURATION In NARRATIVE theory, the relation between the time covered by the STORY or part of it (such as an EVENT) and the 'time' allotted to it by the text (story-time and text-time). Thus three years of story-time may be covered by three pages of text, while further on in the same text one hour of story-time may occupy fifty pages. Unfortunately 'pages' do not give a particularly reliable measure: some readers read more quickly than others and the same reader will read more or less quickly depending upon textual complexity, reader involvement and tension, and so on. As a result many writers on narrative find *speed* or *tempo* more fruitful concepts.

See also p. 113, and compare ISOCHRONY.

ELLIPSIS A gap in the information provided for the reader, which may be permanent (we never learn what Heathcliff did after he left Wuthering Heights and before he returned) or temporary (as with most detective stories, when the missing details about the crime are provided in the book's concluding pages). Ellipses can be marked or unmarked – that is to say the reader may or may not be made aware of the gap. See also p. 112.

EPIC Traditionally a long NARRATIVE poem presenting a heroic subject in an elevated style. Among the earliest epics are the *Odyssey* and the *Iliad*, although earlier examples exist. Some commentators distinguish between primary and secondary epics, where secondary epics have a single author rather than a collective origin, and are written within a literate culture rather than sung or recited in an oral culture. The novel has been approached as a modern epic, and some authors have attempted to give their works something of an epic status, although Mikhail Bakhtin (see p. 6) has argued for a sharp dividing line between epic and novel.

EPISTOLARY NOVEL An epistolary novel is told through letters ('epistles') exchanged between different CHARACTERs. The form flourished in English literature in the eighteenth century. Samuel Richardson's *Pamela* (1740) and *Clarissa* (1747–8), Tobias Smollett's *Humphry Clinker* (1771) and Frances Burney's *Evelina* (1778) are classic epistolary novels. Writers in subsequent periods have made sporadic attempts to adapt the technique to their own needs, and one of the most successful examples of a recent epistolary novel is Alice Walker's *The Color Purple* (1982).

Given how important letters were in English society in the eighteenth century, it is not surprising that the novel should have been heavily influenced by this form of communication in its early development. In his novel *Clarissa*, Samuel Richardson gives a comment to his character Mr Belford, writing to Lovelace about Clarissa, which helps to explain why Richardson (and his readers) favoured the technique:

> *Such a sweetness of temper, so much patience and resignation, as she seems to be mistress of; yet writing of and in the midst of* present *distresses! How* much more *lively and affecting, for that reason, must her style be, her mind tortured by the pangs of uncertainty (the events then hidden in the womb of fate),* than *the dry narrative, unanimated style of a person relating difficulties and dangers surmounted; the relater perfectly at ease; and if himself unmoved by his own story, not likely greatly to affect the reader. (emphases in original)*

Clearly the personal insight, self-display and dramatic effectiveness of the epistolary technique are what appeal to Richardson. On the negative side, a novel told exclusively through letters (Richardson allows himself the occasional authorial footnote and bracketed interpolation) can be unwieldy and inflexible. The characters have to be kept apart (otherwise they have no reason to write to one another), and sometimes this involves artificiality: Richardson's heroines are banished to locked rooms with disturbing regularity. When they actually meet their loved ones Richardson has somehow to arrange for someone else to write a letter about the encounter. Moreover, whatever else the characters do they must always have access to pen and paper. As Clarissa on one occasion writes to Miss Howe: 'And indeed, my dear, I know not how to *forbear* writing. I have now no other employment or diversion. And I must write on, although I were not to send it to anybody.' It was this element in Richardson's *Pamela* that was so cruelly but effectively satirized by Henry Fielding in his parody *An Apology for the Life of Miss Shamela Andrews* (1741), in which the heroine continues to write a letter while the man who is assaulting her virtue climbs into bed with her.

If the 'pure' epistolary novel is rare after the eighteenth century, the technique taught novelists how very useful letters could be as an element within the NARRATIVE variety of a novel. Two good examples are Isabella's long letter about her marriage to Heathcliff in Emily Brontë's *Wuthering Heights*, and Helen's letters to her sister in E.M. Forster's *Howards End*.

EVENT AND EXISTENT Narratologists distinguish between 'existents' (those things that 'are' in a NARRATIVE) and 'events' (those things that are 'done' or that 'occur' in a narrative).

FABLIAU A short medieval tale in verse, usually humorous and satirical and often bawdy. Geoffrey Chaucer's 'The Miller's Tale' from the late fourteenth century is frequently cited as a typical example of the form.

FABULA AND SJUŽET See STORY AND PLOT.

FABULATION AND SURFICTION These two terms are used relatively interchangeably. Both imply an aggressive and playful

luxuriation in the non-representational, in which the writer takes delight in the artifice of writing rather than attempting to describe or make contact with a perceived extrafictional reality. Both terms are normally used in connection with relatively recent fiction.

FACTION The term comes from the American author Truman Capote and is a portmanteau word (= fact + fiction) which describes novels such as his own *In Cold Blood* (1966). In this work primarily novelistic techniques are used to bring actual historical EVENTs to life for the reader. The term has thus come to denote a work that is on the borderline between fact and fiction, concerned primarily with a real event or persons, but using imagined detail to increase readability and verisimilitude.

FANTASTIC Characteristic of the fantastic is that it *hints* at a supernatural explanation without actually confirming that the supernatural has been involved in the EVENTs and experiences described. It thus constitutes one of the more recent movements away from a view associating the novel with a rather more traditional realism. According to some theorists – especially those influenced by Tzvetan Todorov – to be classified as a genuine example of the fantastic, a novel or short story must retain a sense of ambiguity to the end, never allowing the reader finally to establish that the depicted events can only be accounted for by natural or, alternatively, by supernatural, explanations. From this perspective there are few pure examples of the fantastic; according to some (but not all) accounts, one would be Henry James's *The Turn of the Screw*. Recent interest in the fantastic has been encouraged by feminist writers and critics interested in exploring alternative 'realities' in which the gender conventions of past and existing societies are challenged or held up to scrutiny. I discuss the ways in which the new electronic media have developed more traditional forms of the fantastic in Chapter 5.

FICELLE From the French meaning 'string', the term is used by Henry James to denote a minor CHARACTER in a novel whose FUNCTION is that of helping the reader with information, as an anchor-point, and so on.

FICTION See Chapter 1, p. 1.

FIRST PERSON See FOCALIZATION.

FLAT CHARACTER See CHARACTER.

FOCALIZATION A term used by recent theorists of NARRATIVE to specify what used to be known as 'point of view'. See PERSPECTIVE AND VOICE.

FRAME Used within NARRATIVE theory to describe the way in which certain works present the reader with 'narratives within narratives', or *framed* or *nested* narratives. Thus Marlow's telling in Conrad's *Heart of Darkness* is framed by introductory, interjected and concluding comments from an unnamed 'frame NARRATOR'.

FREE INDIRECT DISCOURSE A NARRATIVE technique for providing the reader with a CHARACTER's speech, thoughts or even unconsidered attitudes without the use of direct attribution by tag-phrase ('she thought', 'he said') or even inverted commas. Discussed in more detail on p. 98.

FREQUENCY The numerical relationship between 'EVENTs in a PLOT' and 'events in a STORY'. See p. 113.

FUNCTION According to Vladimir Propp, 'an act of a character, defined from the point of view of its significance for the course of the action'. See p. 106.

GOTHIC NOVEL See *ROMAN NOIR*.

HISTORICAL NOVEL As its name suggests, the historical novel sets its EVENTs and CHARACTERs in a well-defined historical context, and it may include both fictional and real characters. It is often distinguished (in its more respectable forms) by convincing detailed description of the manners, buildings, institutions and scenery of its chosen SETTING, and generally attempts to convey a sense of historical verisimilitude. Its most respected practitioner in Britain has been Sir Walter Scott.

In its more recent popular, 'pulp' and electronic forms it tends to abandon verisimilitude for fantasy, and in some ways can be seen as the present-day version of the ROMANCE, encouraging more an escape from contemporary reality than a critical and imaginative scrutiny of the life that its readers would recognize as their own.

IMAGE AND IMAGERY Terms with a range of meanings in literary critical discussion, but generally implying the use of language to evoke sensuous (often visual) experiences in the reader. More loosely, any examples of figurative language, especially those with a repetitive or cumulative effect in a work. See the discussion on p. 125.

IMPLIED AUTHOR/READER These terms were coined by the American critic Wayne C. Booth. The term 'implied author' is used to refer to that picture of the creating author behind a literary work that a reader builds up solely on the basis of a reading of that work. The term 'implied reader' is used to refer to that sense of the reader that the author (or the work) appears to want – again based solely on 'internal information', that is on the reader who seems to be implied by a sympathetic reading of a work.

INSTALMENT For publication by instalment, see PERIODICAL PUBLICATION.

INTERNAL/INTERIOR DIALOGUE A DIALOGUE between two well-defined voices within the single consciousness of a literary CHARACTER (or, in a wider usage, of a real human being), and the NARRATIVE representation of this process. Interior dialogue involves more than the representation of a character's verbalized thought processes in which questions are asked and answered. To count as genuine interior dialogue the questions and answers must stem from two voices which represent different and as it were *personified* attitudes, beliefs or characteristics. A good example occurs towards the beginning of the tenth chapter of Charlotte Brontë's *Jane Eyre*, in which we have represented a long dialogue between different and personified aspects of Jane Eyre's personality or identity.

INTERNAL/INTERIOR MONOLOGUE A NARRATIVE technique for representing the unexpressed thoughts of a CHARACTER. Strictly speaking, interior monologue, unlike the broader term STREAM OF CONSCIOUSNESS, applies when the words used to express the thoughts are those that the character is assumed to be using for thinking. The term is often used more loosely, however, as a synonym for stream of consciousness. See also p. 97.

INTRUSIVE NARRATOR A NARRATOR who is generally situated outside the world of the action, and who intrudes thoughts, opinions or comments about a CHARACTER or a situation. Thus Lockwood, in *Wuthering Heights*, is not generally thought of as an intrusive narrator in spite of his frequent sentous comments, because he is an intradiegetic narrator (see DIEGESIS AND MIMESIS) narrator, and not situated outside the world of the action. Compare METALEPSIS.

ISOCHRONY Borrowed by recent NARRATIVE theorists from a term used to describe poetic rhythm, isochrony denotes an *unvarying* or an *equal* relationship between narrating-time and STORY-time. The two are not the same: if a story covers three hours and each hour is narrated by means of five thousand words, then the relationship between narrating-time and story-time is unvarying. If a story covers three hours and each hour of the story takes approximately an hour to read, then the relationship between narrating-time and story-time can be said to be equal. The opposite of isochrony is

anisochrony: either a varying or an unequal relationship between narrating-time and story-time – normally the former. Compare DURATION.

ITERATIVE See FREQUENCY.

KÜNSTLERROMAN From the German meaning 'a novel about an artist'. A *BILDUNGSROMAN* which has an artist as its hero or heroine, and which often contains a concealed or partly concealed autobiographical element, can be described as a *Künstlerroman*.

LOCAL COLOUR Realistic detail, often concerned with such matters as dress, scenery, customs, which has no THEMATIC significance but which is there to give the reader a greater sense of verisimilitude.

MAGIC REALISM A blending of the FANTASTIC or fantasy with realism, which today is particularly associated with certain Central and South American novelists such as Gabriel García Márquez and Isabel Allende but which has also been applied to some of the later work of the Kenyan novelist Ngũgĩ Wa Thiong'o and to various European novelists including the German Günther Grass and the British Angela Carter – and even retrospectively to a novel such as Virginia Woolf's *Orlando* (1928) and to the female GOTHIC NOVEL. In Europe the term is particularly associated with certain recent female and feminist novelists. 'Blending' is perhaps misleading; magic realism seems typically to involve the sudden incursion of fantastic elements into an otherwise realistic PLOT and SETTING.

MARVELLOUS A MODE in which the non-realistic and other-worldly is presented in such a way as to exclude any possible REALISTIC or rational explanation.

METAFICTION Literally, fiction about fiction – normally denoting the sort of novel or short story which deliberately breaks fictive illusions and comments directly upon its own fictive nature or process of composition. The English father-figure of metafiction is Laurence Sterne, in whose *Tristram Shandy* (1759–67) the NARRATOR jokes with and teases the reader in various ways – advising him or her to turn back several pages to read a passage afresh, for example (see p. 70). Metafictional techniques are common to much modernist and, especially, postmodernist writing.

METALEPSIS According to Gérard Genette, any transgressing of NARRATIVE levels, such as when Laurence Sterne (or his NARRATOR) implores the reader of *Tristram Shandy* to help the CHARACTER Mr Shandy get back to his bed. Compare INTRUSIVE NARRATOR.

MODE A term that is used in a confusing variety of ways, sometimes as a loose synonym for any sort of 'type', but sometimes with a more precise meaning within NARRATIVE theory, as a rough way of categorizing different sorts of DISTANCE. See also p. 101.

MODERNISM See Chapter 4, p. 61.

MOOD Apart from being used as a rough synonym for 'atmosphere', mood is a term adapted by narratologists from its grammatical sense, which distinguishes between grammatical moods such as the subjective or the indicative. In NARRATIVE theory, mood is roughly equivalent to the old-fashioned 'point of view' (see PERSPECTIVE AND VOICE).

MOTIF In discussion of prose fiction 'motif' is often used as a synonym for *leitmotif*, to refer to recurrent elements that are not quite SYMBOLS or THEMES, but that have a cumulative effect on the reader. Thus Cedric Watts provides the reader of Joseph Conrad's *Lord Jim* in the Penguin edition with a useful list of *leitmotifs*: 'butterflies and beetles'; 'dream, dreams'; 'glimpse (of Jim's character) through mist or fog'; 'in the ranks'; 'jump, leap'; 'nothing can touch me'; 'one of us'; 'romance, romantic'; 'under a cloud'; 'veiled opportunity'.

NARRATEE The 'target' at whom a NARRATIVE is directed. A narratee is not just the individual by whom a narrative is received; there has to be some textual evidence that the narrative is actually intended for a particular person or target for this to count as the (or a) narratee.

NARRATIVE See Chapter 1, p. 6.

NARRATIVE SITUATION Defined according to the NARRATOR's relationship to the narrative and the STORY. Is the narrator diegetic or extradiegetic (see DIEGESIS AND MIMESIS)? Is the NARRATIVE ostensibly spoken or written?

NARRATOLOGY Normally used to refer to the structuralist-inspired theories of NARRATIVE that have flourished in the past three decades, but sometimes used more loosely to describe any body of theory concerned with the analysis of narratives, literary or other. See the discussion in the Introduction, p. vii, and in Chapter 9, p. 173.

NARRATOR The person, voice or language-source that tells the STORY. This awkward formulation stems from the fact that some novels and short stories have no clearly personified or human teller, but it is still conventional to refer to their having a narrator. Some recent theorists have however argued that the term should be reserved for human or personified tellers. See also INTRUSIVE NARRATOR.

NATURALISM Naturalism is a variety of REALISM, and the term is used in much the same way but with a narrower focus. Strictly speaking, naturalism should be restricted to a description of those literary works which were written according to a method founded upon the belief that there is a natural (rather than supernatural or spiritual) explanation for everything that exists or occurs. Naturalist novelists include the Goncourt brothers, Émile Zola, George Moore, the German Gerhard Hauptmann, and Americans such as Theodore Dreiser and Stephen Crane.

NOUVEAU ROMAN (new novel) In the *nouveau roman* the accepted conventions of fictional composition are deliberately distorted or flouted in order to disorient the reader and to foreground certain processes of artistic illusion or NARRATIVE convention. As such it can be seen as a post-Second World War development of MODERNISM. It is associated particularly with France.

The best-known exponents of the *nouveau roman* are Alain Robbe-Grillet (whose book *Pour un nouveau roman* (1963) originated the term), Michel Butor and Nathalie Sarraute. Compare ANTI-NOVEL.

NOUVELLE A *nouvelle* is characterized by a concern with a single episode or state of affairs, although its treatment of this (which conventionally moves to a surprise ending of one sort or another) may cover many pages. The genre is generally agreed to achieve a recognized form in the middle of the sixteenth century, with the publication of *Nouvelles Récréations et Joyeux Devis*, a collection ascribed to Des Périers. The term can be a little treacherous as in some usages it has come to be seen as synonymous with CONTE, while in others it is used interchangeably with NOVELLA.

NOVEL, NOVELLA, SHORT STORY The problems involved in defining these three terms are discussed at length in Chapters 1, 2 and 3. As well as having in common the characteristics of prose and fictionality, all three forms are generally restricted to works with CHARACTERs, action and a PLOT. The terms are conventionally distinguished by reference to their length, and in Chapter 3, I quote Mary Doyle Springer's proposal that a work of fiction of between 15,000 and 50,000 words be categorized as a novella. More than 50,000 words and we have a novel; fewer than 15,000 and we have a short story. Remember however that these are arbitrary and by no means universally accepted distinctions.

NOVELLA See NOVEL, NOVELLA, SHORT STORY.

OBSTINATION The reader's tendency to continue to FRAME a passage of NARRATIVE in a consistent manner (e.g. as Free Indirect Discourse) unless prompted by textual or contextual features to shift to a new frame.

OMNISCIENCE All-embracing, godlike knowledge. Often applied to the NARRATORs of classical realist novels for whom there are no secrets within the created world of the novel. Dorrit Cohn has however cited Gérard Genette's objection to the term, which is that it is absurd: the author has nothing to know because he or she 'invents' everything (Cohn 1999, 175).

PARABLE A short NARRATIVE intended to convey a moral or other lesson. Best known from Christ's biblical parables, but more widespread than is often appreciated. Many modern novelists and (especially) short-story writers have written parable-like works.

PARALEPSIS Presenting more information in a NARRATIVE than is strictly or logically speaking justified by the ostensible NARRATOR and his or her situation. Thus in Joseph Conrad's novel *Under Western Eyes*, the narrator (the 'Teacher of Languages') claims to base his account on the written report of the CHARACTER, Razumov. Yet after Razumov has finished this report and has wrapped it up, the Teacher of Languages continues to describe Razumov's actions and experiences.

PARALIPSIS The omission of certain information that the NARRATOR should in 'real world' terms be aware of.

PARATEXT A coinage of Gérard Genette, used in his work *Seuils* (1987; English translation *Paratexts: Thresholds of Interpretation* (1997)). According to Richard Macksey, the term refers to 'those liminal devices and conventions, both within the book (peritext) and outside it (epitext) that mediate the book to the reader: titles and subtitles, pseudonyms, forewords, dedications, epigraphs, prefaces, intertitles, notes, epilogues, and afterwords – all those framing devices that so engaged Sterne' (Genette 1997, xviii). Thus as Genette explains, 'paratext = peritext + epitext' (1997, 5).

PATRONAGE The specific meaning of this term within the study of literature involves a particular method of financing authorship. Rather than relying upon royalties, or payments from a publisher, an author is supported by a patron, who is rewarded by having his or her name in the eventual book, and perhaps by having his or her person or politics supported within the book. It is generally accepted that an important element in 'the rise of the novel' was the freedom from patronage that the market (i.e. publishers' fees or royalties) gave writers.

PERIODICAL PUBLICATION Normally initial publication of a longer work in instalments in a periodical or magazine. Although periodical publication was an important source of finance for writers in the nineteenth century (periodicals paid well), the constraints it entailed (censorship, division into sections, writing against the clock) did have some negative effects on works and writers.

It is useful to be able to read Henry James's *The Turn of the Screw* (1898) in an edition that marks the division between the instalments of its first published version, as we can then note that James attempts to end each separate instalment at a point of increased tension or dramatic surprise (much like the old film serials for children, each episode of which typically ended with a 'cliff-hanging' finale).

PERSPECTIVE AND VOICE Gérard Genette has drawn attention to the importance of a long-neglected distinction between *Who sees?* and *Who speaks?* I exemplify this distinction by reference to Katherine Mansfield's 'The Voyage' on p. 95.

In Genette's terminology the distinction between *Who sees?* and *Who speaks?* is expressed in terms of the opposition between MOOD and VOICE

(1980, 30). According to him, *mood* operates at the level of connections between STORY and NARRATIVE, while *voice* designates connections both between narrating and narrative, and narrating and story (1980, 32). Others following Genette have preferred to replace *mood* by *perspective*, as the pair 'perspective and voice' matches up more neatly with 'who sees/who speaks'. If 'who sees' = perspective and 'who speaks' = voice, then a single narrative passage may combine the voice of one character or position and the perspective of another character or position.

The matched terms 'perspective' and 'voice' thus provide a more fine-tuned way of investigating what was traditionally known as 'point of view' in the days prior to the emergence of modern NARRATOLOGY.

PICARESQUE NOVEL A 'picaro' in Spanish is a rogue, and the picaresque novel is built on the tradition of the sixteenth-century Spanish picaresque NARRATIVE, which typically portrayed a sharp-witted rogue living off his wits while travelling through a variety of usually low-life SETTINGS. The picaro typically lives by begging or by minor theft; he is cynical in his attitude to the softer emotions, especially love; and through witty and satirical comments he questions established beliefs and customs. Critics frequently relate the emergence of the picaro to the break-up of the feudal world, and his open-minded, self-interested, geographical and intellectual wandering and questing are seen by many to merge into the spirit of possessive individualism that is ushered in with the growth of capitalist social relations.

The picaresque novel is typically *episodic*, lacking a sophisticated PLOT and psychologically complex – or developing – CHARACTERs.

Part of the appeal of the picaresque lies in its concern with the ordinary and the trivial, a concern which sets the picaresque apart from the ROMANCE, and which explains the historical importance accorded the picaresque in the history of the novel's emergence and development.

See the discussion of CYBERPUNK/ CYBERFICTION above for comment on picaresque elements in cyberpunk.

PLOT See STORY AND PLOT.

POINT OF VIEW See PERSPECTIVE AND VOICE.

POSTMODERNIST NOVEL During the last two or three decades 'postmodernism' has emerged as the umbrella term which is most frequently used to describe a range of formal and technical experiments that are linked to theories about reality in general and the modern world in particular. In his *Postmodernist Fiction*, Brian McHale distinguishes postmodernism from MODERNISM by differentiating between a poetics (or systematized theory of literature) dominated by ontological issues (meaning a concern with the nature of reality in general), and a poetics dominated by epistemological issues (meaning how and if we know the world or 'the real') (1987, xii). Postmodernism is seen by many to involve (among other things) the taking of certain modernist techniques to an extreme, and the more extended consideration of modernism and postmodernism in Chapter 4 should be consulted for further discussion. Prominent American postmodernists are Donald Barthelme, Ronald Sukenick, John Barth and Walter Abish, but British novelists such as B.S. Johnson and Christine Brooke-Rose, the Colombian Gabriel García Márquez, and many others are now regularly described as postmodernist novelists.

POST-STRUCTURALISM See the discussion in Chapter 7, p. 173.

PROLEPSIS See ANALEPSIS AND PROLEPSIS.

REALISM See Chapter 4, p. 57.

REGIONAL NOVEL The regional novel involves an especial focus of attention on the life of a particular, well-defined geographical region. Traditionally the region in question will be rural rather than urban (thus it would be distinctly odd to refer to Charles Dickens as a regional novelist, in spite of the fact that so many of his novels explore London life in such intimate detail). Very often a 'regional novelist' will write a number of books all involving the same territory or place – as with Thomas Hardy's 'Wessex' and William Faulkner's 'Yoknapatawpha County'. Both of these 'regions' are closely modelled on particular areas of England and the United States, in spite of their fictitious names (and, ironically, the popularity of Hardy's novels has led to the term 'Wessex' being used to denote that part of England upon which it is based).

ROMAN À CLEF The *roman à clef* is the sort of novel that can be 'unlocked' given the right 'key' – in other words one which refers to real people, places or EVENTs in disguised form so that once one realizes what the work is about, the hidden references all become apparent. Thomas Love Peacock wrote several humorous novels in the early nineteenth century in which thinly disguised portrayals of contemporary individuals such as Shelley and Coleridge appeared.

We do not call a novel a *roman à clef* simply because it contains one thinly disguised portrayal of a real person. Thomas Mann's *The Magic Mountain* (1924) was much admired by the Hungarian Marxist critic Georg Lukács, who apparently did not recognize what is allegedly the case – that the highly unpleasant CHARACTER Naphta in the novel was based upon himself.

ROMAN À THÈSE/TENDENZROMAN The *roman à thèse* has, as the term suggests, a particular thesis or argument underlying it. It is typically a novel concerned to encourage social reform, or the correction of a particular abuse or wrong. Central to the definition is the idea of a dominant and usually a simple and uncomplicated thesis. (See p. 122 for the distinction between 'thesis' and 'theme'.) Harriet Beecher Stowe's *Uncle Tom's Cabin* (1852), which is structured around an attack upon the institution of slavery in the United States, is a classic *roman à thèse*. A novel like Thomas Hardy's *Jude The Obscure* (1896), in contrast, although it undeniably involves an attack upon certain social conventions which are seen as repressive and although in a sense it clearly 'calls for' a change in society so that women and working people have greater opportunities for self-development and for education, is too complex and involved a novel to be termed a *roman à thèse*.

ROMANCE The medieval romance is discussed at length in Chapter 2. The modern use of the term denotes a type of formulaic prose fiction aimed at women readers and focused on courtship and marriage seen from a woman's point of view. Although many differences exist, there are arguably lines of continuity linking the medieval romance with its modern namesake.

ROMAN FEUILLETON This is a novel that is published in instalments in unabridged form by a daily newspaper – a practice that was common in the nineteenth century. The method of publication is unusual today for a novel, although it is becoming more and more fashionable for certain sorts of non-fictional work to be published in abridged form in newspaper instalments.

ROMAN-FLEUVE This term denotes a series of sequence or novels which can be read and appreciated individually but which deal with recurring CHARACTERs and/or common EVENTs and which form a sequence or complement one another. Perhaps the best-known example is Balzac's *La Comédie humaine*, but Anthony Powell's *A Dance to the Music of Time* (1951–75) is a more recent example. The *roman-fleuve* is closely related to what is called the *saga novel* – a series of novels about a large family each of which

concentrates upon different branches of the family or different events in which it is implicated. Thomas Mann's tetralogy *Joseph and his Brothers* (1933–43) is one twentieth-century example; John Galsworthy's *Forsyte Saga* (1906–35) is another.

ROMAN NOIR /GOTHIC NOVEL The more usual term in English is 'gothic novel'. The term denotes a type of fiction that was ushered in by Horace Walpole's *The Castle of Otranto* (1764). Walpole was much influenced by the revival of interest in the gothic that occurred in the later eighteenth century, a revival that can be seen as a precursor of aspects of Romanticism in its predilection for the wild, the uncanny and the horrific – all of which were associated by the pre-Romantics with the medieval period. The gothic novel introduced stock CHARACTERs, situations and SETTINGs that still survive in the modern horror film: gloomy medieval settings (especially ancient castles), sinister or tortured characters with guilty secrets, and a strongly supernatural element. The gothic novel proper flourished for a limited period, and was more or less a thing of the past by the early nineteenth century, but gothic elements can be found in a wide range of fiction during the nineteenth and even twentieth centuries. Jane Austen parodies aspects of the gothic novel in *Northanger Abbey* (begun in 1798 and published in 1816). The term 'gothic' has been applied to the works of Mervyn Peake much more recently, and the survival of the gothic in popular film and literature, and computer games, probably guarantees that it will remain a continuing influence on serious literature.

The work of certain recent women writers such as Angela Carter and Sylvia Plath has been claimed to contain gothic elements, and a revival of interest in the gothic has been encouraged by a feminist interest in the way in which gothic formulae can be seen both to encapsulate certain stereotypical masculine fears about women and also to allow women the space to explore hidden aspects of gender formation.

ROUND CHARACTER See CHARACTER.

SAGA NOVEL See *ROMAN-FLEUVE*.

SATIRICAL NOVEL Satire does not have to be either in prose or fictional, although there is a sense in which the exaggeration upon which it typically depends necessarily involves a certain amount of fictive imagining. There is a tradition of satire which is independent of the novel and which stretches back to antiquity, and aspects of this tradition have been important influences upon the novel. Satire attacks alleged vices and stupidities – either of individuals or of whole communities or groups – and its tools are ridicule, exaggeration and contempt.

Jonathan Swift's satirical writings – and especially his *Gulliver's Travels* (1726) – are extremely important staging-posts for the novel, although most commentators have been unwilling to allow that any of these works themselves merit the title 'novel'. If we think of Mark Twain's *The Adventures of Huckleberry Finn* (1884), we can see how the mature novel of the nineteenth century was able to incorporate important satirical techniques from earlier writers within a much more REALISTIC framework than Swift, for example, provides. The use of a naive NARRATOR travelling among people whose strange ways he describes innocently while at the same time conveying his creator's biting satire of what they stand for is one element which unites Swift's and Twain's major works.

The satirist is by definition more concerned to draw our attention to what he or she is attacking than to create CHARACTERs, SITUATIONs and EVENTs that are believable in and for themselves. A novelist may however include satirical elements in works that do not, overall,

merit the term 'satirical novel' (and indeed most novelists do). Thus E.M. Forster's *Howards End* is not usually categorized as a satirical novel, but it does include a distinctively satirical vein in its treatment of various characters. Take the following passage from the end of the first paragraph of Chapter 3. Mrs Munt is considering her responsibilities towards the two Schlegel sisters, Helen and Margaret:

> Sooner or later the girls would enter on the process known as throwing themselves away, and if they had delayed hitherto it was only that they might throw themselves more vehemently in the future. They saw too many people at Wickham Place – unshaven musicians, an actress even, German cousins (one knows what foreigners are), acquaintances picked up at continental hotels (one knows what they are too). It was interesting, and down at Swanage no one appreciated culture more than Mrs Munt; but it was dangerous, and disaster was bound to come.

The passage is clearly satirical: it attempts to diminish a set of beliefs by making it appear ridiculous. Although the passage is ostensibly related to us from the viewpoint of Forster's narrator, it mimics Mrs Munt and makes her views seem absurd by pretending to adopt them. (Forster makes use of FREE INDIRECT DISCOURSE here.)

If we compare *Howards End* with Joseph Heller's *Catch-22* (1961), we will appreciate that the latter can more properly be termed a satirical novel than the former. Heller's dominating concern is clearly to diminish war and the military in our eyes by making them appear ridiculous and vain; his major aim in the novel is, in other words, satirical.

SCIENCE FICTION Some definitions link science fiction with FANTASTIC literature, and the two are clearly closely related.

The fantastic normally invokes the strong possibility (but not certainty) of supernatural agencies, however, while science fiction does not generally do this. Science fiction is rather characterized by SETTINGS involving interplanetary travel and advanced technology, and is typically set in the future. In contrast to fantasy literature, its settings and EVENTs are often conceivable but not actual.

Jules Verne and H.G. Wells are each sometimes granted the title of the father of science fiction (its most celebrated authors tend to be male), and its best-known practitioners today are Ray Bradbury, Arthur C. Clarke and Isaac Asimov.

It is possible to relate science fiction to a work such as Swift's *Gulliver's Travels*, and clearly science fiction can have a 'pastoral' element: commenting upon one society or community under the pretext of describing another, imagined one. Often abbreviated to SF, the tradition is an important source of CYBERPUNK and of various forms of electronic fiction (see Chapter 5).

SETTING See p. 120.

SHORT STORY See NOVEL, NOVELLA, SHORT STORY.

SILVER FORK NOVEL A now archaic term used to refer to a particular sub-genre of the novel, popular in the early years of the nineteenth century, that focused on the lives and preoccupations of high society and that included much LOCAL COLOUR of the 'silver fork' variety. The novels of Benjamin Disraeli are sometimes so categorized.

SKAZ A MODE or technique of narration that mirrors oral NARRATIVE. The term comes from the Russian, as Russian formalist theorists were the first to tackle the issues raised by *skaz*, but there are many non-Russian examples. For example, from a technical point of view much of Joseph Conrad's *Heart of Darkness* can be described as *skaz*, as a large part of what we read represents the CHARACTER Marlow's oral address to listeners. The technique allows for the depiction of such things as hesitation, tone of voice, slips of the tongue, self-correction and interaction with a depicted intradiegetic (see DIEGESIS AND MIMESIS) audience.

STORY AND PLOT A distinction related to that made by the Russian formalists between fabula (story) and sjužet (plot). 'Story' is used to refer to the events of a NARRATIVE in the order in which they happened (or in an order determined by cause and effect), while 'plot' is used to refer to the events of a narrative as they are ordered and presented artistically, in the work. See Chapter 6, p. 111.

STREAM OF CONSCIOUSNESS The representation in words of a succession of thoughts in a CHARACTER's mind, typically when the character is alone and is allowing thought to follow thought without external prompting. Strictly speaking, stream of consciousness is the umbrella term within which INTERNAL MONOLOGUE (which requires that the words used be those that the character thinks by means of) is a subordinate category. The two terms are however often used as synonyms. See the discussion on p. 97.

STRUCTURALISM See the Introduction, p. 1, and Chapter 7, p. 172.

SUB-PLOT The term is more commonly applied to classical drama, as in a Shakespearian tragedy, for example, where it denotes a 'second and subordinate story' which accompanies or runs alongside the main STORY of the fall of a person of high estate. It is sometimes applied to fiction, although, because the novel often involves very many PLOT 'threads', it is less appropriate to this genre.

Cedric Watts has coined the term 'covert plot' to describe those sub-plots that are concealed and become apparent only after being teased out during a second or subsequent reading.

SUBSCRIPTION A method of financing publication which requires prospective buyers of the work to pay in advance for a copy of the published work. Along with PATRONAGE, this is a method of financing authors which was largely replaced by publishers' fees and royalties ('the market') in the course of the eighteenth century. Like patronage, of which it can be seen to be a variant, subscription freed the author from the need to sell lots of copies of a work and it provided income while the work was being written (like an 'advance on royalties'), but it required the author to stay on good terms with the source of his or her income.

SYLLEPSIS In traditional usage, another term for 'zeugma', or the joining of very different elements together in a single phrase, as in Pope's 'Or stain her honour, or her new brocade' (*The Rape of the Lock* (1714)). In NARRATOLOGY, a cluster or gathering (of EVENTs, circumstances, experiences, and so on) ordered according to some principle other than temporal unity or sequence. Thus 'John told her all the things that had happened in his mother's house' is a syllepsis based on situational coherence.

SYMBOL A unit (linguistic or otherwise) which either conventionally or naturally represents something apart from itself. A white wedding dress conventionally symbolizes virginity; blood naturally symbolizes violence. See the extended discussion on p. 123

TELLING AND SHOWING A term used to distinguish two ways of providing the reader with relevant information. Telling is seen as the cruder technique, involving overt statement on the part of NARRATOR or CHARACTER. Showing is more subtle and indirect, presenting scenes of DIALOGUE, thought or action and allowing the reader to draw certain conclusions him- or herself. See also p. 7 and the longer discussion on p. 107

THEME In traditional literary-critical usage the term 'theme' suffers from a certain ambiguity. Whereas for some critics it implies a certain claim, doctrine or argument raised either overtly or implicitly throughout a literary work (or by the work as a whole), for others the term 'thesis' is used with this meaning, and theme is reserved for what one can better call an issue. A theme is generally also distinguished from a motif (or *leitmotif*) by its greater abstraction: motifs are generally linked to specific, concrete forms of manifestation. See the discussion on p. 121, and the entry for MOTIF.

THIRD PERSON Traditionally used to indicate a narrator who is in some sense outside of the story told, and who typically refers to characters within the story as 'he', 'she' or 'they' but not 'I' or 'we'. See the comments on pp. 82–4.

TRIPLE-DECKER During the Victorian period, publication of a novel in book form (rather than in instalments in a periodical) commonly involved the production of a triple-decker, that is to say a novel produced in three volumes. Such triple-deckers were generally borrowed from one of the circulating libraries such as Mudie's. Publication aimed at personal sales usually followed triple-decker publication, and was normally in the form of a single volume. Because circulating libraries exercised forms of censorship on authors, it is important to know whether a novel was first published in this form.

TONE The sense of an author's or narrator's attitude to his or her character, situation or subject, as conveyed by the words he or she chooses. Sometimes used in a wider sense to describe the mood engendered in a reader by a particular work. See the discussion on p. 121.

UNCLE CHARLES PRINCIPLE See COLOURING.

VOICE See PERSPECTIVE AND VOICE, and the discussion in Chapter 6, p. 95.

Annotated bibliography

Alexander, Marguerite (1990). *Flights from Realism: Themes and Strategies in Postmodernist British and American Fiction*. London: Edward Arnold.
If you are curious about the form that postmodernism in fiction takes, and wish to read a sensible discussion of the work of such writers as Faulkner, Beckett, Pynchon and Vonnegut, this is a good place to start.

Anand, Mulk Raj (1946). *Indian Fairy Tales*. Bombay: Kotub Publishers.

Andrew, Dudley (1992). Adaptation. First published in Dudley Andrew, *Concepts in Film Theory* (Oxford: Oxford University Press, 1984). Reprinted in Gerald Mast, Marshall Cohen and Leo Braudy (eds) (1992), *Film Theory and Criticism* (New York and Oxford: Oxford University Press), 420–8.

Armitt, Lucie (1996). *Theorising the Fantastic*. London: Arnold.
Both an investigation into and development of theories of the literary fantastic, and a collection of useful studies of individual texts. Includes discussion of (among others) Lewis Carroll's Alice *texts, Stevenson's* The Strange Case of Dr Jekyll and Mr Hyde, *Charlotte Perkins Gilman's* The Yellow Wallpaper, *and Angela Carter's* The Passion of New Eve.

Armstrong, Nancy (1987). *Desire and Domestic Fiction: A Political History of the Novel*. New York and Oxford: Oxford University Press.
Armstrong associates the novel with 'the rise of the domestic woman', and uses the theories of Michel Foucault as the basis for a view of the novel as involved in social change in more complex ways than are covered by patterns of simple cause and effect. Includes useful discussion of Richardson's Pamela, *Jane Austen's* Emma, *and the Brontës.*

Atkins, Barry (2003). *More than a Game: The Computer Game as Fictional Form*. Manchester and New York: Manchester University Press.

Atwood, Margaret (1991). Weight. In *Wilderness Tips*. London: Bloomsbury, 177–93.

Azim, Firdous (1993). *The Colonial Rise of the Novel*. London: Routledge.

Bakhtin, M.M. (1981). *The Dialogic Imagination: Four Essays*. Translated by Caryl Emerson and Michael Holquist. Austin: University of Texas Press.
Bakhtin's work has been very influential in European and North American academic circles since it started to appear in translation. This volume represents the most important collection of essays so far as students of the novel are concerned, with pieces on 'Epic and Novel', 'From the Prehistory of Novelistic Discourse', 'Forms of Time and Chronotope in the Novel' and 'Discourse in the Novel'.

Bal, Mieke (1985). *Narratology: Introduction to the Theory of Narrative*. Translated by Christine van Boheemen. Toronto and London: University of Toronto Press.

Now available in a revised second edition (1997; paperback 1998). This and Shlomith Rimmon-Kenan's Narrative Fiction: Contemporary Poetics *(see below) are recommended as accessible but sophisticated introductions to narrative theory.*

Banfield, Ann (1982). *Unspeakable Sentences: Narration and Representation in the Language of Fiction.* London: Routledge.
An advanced and often difficult book that has been very influential in the debate around the topic of Free Indirect Discourse. Banfield is concerned with FID as a technique that can be used to present information that is, paradoxically, 'unspeakable'. See my comments on p. 88.

Barthes, Roland (1974). *The Pleasure of the Text.* Trans. Richard Miller. New York: Hill and Wang.

Beale, Antony (ed.) (1961). *Selected Literary Criticism: D.H. Lawrence.* London: Mercury Books.

Booth, Austin and Mary Flanagan (eds) (2002). *Reload: Rethinking Women + Cyberculture.* With an introduction by the editors. Cambridge, Mass. and London: MIT Press.

Booth, Wayne C. (1961). *The Rhetoric of Fiction.* Chicago: University of Chicago Press.
A study that really initiated the new wave of interest in narrative technique in the English-speaking world. Booth is a stimulating and accessible critic, and his book has been enormously influential. The second edition contains a useful afterword.

Boumelha, Penny (1988). Jane Eyre, Jamaica and the Gentleman's House. *Southern Review*, 21(2), July, 111–22.

Bowen, Elizabeth (1976). Introduction to *The Faber Book of Modern Short Stories.* First published in 1936. Reprinted in May 1976, 152–8.

Bradbury, Malcolm (ed.) (1990). *The Novel Today: Contemporary Writers on Modern Fiction.* Revised edition. Glasgow: Fontana.
A very useful collection of essays by practising novelists writing about their own and others' fiction. Essential for any student interested in modernism and postmodernism in the novel. The 1990 edition includes a new introduction, a new piece by Italo Calvino, and an interview with Milan Kundera by Ian McEwan.

Bradbury, Malcolm (2002) *The Modern British Novel 1878–2001.* Harmondsworth: Penguin.

Brecht, Bertolt (1977). Against Georg Lukács. Translated by Stuart Hood. In Ernst Bloch, Georg Lukács, Bertolt Brecht, Walter Benjamin and Theodor Adorno, *Aesthetics and Politics.* London: New Left Books, 68–85.
This consists of four pieces written by Brecht in the late 1930s.

Brooke-Rose, Christine (1981). *A Rhetoric of the Unreal: Studies in Narrative and Structure, Especially of the Fantastic.* Cambridge: Cambridge University Press.

Burke, Peter (1997). Representations of the Self from Petrarch to Descartes. In Roy Porter (ed.), *Rewriting the Self: Histories from the Renaissance to the Present.* London: Routledge.

Butler, Andrew M. (2000). *Cyberpunk.* Harpenden: Pocket Essentials.

Butler, Christopher (1984). The Pleasures of the Experimental Text. In Jeremy Hawthorn (ed.), *Criticism and Critical Theory*. London: Edward Arnold.

Calisher, Hortense (1964). *Extreme Magic: A Novella and Other Stories*. Boston: Little, Brown.

Carey, Charles Stokes (ed.) (1912). *Letters Written by Lord Chesterfield to his Son*. Volume 1. London: Wm. Reeves.

Carlier, J.C. (2000). Roland Barthes' Resurrection of the Author and Redemption of Biography. Translated from the French by C.T. Watts. *The Cambridge Quarterly*, 29(4), 386-93.

Chatman, Seymour (1990). *Story and Discourse: Narrative Structure in Fiction and Film*. Ithaca, NY and London: Cornell University Press.

Cohen, Margaret and Carolyn Dever (eds) (2002). *The Literary Channel: The Inter-National Invention of the Novel*. Princeton and Oxford: Princeton University Press.

Cohn, Dorrit (1999). *The Distinction of Fiction*. Baltimore and London: Johns Hopkins University Press.
Cohn argues strongly for literary fiction as a distinct category, one that must be distinguished from narrative in general. The final chapter, 'Optics and Power in the Novel', takes up a determined opposition to recent attempts to see fictional narrators in terms of Michel Foucault's extension of Jeremy Bentham's idea of the 'Panopticon'.

Conrad, Joseph (1971). *Heart of Darkness*. Edited by Robert Kimbrough. Norton Critical Edition. Second edition. (Third edition 1988.) New York and London: W.W. Norton.

Cornwell, Neil (1990). *The Literary Fantastic: From Gothic to Postmodernism*. Hemel Hempstead: Harvester Wheatsheaf.

Cranny-Francis, Anne (1990). *Feminist Fiction: Feminist Uses of Generic Fiction*. Cambridge: Polity Press.
This is an intelligent study of what is claimed to be a range of feminist genres: feminist science fiction, fantasy, utopias, detective fiction and romance. If you are interested in what a feminist investigation into these areas, and into the work of important recent writers such as Angela Carter, Marge Piercy, Valerie Miner and others, looks like, then this is a good place to start. The book also contains a useful concluding chapter on 'Gender and Genre'.

Curle, Richard (ed.) (1928). *Conrad to a Friend: 150 Selected Letters from Joseph Conrad to Richard Curle*. London: Sampson Low.

Currie, Gregory (1990). *The Nature of Fiction*. Cambridge: Cambridge University Press.

Day, Geoffrey (1987). *From Fiction to the Novel*. London: Routledge.

Doody, Margaret Anne (1996). *The True Story of the Novel*. New Brunswick, NJ: Rutgers University Press.

Downie, J.A. (2000). Mary Davy's 'Probable Feign'd Stories' and Critical Shibboleths about 'The Rise of the Novel'. In *Reconsidering the Rise of the Novel*. Special issue of *Eighteenth-Century Fiction*, 12(2–3), January–April, 309–26.

Ferguson, Suzanne (1989). The Rise of the Short Story in the Hierarchy of Genres. In Lohafer and Clarey 1989, 176–92.

Fludernik, Monika (1993). *The Fictions of Language and the Languages of Fiction*. London: Routledge.
Along with Ann Banfield's Unspeakable Sentences *(see above and also p. 88), on which it builds but with which it takes issue on a number of points, probably the most exhaustive and demanding study of Free Indirect Discourse available. Not recommended as an introductory text, but very rewarding for the reader prepared to grapple with its difficulties.*

Forster, E.M. (1962). *Aspects of the Novel*. First published 1927. Harmondsworth: Penguin.
In spite of its chatty tone and of the fact that criticism of the novel has refined and expanded its repertoire of terms and concepts since 1927, this is a study that is still worth reading. Full of shrewd insights and illuminating asides on particular novels.

Fox, Ralph (1979). *The Novel and the People*. First published 1937. London: Lawrence & Wishart.

Friedman, Norman (1976). What Makes a Short Story Short? First published 1958. Reprinted in May 1976, 131–46.

Friedman, Norman (1989). Recent Short Story Theories: Problems in Definition. In Lohafer and Clarey 1989, 13–31.

Frow, John (1997). *Time and Commodity Culture*: *Essays in Cultural Theory and Postmodernity*. Oxford: Clarendon Press.

Gasiorek, Andrzej (1994). *Post-War British Fiction: Realism and After*. London: Arnold.
A stimulating book that makes a sophisticated case for the continued relevance of 'realism' to novelists writing since 1945 – including those often labelled 'postmodernist'.

Genette, Gérard (1980). *Narrative Discourse: An Essay in Method*. Translated by Jane E. Lewin. First published in French 1972. Ithaca, NY: Cornell University Press.
Perhaps the most influential of the first wave of structuralist studies of narrative. There are more accessible introductions, and sometimes Genette's use of the linguistic paradigm (or analogy) makes for difficulties of terminology and comprehension, but this is a book rich in local insights and conceptual innovations.

Genette, Gérard (1997). *Paratexts: Thresholds of Interpretation* (*Literature, Culture, Theory*, 20; first published in French, 1987). Translated by Jane E. Lewin. Cambridge: Cambridge University Press.

A fascinating account of such things as titles, prefaces, forewords, and so on, and their effect upon the works they are attached to.

Gilbert, Susan M. and Susan Gubar (1979). *The Madwoman in the Attic: The Woman Writer and the Nineteenth-century Literary Imagination*. New Haven, Conn.: Yale University Press.
An extremely influential account of recurrent themes and stereotypes of women as represented in nineteenth-century literature. Gilbert and Gubar devote considerable attention to prose fiction.

Gilmour, Robin (1986). *The Novel in the Victorian Age*. London: Edward Arnold.
This is one of the best introductions to the Victorian English novel, intelligently blending information about the age with detailed commentary on individual novelists and novels.

Gombrich, Ernst (1960). *Art and Illusion*. New York: Pantheon.

Good, Graham (1994). Notes on the Novella. First published in 1977. In May 1994, 147–64.

Goring, Paul, Jeremy Hawthorn and Domhnall Mitchell (2001). *Studying Literature: The Essential Companion*. London: Arnold.

Harvey, David (1989). *The Condition of Postmodernity*. Oxford: Blackwell.
Perhaps the most accessible introduction to ideas about the postmodern.

Hassan, Ihab (1985). The Culture of Postmodernism. *Theory, Culture and Society*, 2(3), 119–31.

Hawthorn, Jeremy (1998). Repetitions and Revolutions: Conrad's Use of the Pseudo-iterative in *Nostromo*. In *Joseph Conrad 1*, special Conrad issue of *La revue des lettres modernes*. Paris: Editions Minard, 125–49.

Hunter, J. Paul (1990). *Before Novels: The Cultural Contexts of Eighteenth-century English Fiction*. New York: W.W. Norton.
I refer repeatedly to this book in Chapter 2. It contains a wealth of detailed information about social and literary contexts within which the modern novel emerged.

Huyssen, Andreas (1988). *After the Great Divide: Modernism, Mass Culture and Postmodernism*. London: Macmillan.

Isherwood, Christopher (1977). *Christopher and his Kind: 1929–1939*. London: Methuen.

Jakobson, Roman (1971). On Realism in Art. Translated by Karol Magassy. In Ladislav Matejka and Krystyna Pomorska (eds), *Readings in Russian Poetics: Formalist and Structuralist Views*. Cambridge, Mass.: MIT Press, 38–46.

Jameson, Fredric (1991). *Postmodernism, or, The Cultural Logic of Late Capitalism*. Durham, NC: Duke University Press.

Johnson, B.S. (1973). *Aren't You Rather Young to be Writing Your Memoirs?* In Bradbury 1990, 151–68. First published in 1973.

Karl, Frederick and Laurence Davies (eds) (1986). *The Collected Letters of Joseph Conrad.* Volume 2, 1898–1902. Cambridge: Cambridge University Press.

Kermode, Frank (2004). Retripotent. (Review of Jonathan Coe, *Like a Fiery Elephant: the Story of B. S. Johnson,* and of B. S. Johnson, *Trawl, Albert Angelo* and *House Mother Normal.*) *London Review of Books,* 26(15), 5 August, 11–13.

Kettle, Arnold (1967). *An Introduction to the English Novel.* Second edition. Volume 1. London: Hutchinson.

Kundera, Milan (1988). *The Art of the Novel.* Translated by Linda Asher. First published in French in 1986. London and Boston: Faber.

Lamarque, Peter (1996). *Fictional Points of View.* Ithaca, NY: Cornell University Press.

Lamarque, Peter and Stein Haugom Olsen (1994). *Truth, Fiction, and Literature: A Philosophical Perspective.* Oxford: Clarendon Press.

Landow, George (1992). *Hypertext: The Convergence of Contemporary Critical Thought and Technology.* Baltimore, MD: Johns Hopkins University Press.

Lawrence, James Cooper (1976). A Theory of the Short Story. First published in 1917. In May 1976, 60–71.

Leader, Zachary (ed.) (2003). *On Modern British Fiction.* Oxford: Oxford University Press.

Leavis, F.R. (1969). *English Literature in our Time and the University.* London: Chatto & Windus.

Leech, Geoffrey N. and Michael H. Short (1981). *Style in Fiction: A Linguistic Introduction to English Fictional Prose.* London: Longman.
Those who have tried to read accounts of prose fiction by linguisticians and who have determined not to try again should relent and read this book. The authors yield nothing to literary specialists in their sensitivity to fictional texts and passages, and are able to present a conception and analysis of style which any student of the novel will find invaluable. Well provided with sensible and well-illustrated examples.

Leitch, Thomas M. (1989). The Debunking Rhythm of the American Short Story. In Lohafer and Clarey 1989, 130–47.

Levenson, Michael (1991) *Modernism and the Fate of Individuality: Character and Novelistic Form from Conrad to Woolf.* Cambridge: Cambridge University Press.

Little, T.E. *The Fantasts* (1984). Avebury: Amersham.

Lodge, David (1992). *The Art of Fiction.* Harmondsworth: Penguin.
A collection of short articles originally published in the Independent on Sunday, *offering both accessible and authoritative accounts of fifty different terms and concepts ranging from 'Beginning' to 'Ending' and taking in others such as suspense, stream of consciousness, defamiliarization, repetition, showing and telling, symbolism, allegory, epiphany, metafiction, aporia and the Uncanny. All are illustrated with extracts from either classic or modern texts.*

Lohafer, Susan and Jo Ellyn Clarey (eds) (1989). *Short Story Theory at a Crossroads*. Baton Rouge and London: Louisiana State University Press. *A most useful collection of extracts and articles concerned to define and discuss the short story. Updates and extends May 1976 (see below).*

Lothe, Jakob (1989). *Conrad's Narrative Method*. Oxford: Clarendon Press.

Lothe, Jakob (2000). *Narrative in Fiction and Film: An Introduction*. Oxford: Oxford University Press.
A very readable and stimulating introduction to the differences between narrative in prose fiction and in film. Detailed and rewarding discussion of theoretical issues and of film adaptations of Kafka's The Trial, *James Joyce's 'The Dead', Joseph Conrad's* Heart of Darkness *(Francis Ford Coppola's* Apocalypse Now*) and Virginia Woolf's* To the Lighthouse.

Lubbock, Percy (1921). *The Craft of Fiction*. London: Jonathan Cape.

Lugowski, Clemens (1990). *Form, Individuality and the Novel*. Revised edition. Translated by John Dixon. First published in German 1932 (revised edition 1976). Cambridge: Polity Press.

Lukács, Georg (1969). *The Historical Novel*. Translated by Stanley and Hannah Mitchell. First published in Russian 1937, and in English 1962. Harmondsworth: Penguin.
An important book on a somewhat unfashionable topic (the historical novel is looked down upon by some recent academics, and it has often had a higher reputation in Continental Europe than in Britain and Ireland).

Luria, A.R. (1976). *Cognitive Development*. Cambridge, Mass.: Harvard University Press.

Margolies, David (1985). *Novel and Society in Elizabethan England*. Beckenham: Croom Helm.

Marías, Javier (1995). *All Souls*. Translated from the Spanish by Margaret Jull Costa. First published in Spanish 1989 and in English in 1992. London: The Harvill Press.

Marías, Javier (1997). *Tomorrow in the Battle Think on Me*. Translated from the Spanish by Margaret Jull Costa. First published in Spanish 1994 and in English 1996. New York: New Directions.

Maupassant, Guy de (1975). *Bel-Ami*. Translated by Douglas Parmée. Harmondsworth: Penguin.

May, Charles E. (ed.) (1976). *Short Story Theories*. Athens: Ohio University Press.
Like Lohafer and Clarey 1989 (see above), this provides a most useful collection of extracts and articles concerned with theories of the short story.

May, Charles E. (ed.) (1994). *The New Short Story Theories*. Athens: Ohio University Press.

McGann, Jerome J. (1991). *The Textual Condition*. Princeton: Princeton University Press.

McHale, Brian (1978). Free Indirect Discourse: A Survey of Recent Accounts. *Poetics and Theory of Literature* 3, 249–87.

McHale, Brian (1987). *Postmodernist Fiction*. London: Methuen.
McHale's study is extremely wide-ranging, including authors and texts from several continents, and theoretically penetrating and insightful. The author is very well versed in modern narrative theory, but he brings other theoretical perspectives to bear on his analyses.

McKeon, Michael (1987). *The Origins of the English Novel 1600–1740*. Baltimore: Johns Hopkins University Press.
In common with J. Paul Hunter's study (see above), this is an indispensable enquiry into where the English novel came from. Contains many thought-provoking arguments about such things as the relationship between the novel's linear order and a 'quasi-Calvinist' view of the linear life of the hard-working middle classes.

Meek, James (2004). Get a Life. *Guardian*, 3 August. Accessed on <http://www.guardian.co.uk/online/story/0,3605,1274808,00.html>, 30 August 2004.

Millett, Kate (1971). *Sexual Politics*. First published 1970. London: Sphere Books.

Montfort, Nick (2003). *Twisty Little Passages: An Approach to Interactive Fiction*. Cambridge, Mass. and London: MIT Press.

Moretti, Franco (1998). *Atlas of the European Novel 1800–1900*. London and New York: Verso.
This is a book that is full of useful information about a range of important issues. Which places and geographical areas are referred to by novelists, and do they change over time? Where are books published? Which books do people have in their homes? What percentage of library books are novels – and what did nineteenth-century librarians think of this?

Newman, Judie (1995). *The Ballistic Bard: Postcolonial Fictions*. London: Arnold.

Ngugi, James (1972). *Weep Not, Child*. First published 1964. London: Heinemann Educational. (See also Thiong'o, Ngũgĩ Wa.)

Novak, Maximilian E. (1991). Review of J. Paul Hunter, *Before Novels: The Cultural Contexts of Eighteenth-century English Fiction*. *Times Literary Supplement*, no. 4582, 25 January, 8.

O'Connor, Frank (1963). *The Lonely Voice: A Study of the Short Story*. London: Macmillan.
A quirky but insightful account of the short story, written by one of its leading practitioners.

O'Faolain, Sean (1972). *The Short Story*. First published 1948. Cork: The Mercier Press.

O'Rourke, William (1989). Morphological Metaphors for the Short Story: Matters of Production, Reproduction, and Consumption. In Lohafer and Clarey 1989, 193–205.

Page, Norman (1988). *Speech in the English Novel*. Second edition. London: Macmillan.
A very useful account that covers such issues as methods of speech presentation, dialect and idiolect. Also contains a number of case studies, and a concluding chapter on 'Dickens and Speech'.

Pearce, Lynne (1994). *Reading Dialogics*. London: Arnold.
For those interested in a recent application of Mikhail Bakhtin's theories of dialogism to a range of texts, this book is recommended. Pearce includes both readings of individual works (including Wuthering Heights, The Waves, Sexing the Cherry *and* Beloved*) and an extended theoretical discussion of dialogue and the dialogic.*

Plain, Gill (1996). *Women's Fiction of the Second World War: Gender, Power and Resistance*. Edinburgh: Edinburgh University Press.
An interesting feminist study of the different ways in which women writers respond to that 'crisis of patriarchy' which is war. Includes commentary on the work of Dorothy L. Sayers, Stevie Smith, Virginia Woolf, Naomi Mitchison and Elizabeth Bowen. A useful bringing together of two contexts: that of socio-historical crisis, and that of the community of women novelists.

Price, Leah (2000). *The Anthology and the Rise of the Novel: From Richardson to George Eliot*. Cambridge: Cambridge University Press.

Propp, Vladimir (1968). *Morphology of the Folktale*. Revised edition. Translated by Laurence Scott. Austin: University of Texas Press.

Reconsidering the Rise of the Novel (2000). Special issue of *Eighteenth-Century Fiction*, 12(2–3), January–April.
A collection of essays all of which attempt to engage with, respond to or counter the arguments in Ian Watt's influential The Rise of the Novel. *Essential for those interested in the debates around the emergence of the modern English novel.*

Rimmon-Kenan, Shlomith (1983). *Narrative Fiction: Contemporary Poetics*. London: Methuen.
Still probably the best place to start for those requiring an introduction to structuralist-influenced theories of narrative. Clearly and concisely written, and very fully illustrated with examples from a range of texts. Its only competitor as an introductory text is Mieke Bal's Narratology: Introduction to the Theory of Narrative *(see above).*

Ryan, Marie-Laure (2001). *Narrative as Virtual Reality: Immersion and Activity in Literature and Electronic Media*. Baltimore and London: Johns Hopkins University Press.

Saussure, Ferdinand de (1974). *Course in General Linguistics*. Edited by Charles Bally and Albert Sechehaye. Translated by Wade Buskin. Revised edition. London: Peter Owen.

Sedgwick, Eve Kosofsky (ed.) (1997). *Novel Gazing: Queer Readings in Fiction*. Durham, NC and London: Duke University Press.

A wide-ranging selection of essays demonstrating the sorts of reading that Queer Theory (see p. 181) can generate when applied to the novel.

Seidel, Michael (2000). The Man Who Came to Dinner: Ian Watt and the Theory of Formal Realism. In *Reconsidering the Rise of the Novel*. Special issue of *Eighteenth-Century Fiction*, 12(2–3), January–April, 193–212.

Sell, Roger (1983). Projection Characters in *David Copperfield*. *Studia Neophilologica*, 55, 19–30.

Seymour-Smith, Martin (1980). *Novels and Novelists: A Guide to the World of Fiction*. New York: St Martin's Press.

Shaw, Valerie (1983). *The Short Story: A Critical Introduction*. London and New York: Longman.

A study based upon an extremely wide-ranging knowledge of the short story; full of detailed references to key writers and texts.

Skinner, John (2001). *An Introduction to Eighteenth-century Fiction: Raising the Novel*. Basingstoke: Palgrave.

A very useful study that opens with a discussion of theoretical and critical issues, the formation of a canon and the issue of gender, and then devotes chapters to the work of a range of canonical and less well known novelists, ending with Jane Austen.

Spender, Dale (1986). *Mothers of the Novel: 100 Good Women Writers Before Jane Austen*. London: Pandora Press.

The title is self-explanatory: this is an attempt to reclaim the work of many 'forgotten' female contributors to the development of a genre which owes an enormous debt to the female sex.

Spilka, Mark (ed.) (1977). *Towards a Poetics of Fiction*. Bloomington: Indiana University Press.

This book contains essays from the journal Novel *from the period 1967–76, and includes many fine theoretical and interpretative pieces by well-known writers. Wayne C. Booth and Ian Watt comment, respectively, on their influential books* The Rhetoric of Fiction *and* The Rise of the Novel. *There are also studies of the criticism of Georg Lukács, Wayne C. Booth and F.R. Leavis, and an essay on the contributions of formalism and structuralism to the theory of fiction.*

Spoto, Donald (1983). *The Dark Side of Genius: The Life of Alfred Hitchcock*. Boston: Little, Brown and Company.

Springer, Mary Doyle (1975). *Forms of the Modern Novella*. Chicago and London: University of Chicago Press.

Stam, Robert (2000). Beyond Fidelity: The Dialogics of Adaptation. In James Naremore (ed.), *Film Adaptation*. New Brunswick, NJ: Rutgers University Press, 54–76.

Stevenson, Randall (1997). *Modernist Fiction*. Revised edition. Harlow: Longman.

Concentrates on major figures such as Henry James, Joseph Conrad, Ford Madox Ford, D.H. Lawrence, Wyndham Lewis, Virginia Woolf and James Joyce. Informed both by a strong sense of history and by recent developments in narrative theory.

Thiong'o, Ngũgĩ Wa (1987). *Devil on the Cross.* First published in Gĩkũyũ in 1980, and in the author's English translation in 1982. London: Heinemann Educational. (See also Ngugi, James.)

Thomas, Brook (1991). *The New Historicism: And Other Old-fashioned Topics.* Princeton: Princeton University Press.

Thomson, A.W. (1965). *The Turn of the Screw*: Some Points on the Hallucination Theory. *Review of English Literature* VI(4), 26–36.

Todorov, Tzvetan (1984). *Mikhail Bakhtin: The Dialogical Principle.* Minneapolis: University of Minnesota Press.
An excellent introduction to the work and ideas of a writer who has had a profound influence on our ideas about the novel.

Toker, Leona (1993). *Eloquent Reticence: Withholding Information in Fictional Narrative.* Lexington: University Press of Kentucky.
A must for anyone interested in how the creative powers of readers contribute to the experience of reading novels. Toker takes a number of examples in which the reader has to 'fill in' missing or delayed information. There are excellent chapters on The Sound and the Fury, Nostromo, Bleak House, Emma, Tom Jones, A Passage to India *and* Absalom, Absalom!

Tomkins, J.M.S. (1932). *The Popular Novel in England 1770–1800.* London: Constable.
A book that has dated very little, and essential reading for those interested either in the importance to the novel of women as writers and readers or in the whole complex issue of the novel and 'the popular'. Particularly interesting on such matters as the theme of incest in early modern novels and the symbolic importance of the brother–sister relationship to early women novelists.

Toolan, Michael J. (1988). *Narrative: A Critical Linguistic Introduction.* London: Routledge.
An accessible introduction to narrative theory which includes a concern not just with literary narratives but also with oral narratives and narratives in newspapers, law courts and elsewhere. Although Toolan's emphasis is a linguistic one, he is good on the ideological and political ramifications of narrative choices.

Truffaut, François (1986). With the collaboration of Helen G. Scott. *Hitchcock.* Revised edition. First published 1968. London: Paladin.

Various authors (1956). *Did It Happen? Stories.* London: Oldbourne Press.

Warner, William B. (1998). *Licensing Entertainment: The Elevation of Novel Reading in Britain, 1694–1750.* Berkeley: University of California Press.

Watt, Ian (1963). *The Rise of the Novel.* First published 1957. Harmondsworth: Penguin.
In spite of repeated attempts to qualify, rebuff or supersede Watt's arguments (see for example Reconsidering the Rise of the Novel, *above), this is a book that continues to require and repay attention.*

Watt, Ian (1980). *Conrad in the Nineteenth Century.* London: Chatto & Windus.

Watts, Cedric (1984). *The Deceptive Text: An Introduction to Covert Plots.* Brighton: Harvester.

Woolf, Leonard (ed.) (1972). *A Writer's Diary: Being Extracts from the Diary of Virginia Woolf.* London: Hogarth Press.

Woolf, Virginia (1966a). *Collected Essays.* Volume 1. London: Hogarth Press.

Woolf, Virginia (1966b). *Collected Essays.* Volume 2. London: Hogarth Press.

Woolf, Virginia (1967). *A Room of One's Own.* First published 1929. London: Hogarth Press.

Wyndham, Francis and Diana Melly (eds) (1984). *Jean Rhys: Letters 1931–1966.* London: André Deutsch.

Index

All main glossary terms are shown in **bold**.